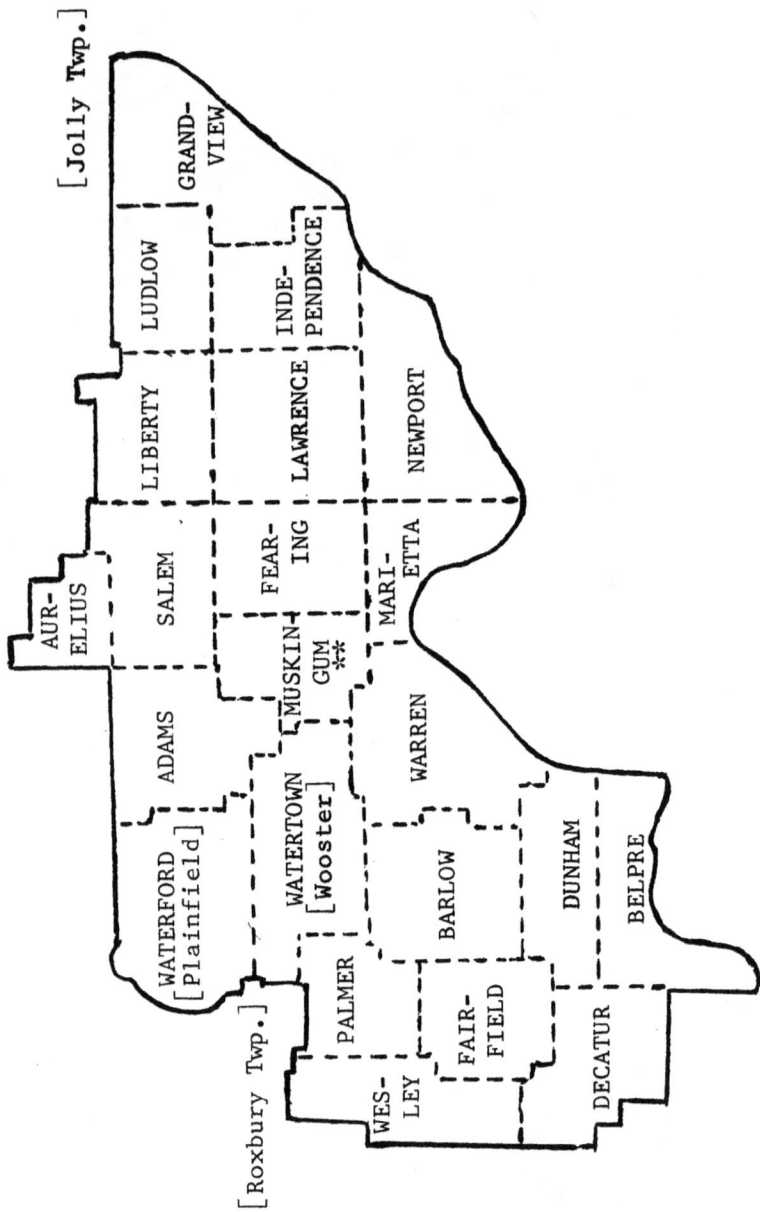

Township outline WASHINGTON COUNTY, OHIO

—Showing areas of extinct townships: Jolly, Roxbury, Wooster; location of Plainfield (same area for Millburg), and (**) center of Union Twp.

WASHINGTON COUNTY, OHIO

Marriages
1789 – 1840

Compiled by

Bernice Graham *&* Elizabeth S. Cottle

CLEARFIELD

Reprinted for
Clearfield Company by
Genealogical Publishing Co.
Baltimore, Maryland
2000, 2007

Originally published: Marietta, Ohio, 1976
Reprinted in a new format by
Genealogical Publishing Company
Baltimore, 1989

Library of Congress Catalogue Card Number 88-82648
ISBN-13: 978-0-8063-1232-3
ISBN-10: 0-8063-1232-7

Made in the United States of America

TABLE OF CONTENTS

INTRODUCTION

In response to an urgent need for pertinent data concerning early marriages of this area by family historians and genealogical researchers, we have prepared names of the brides and grooms, both indexed, their residences when given, the dates of marriage, names of persons performing the ceremonies with their offices, and the page references in the original books where they may be found, from 1789 through 1840.

The earliest book bearing the dates 1789-1803 contains records made when Washington County covered a large section of the Northwest Territory, that vast area "north and west of the River Ohio" later to be carved into five states. For convenience we call it the Northwest Territory Book. Several of the early townships such as Gallipolis, Tuskarawa and Middleton are now in other Ohio counties.

On one of the last pages of the NW book (1789-1803) are the following inscriptions:

"Marietta, Ohio, August 1, 1873.

"This book found among the old papers of my grandfather, Dudley Woodbridge, Scqe and examined with great interest. Loaned to Mr. Anselm T. Nye. I am in some doubt about the place in which to deposit it. Formerly all records of marriage were kept by the Clerk of the Court of Common Pleas, but more recently by the Judge of Probate.

"Should it not be deposited at once, I trust care will be taken of it and it be left in the office of the Probate Court of Washington County.

George M. Woodbridge"

"About the year 1873, Mr. Anselm T. Nye was shown this book by George M. Woodbridge. At no time did Mr. Nye have the book in his possession for over a day when it was returned to Mr. Woodbridge.

August 12, 1897.   Mary C. Nye"

Book I began with statehood and continued to 1840 with a handful of entries for 1841. We have here listed every marriage in Book I and, in addition, have gone into Book II to pick up the 1840 marriages only.

iii

WASHINGTON COUNTY MARRIAGES

The references given to Book I are by page number only, but the other references give the volume also. Thus, NW-3 means Northwest Territory book, page 3 and II-14 means volume II, page 14.

According to the *Inventory of the County Archives of Ohio* prepared by The Historical Records Survey, Division of Women's Professional Projects, Works Progress Administration, No. 84, Washington County (Marietta), at Columbus, Ohio, in April, 1938, "the Probate Court was established by an act of the Northwest Territory on August 30, 1788, and consisted of a probate judge with jurisdiction in probate, testamentary and guardianship matters, and two judges of the court of common pleas, who sat with him and ruled on contested points, defective sentences and final judgments."

The judicial system established under the first constitution of Ohio in 1802 did not provide for a probate court but vested the court of common pleas with such powers as had been exercised by the court in the territorial period. The constitution of 1851 re-created the probate court and gave it original jurisdiction in probate and testamentary matters, the appointment of administrators and guardians, the settlement of the accounts of executors, administrators and guardians, etc. It was not until 1851 that a separate court was formed and the records formerly kept in the court of common pleas transferred to the new office. This included marriage records.

In the probate office there is also an index volume for books I, II and III in which are noted a few marriages for which there are said to be original certificates. The year but not the exact date is given which will have to suffice until these certificates are located.

This publication contains more than 3600 marriage records of Washington County, over a period of slightly more than fifty years. All of these records are handwritten and sometimes difficult to interpret, but since this was done by a pair, consultation was always available. Occasionally we have marked a name with a question mark when its reading was not clear. Similarly a marriage date which was recorded a year before the fact doesn't make sense and also bears a question mark. For the few missing pages we have used information supplied in earlier readings by Mrs. Helen Hill Sloan or by Ralph L. Schroeder.

We were privileged to check through a package of original certificates which had been taken to Campus Martius Museum Library while Mrs. Edith S. Reiter was curator, at a time when someone feared destruction of the papers at the court house. We found three marriages which had never been recorded. These will be labeled O.C. These records were for (1) Richard Greene and Bathsheba Rouse; (2) William Smith and Sabra Gates; (3) Seth Washburn and Bathsheba Loring.

A few marriages (labelled E.C.) are listed which were found in the Ephraim Cutler Account Book in the Special Collections of the Dawes Memorial Library at Marietta College.

Not recorded in the original books, also, are the first two marriages which took place in Marietta after the April 7th, 1788 settlement. The first was that of the Hon. Winthrop Sargent, secretary of the Northwest Territory, and Miss Rowena Tupper by General Rufus Putnam on February 6, 1789. This is mentioned in *The History of Washington County, Ohio* by H. Z.

Williams (1881). The following copy of a permit granted for the marriage by Arthur St. Clair, Governor of the Northwest Territory, is from the manuscripts of the Special Collections in the Marietta College Library.

"TO WHOM IT MAY CONCERN:
"Know ye that license is hereby granted for Winthrop Sargent, Esqe, and Miss Rowena Tupper to be united as Husband and Wife--and either of the judges of the Territory, Court of Common Pleas or others authorized by law to solemnise Marriages are empowered and directed upon application of the parties to perform the Marriage Ceremonies--for which this shall be their sufficient warrant. Given under my hand and Seal in the County of Washington, Territory of the United States North West of the River Ohio, this 20th day of January, AD 1789 and in the thirteenth year of the Independence of the United States.
A. T. St. Clair"

The second marriage in Marietta was that of Captain David Ziegler and Miss Lucy Coggeshell Sheffield, 22 February, 1789. This marriage is mentioned in the Military Journal of Major Ebenezer Denny, an officer in the Revolutionary and Indian Wars, with an introductory Memoir. On page 131 is written:

"Feb. 22nd, 1789. Married this evening, Capt. David Ziegler of the first regiment, to Miss Sheffield, only single daughter of Mrs. Sheffield of Campus Martius, city of Marietta. On this occasion I played the Captain's aid, and at his request, the memorandums made. I exhibited a character not more awkward than strange, at the celebration of Captain Ziegler's nuptials, the first of the kind I had been a witness to."

A few marriages are included in these records which represent Marietta or Washington County men who married women from outside this area and they therefore secured permits from the court of the bride's residence area. These were usually reported in the local newspaper here, such as the *American Friend* and the *Marietta Gazette.* They also may be found in the Special Collections of Marietta College Library. This is a random selection and does not claim to be all-inclusive.

Another source is a collection of records of the First Religious Society which was organized December 4, 1796 by early settlers here. They met in Campus Martius and drew members from a wide area, including Vienna, (W.) Va., Waterford and Belpre. Their records include minutes of meetings and several marriages of members. The original copy is now in possession of the First Congregational Church in Marietta. There is also a typed copy of the same in the files of Campus Martius Museum Library.

It is important for you to realize that spelling was a phonetic art and that names have changed over the years. A few examples will illustrate this in the following pairs or groups of equivalent names.

Allison - Ellison	Rarden, Rardin, Rardon, Raredon, Rarredon
Beaver - Bever	Kenada, Kenady, Kennedy
Hoff - Hough	Marhew - Mayhew
Hewett - Huet	Perdieu, Perdew, Perdue
Hais - Hayes	Rude - Rood
Gold - Gould	Ryon, Rion, Ryan
Watrous - Waters	Sedlift - Sutliff
Spacht - Speck	

If you will pronounce each name you will find similarities which the eye may not detect.

Special credit should be given to Ralph L. Schroeder, President of the Washington County Historical Society, who supplied the original format for these records and researched the history of the townships of Washington County which follows. Owen Hawley, Treasurer and Bulletin Editor of this same society was very helpful in setting up the code numbers and abbreviations while both were consultants in all the details of getting this ready for publication.

Thanks are also due to a group of DAR members who helped with the alphabetization; namely, Mrs. Robert C. Blake, Mrs. Lester H. Butler, Mrs. Benjamin P. Bragg, Mrs. Ray Curtis, Miss Rowena Rood and Mrs. Carl Douglass, Regent of the Marietta Chapter, DAR. Mr. Ralph Schroeder also joined us in the alphabetization activity.

The compilers are members of the Marietta Chapter DAR and also of the Washington County Historical Society which organizations are joint sponsors of this publication.

Elizabeth S. Cottle, Bernice Graham

CHRONOLOGICAL FORMATION OF TOWNSHIPS
WASHINGTON COUNTY, OHIO

Compiled by -- Ralph L. Schroeder

Those townships that have survived (currently in existence), are in italics. Total 23. Survey descriptions are not included here. To start with the original descriptions and to progress, showing their alterations or reductions, would be meaningless verbiage without overlay maps, for persons untutored in such terminology. The reader may refer to the accompanying map of Washington County for the lay of its current townships.

1. 1790 (20 Dec.) *MARIETTA*
2. 1790 (20 Dec.) *BELPRE* Its lines remained intact until 1856 when the northern division was incorporated into Dunham Twp. (Wms. p. 497)
3. 1790 (20 Dec.) *WATERFORD* (Plainfield)
4. _____ WARREN This Twp. adjoined the Pennsylvania line and was taken off in 1797 by the establishment of Jefferson County. (Wms. p. 109)

5. _____ MIDDLETOWN This Twp. lay west of Warren and was also taken off by the creation of Jefferson County.
6. 1797 (March) *ADAMS* See No. 21 below.
7. 1797 (March) GALLIPOLIS In essence represents what became Gallia County.
8. 1797 (5 Dec.) *SALEM*
9. 1798 (Dec.) MIDDLETOWN (Middleton) Second usage of the name and embraced almost all of what is now Athens Twp., Athens County. (Wms. 109)
10. 1798 (Dec.) NEWTOWN (Newton) It was formed from the north part of Waterford and lay outside of what is now Washington County proper. Presently it is the southwest corner of Muskingum County.
11. 1798 (Dec.) *NEWPORT*
12. 1802 _____ AMES Included what became Ames Twp., Athens County; and especially the area that was eventually taken off of Ames to create Dover Twp.
13. 1802 _____ HOCKHOCKING ("Bottle River") Probably the area that became Orange and Olive Twps., Meigs County.
14. 1802 _____ TUSKARAWA ("Open Mouth") In 1808 became part of Tuscarawas County, and in 1811 part of it went into the formation of Coshocton County.
15. 1802 _____ *GRANDVIEW*
16. 1806 (4 June) WOOSTER (Watertown) Name changed to Watertown 6 Dec. 1824. (Wms. 621)
17. 1806 _____ ROXBURY In 1851 Roxbury was lost by the creation of Noble County. A portion of it was annexed to Morgan County. The remainder was absorbed by the then newly created Palmer Twp. (Wms. 670)
18. 1808 (8 March) *FEARING*
19. 1810 (12 Aug.) *WESLEY* This was created out of parts of Wooster and Roxbury.
20. 1810 (10 Sept.) *WARREN* This is the second use of this name, and here it is in Washington County proper. See No. 21 below.
21. 1812 _____ UNION September 1813 part of Union was annexed to Wooster. (Wms. 621) In 1877 it was eliminated by being divided among Adams, Muskingum, Warren and Watertown.
22. 1812 (July) DEERFIELD Lost by creation of Morgan County 1819.
23. 1815 (April) MEIGSVILLE to Morgan County 1819.
24. 1815 (June) *LAWRENCE*
25. 1817 (June) OLIVE – GREEN to Morgan County 1819, now Jackson Twp., Noble County.
26. 1818 (July) MORGAN to Morgan County 1819.
27. 1818 (July) *BARLOW*
28. 1818 (15 Dec.) *AURELIUS*
29. 1819 (17 July) *LUDLOW*
30. 1820 (30 Nov.) *DECATUR*
31. 1824 (6 Dec.) *WATERTOWN* See Nos. 16 and 21 above.
32. 1832 (15 March) *LIBERTY*

33. 1840 (3 June) *INDEPENDENCE*
34. 1840 _____ JOLLY A part of it was added to Monroe County, 1851, the rest to Grandview, 1859.
35. 1851 (19 May) *PALMER* See No. 17 above.
36. 1851 (Dec.) *FAIRFIELD*
37. 1855 (15 June) *DUNHAM* See No. 2 above.
38. 1861 (18 April) *MUSKINGUM* See No. 21 above.
39. 1967 (6 June) *PIONEER* Embraces the City of Marietta proper.

Formation of Counties Relative to Washington County:

1788 (26 July) Washington, the parent county, was established by Proclamation of Gov. Arthur St. Clair. This included nearly half of the present State.

    1797 -- Jefferson (8th county in the Territory)
    1798 -- Ross
    1800 -- Trumbull
    1801 -- Belmont
    1803 -- Gallia
    1804 -- Muskingum
    1805 -- Athens
    1808 -- Tuscarawas
    1810 -- Guernsey
    1811 -- Coshocton
    1815 -- Monroe
    1818 -- Hocking
    1819 -- Morgan
    1819 -- Meigs
    1850 -- Vinton
    1851 -- Noble

City of Marietta (originally called Adelphia), named 2 July 1788; incorporated 2 Dec. 1800 (Andrews 31)
Athens incorporated 6 December 1800
Cincinnati incorporated 1 January 1802
Chillicothe incorporated 4 January 1802
French Settlement of Gallipolis, 19 October 1790.

Bibliography:

H. Z. Williams: *History of Washington County, Ohio* (1881) (Wms.)
I. W. Andrews: *Washington County and the Early Settlement of Ohio* (1877)
Census Records of Washington County, Ohio -- 1800, 1803
Washington County Ohio County Commissioners Journal 1810-1831

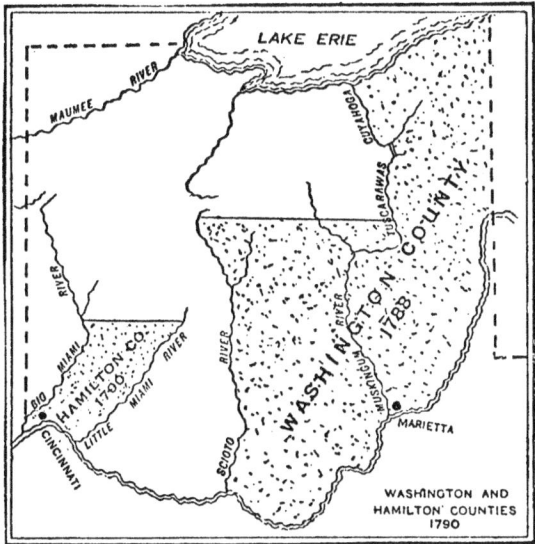

First Counties Established in the Northwest Territory

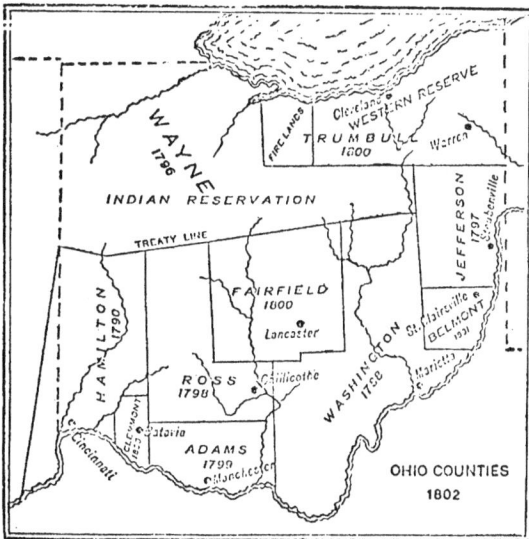

Maps showing Ohio counties for 1790 and evolution of counties by 1802.

These maps are from Ohio Archaeological & Historical Quarterly, Vol. V, pp. 329 and 349. They also appeared in Tallow Light, Vol. 10, No. 3, pp. 59 and 60.

How Ohio Appeared when the State was Formed

ABBREVIATIONS
(for Marriage Records)

A. - Athens, Ohio
A.C. - Athens County, Ohio
Ad - Adams Twp.
A.F. - *American Friend*
Ala. - Alabama
Alx. - Alexandria, Va.
Am - Ames Twp.
Au - Aurelius Twp.
Ba - Barlow Twp.
B.C. - Belmont County, Ohio
Be - Belpre (Belleprie) Twp.
Bev. - Beverly, (W.C.)
Br.C. - Brown County, Ohio
Bu.C. - Butler County, Ohio
Ch. - Charleston, (W) Va.
Chs. - Chester, Meigs County, Ohio
Cin. - Cincinnati, Ohio
Col. - Columbus, Ohio
Cr.C. - Crawford County, Ohio
Ct. - Connecticut
Cuy.C. - Cuyahoga County, Ohio
De - Decatur Twp.
Df - Deerfield Twp.
Du - Dunham Twp.
E.C. - Ephraim Cutler's Account
        Book
Fa - Fairfield Twp.
Fa.C. - Fairfield County, Ohio
Fe - Fearing Twp.
Ga - Gallipolis Twp.
G.C. - Gallia County, Ohio
Gn - Gnadenhutten, Ohio
Gr - Grandview Twp.
Grl - Granville, Ohio
Gu.C. - Guernsey County, Ohio
Guy. - Guyandotte, Va.
Ha - Harmar Village, (W.C.)
H.C. - Hamilton County, Ohio
Hk.C. - Hocking County, Ohio
Ho - Hockhocking Twp.
Hr.C. - Harrison County, Ohio
Hu.C. - Huron County, Ohio
IL - Illinois
In - Independence Twp.
Ja.C. - Jackson County, Ohio

Jo - Jolly Twp.
K.C. - Knox County, Ohio
Ken.C. - Kenhawa County, Va.
Ky. - Kentucky
La - Lawrence Twp.
Lan - Lancaster, Ohio
L.C. - Licking County, Ohio
Li - Liberty Twp.
Lo.C. - Logan County, Ohio
Low. - Lowell, (W.C.)
Lu - Ludlow Township
M - page missing
Ma - Marietta City and Township
Mad.Ia. - Madison, Iowa
Me.C. - Meigs County, Ohio
M.G. - *Marietta Gazette*
Mg.C. - Morgan County, Ohio
Mgt.Va. - Morgantown, Va.
M.I. - *Marietta Intelligencer*
Mich. - Michigan
Mi - Middleton (Middletown) Twp.
Mn.C. - Monroe County, Ohio
Mon.C. - Monongahela County, Va.
Ms. - Mississippi Territory
Mtg.C. - Montgomery County, Ohio
Mu - Muskingum Twp.
Mu.C. - Muskingum County, Ohio
Mvl - Meigsville Twp.
N.H. - New Hampshire (Boscawen)
Np. - Newport Twp.
Nt - Newtown (or Newton) Twp.
N.W. - Northwest Territory
O.C. - Original Certificate
O.G. - Olive Green Twp., (W.C.)
O.G., Mg.C. - Olive Green Twp.,
        Morgan County, Ohio
Oh - Ohio
Oh.C. - Ohio County, Va.
Pa. - Pennsylvania
Pe.C. - Perry County, Ohio
Pit. - Pittsburgh, Pa.
Pkb. - Parkersburg, Va.
Pk.C. - Pickaway County, Ohio
Po.C. - Portage County, Ohio
Pr. - Palmer Twp.

WASHINGTON COUNTY MARRIAGES

R. - First Religious Society
r - Recorded date, rather than
    actual
Ra - Rainbow, Ohio (W.C.)
Ro - Roxbury Twp.
Rs.C. - Ross County, Ohio
Sa - Salem Twp.
Sh.M. - Shrewsbury, Mass.
Sp. - Springfield, Ohio
Sp.M. - Springfield, Mass.
St.C. - Stark County, Ohio
St. L. - St. Louis, Mo.
Tr.C. - Trumbull County, Ohio
Tu - Tuskarawa Township
Twp. - Township, when not other-
    wise designated refers to
    Washington County
Ty.C. - Tyler County, Va.
Un - Union Twp.
Va. - Virginia and parts later W.Va.
Vt. - Vermont

Wa.Pa. - Washington County, Pa.
Way.C. - Wayne County, Ohio
W.C. - Washington County, Ohio
Wd.C. - Wood County, Va.
We - Wesley Twp.
Wec.N.Y. - Westchester, N.Y.
Wf - Waterford Twp.
Wh - Wheeling, Va.
Wn - Warren Twp.
Wo - Wooster Twp.
Wr.,Vt. - Wardsborough, Vt.
Wt. - Watertown Twp.
X - Index
Za - Zanesville, Ohio
* - First Marriage in the Northwest
    Territory
** - Second Marriage in Northwest
    Territory
II - Volume 2 of Washington County
    Marriages in the Court
    House

ABBREVIATIONS
(for Marrying Officials list)

Bapt. - Baptist
Cong. - Congregational
Ch. - Church
Chr. - Christian
Elder - Church Elder
Epis. - Episcopal
J.C.C.C.P. - Judge of County Court
    of Common Pleas
J.P. - Justice of the Peace

J.T.N.W.R.O. - Judge of Territory
    Northwest of the River Ohio
M.E. - Methodist Episcopal
Meth. - Methodist
Pas. - Pastor
Presb. - Presbyterian
R.C. - Roman Catholic
Rev. - Reverend
U.B. - United Brethren
Univ. - Universalist

MARRYING OFFICIALS

1. Allen, Diarca (Rev.)
2. Allison, Andrew, J.P., Adams Twp.
3. Ames, Cyrus, J.P., Belpre Twp.
4. Ames, Jesse M., J.P., Belpre Twp.
5. Archbold, Israel, Meth. Min.
6. Armstrong, Richard, Presb. Min.
7. Arnold, Levi, J.P.
8. Athey, Walter, Meth. Min.

9. Baker, Isaac, J.P.
10. Baker, Seth, J.P., Waterford Twp.
11. Barber, Levi, J.P.
12. Barker, Col. Joseph Sr., (1765-1843) J.P.
12. Barker, Joseph Jr., (1790-1860), J.P., Newport
13. Bartlett, Levi, J.P.
14. Bartlett, Smith, J.P.
15. Batchelder, Ebenezer, J.P.
16. Battelle, Ebenezer, J.P.
17. Beach, Hiram, J.P.
18. Beach, Samuel, J.P., Waterford
19. Beecher, Lyman (Rev.)
20. Berkley, Reuben, Elder Bapt. Ch., Wesley Twp.
21. Bingham, Alvan A., J.P.
22. Bingham, Luther G., Min. First Religious Soc.
23. Blue, Gilbert, Meth. Min.
24. Blue, Samuel (Rev.)
25. Boies, William, Min. Presb. Ch., Waterford
26. Bonnar, James, Rector, St. Lukes, Marietta (Epis.)
27. Booth, James M., J.P., Marietta
28. Bradford, Robert, J.P.
29. Bridges, Jacob, J.P., Warren Twp.
30. Brough, Jacob, J.P.
31. Brough, John, J.P.
32. Brown, Alva, J.P.
33. Brown, Arza, Meth. Min.
34. Brown, Benjamin M., J.P., Wesley Twp.
35. Brown, John (Rev.)
36. Brown, Samuel, J.P.
37. Browning, William, J.P.
38. Buell, Daniel H., J.P., Marietta
39. Buell, Joseph, J.P.
40. Buell, Perez Barnum, J.P., Adams Twp.
41. Burnham, William, J.P., Waterford
42. Burroughs, William, J.P.
43. Burton, Jeremiah (Rev.)
44. Cambell, Richard, J.P., Salem Twp.
45. Carhart, Seth, J.P.
46. Carper, Joseph, Meth. Min.
47. Chamberlain, John D., J.P., Wooster Twp.
48. Chamberlain, Judah M., J.P.
49. Chapman, Joseph, J.P.
50. Chase, Philander, Epis. Bishop of Ohio
51. Cheadle, Asa, J.P.
52. Cheadle, Richard, J.P.
53. Churchill, Jacob, J.P.
54. Clark, Seneca, J.P.
55. Cogswell, Eli, J.P.

56. Cole, Elias, J.P.
57. Cole, Philip, J.P., Warren Twp.
58. Collins, Elliott H., J.P.
59. Collins, John, J.P.
60. Conger, Elias, J.P.
61. Cook, Pardon, Meth. Min.
62. Cook, Salmon N., J.P.
63. Cook, Silas, J.P., Marietta Twp.
64. Cooley, Asahel, J.P.
65. Corp, John S., Meth. Min. and J.P., Aurelius Twp.
66. Cory, Charles S., J.P.
67. Cradlebaugh, Frederic, J.P., Wesley Twp.
68. Crandall, Lester R., J.P.
69. Crawford, Calvin, J.P., Aurelius Twp.
70. Crawford, John, J.P.
71. Crawford, William, J.P.
72. Culbertson, James (Rev.)
73. Cunningham, James (Rev.)
74. Curtis, Horace, J.P.
75. Curtis, John, J.P.
76. Curtis, Walter, J.P.
77. Cushing, Nathaniel, J.P.
78. Cutler, Ephraim, J.C.C.C.P.; J.P.
79. Dale, Jeremiah, Pastor, Marietta Bapt. Ch.
80. Dana, Alfred, Min. Bapt. Ch.
81. Dana, Edmund B., J.P.
82. Dana, George, J.P.
83. Dana, Luther, J.P.
84. Dana, William, J.P.
85. Daniels, Abraham, Meth. Min.
86. Dare, Jeremiah, J.P.
87. Darrow, Allen, Min. Bapt. Ch.
88. Davis, Daniel, J.P., Adams Twp.
89. Davis, David, J.P.
90. Davis, Dudley, J.P., Salem Twp/
91. Davis, Nehemiah, Baptist Min.
92. Davis, William, Min. Bapt. Ch., Roxbury
93. Deming, Simeon, J.P.
94. Devol, Daniel, J.P.
95. De Witt, Levi, J.P.
96. De Witt, Luke (Rev.)
97. Dickerson, Joseph, J.P.
98. Dickey, Solomon, J.P.
99. Doan, Orgillous, J.P.
100. Donahoo, James F., Meth. Min.
101. Donihu, Daniel, J.P.
102. Drown, Notley, J.P.
103. Dunham, Amos, J.P.

WASHINGTON COUNTY MARRIAGES

104. Dunham, Jonathan, J.P.
105. Dunham, Samuel P., Pastor Presb. Ch., Barlow
106. Dunham, William, J.P.
107. Dunlevy, George, J.P.
108. Dunsmore, Hiel, J.P.
109. Dye, Samuel, J.P., Lawrence Twp.
110. Earhart, Jacob, J.P.
111. Edwards, David, Meth. Min.
112. Elliott, Aquilla (Rev.)
113. Emery, Nathan, Meth. Min.
114. Ewart, Robert K., J.P., Grandview Twp.
115. Fairlamb, Samuel, J.P.
116. Ferguson, Thomas, J.P.
117. Fisher, Nathaniel W., Presb. Min.
118. Flagg (Flack), James, J.P.
119. Flint, Daniel, J.P.
120. Foster, Amos, J.P.
121. Foster, Peregrine, J.C.C.C.P.
122. Fox, Absolom D., Meth. Min., Marietta
123. Frisbey, George P., J.P., Roxbury Twp.
124. Frye, Joseph, J.P.
125. Fuller, J., J.P.
126. Fuller, Thomas, J.P.
127. Gard, Hiram, J.P.
128. Gates, Timothy M., J.P.
129. Gear, Hiram, Min, Marietta Bapt. Ch.
130. Gilbert, Eli, J.P.
131. Gilbert, John W., Elder, Meth. Ch.
132. Gilman, Joseph, J.C.C.C.P.
133. Goodno, Daniel, J.P.
134. Goss, Solomon, Min. M.E. Church
135. Graham, James, J.P.
136. Gray, Matthew, J.P.
137. Gray, William, J.P.
138. Green, John, J.P., Adams Twp.
139. Green, Smith, J.P.
140. Greene, Griffin, J.P. and J.C.C.C.P.
141. Greene, John (Rev.)
142. Greene, Philip, Min. M.E. Ch., Newport
143. Greenman, Jeremiah, J.P.
144. Guthrie, Erastus, J.P.
145. Guthrie, Stephen, J.P.
146. Haensel, C. L. F., Epis. Min.
147. Hamilton, Nathaniel, J.P.
148. Hamilton, Samuel, Elder M.E. Ch.
149. Hanby, William, U.B. Min.
150. Handlin, Felix, J.P.
151. Harper, William, J.P.

152. Harris, Timothy, J.P.
153. Harvey, Stillman, J.P.
154. Hastings, Royal, Elder, U.B. Ch.
155. Haynes, Sylvester, J.P.
156. Hendershot, David, J.P.
157. Henry, John, J.P., Watertown Twp.
158. Herr, William, Min. Meth. Ch.
159. Hewitt, Henry (Rev.)
160. Hill, Ira, J.P.
161. Hill, Jesse, J.P.
162. Hobby, Silas, J.P., Fearing Twp.
163. Hoge, James (Rev.)
164. Hooper, Israel (Rev.)
165. Houghland, Cornelius, J.P.
166. Howe, Hiram (Rev.)
167. Howe, Peter, J.P.
168. Howe, Rufus W., J.P., Belpre Twp.
169. Hubner, Lewis, U.B. Min., Gnadenhutten
170. Humphreys, Isaac, J.P., Warren Twp.
171. Hursey, Ariel (Rev.)
172. Hutchins, Hollis, J.P.
173. Jewell, Levi (Rev.)
174. Johnson, Francis H., Univ. Min., Belpre
175. Johnson, John, J.P.
176. Jolly, Henry, J.P.
177. Jolly, William H. (Rev.)
178. Jones, Samuel D. (Rev.)
179. Kenney, John W. (Rev.)
180. Keene, Samuel, J.P., Ludlow Twp.
181. Kent, William J., Min. M.E. Ch.
182. Kimbal, Peter (Rev.)
183. Kimball, Titan, J.P.
184. Kingsbury, Addison, Pastor of Congregational Ch., Belpre and pastor
    Presb. Ch., Warren
185. Knapp, Artemas, J.P.
186. Laflin, Harley, J.P., Barlow Twp.
187. Lambdin, William (Rev.)
188. Langdon, Solomon, Meth. Min.
189. Lawrence, Ami, J.P.
190. Laws, James, Min. Meth. Ch.
191. Learned, Horace, J.P.
192. Leget, Robert, J.P.
193. Lewis, David, Min. Meth. Ch.
194. Limerick, Daniel, Elder Meth. Ch.
195. Lindley (Linsly), Jacob (Rev.)
196. Lindsey, Marcus, Meth. Min.
197. Lindsley (Lindley), Stephen, Presb. Min.
198. Linsley, Joel Harvey (Rev.)

199. Lippett, Abraham, Min. M.E. Church
200. Little, James, J.P.
201. Little, William, J.P.
202. Lord, Thomas, J.P.
203. Loring, Daniel, J.C.C.C.P./and J.P.
204. Low, John, J.P.
205. McAboy, James, Min. Bapt. Ch.
206. McCaffrey, James, R.C. Pastor, Marietta
207. McClanathan, L.C., J.P.
208. McCleary, Thomas, Min. M.E. Ch., Newport
209. McCollum, Samuel (Rev.)
210. McFarland, Osgood, J.P.
211. McGinnis, Edwin, J.P., Middletown Twp.
212. McGowan, Peter M., Min. M.E. Ch., Newport
213. McIntire, David, J.P.
214. McMahon, John (Rev.)
215. Maltby, Erastus (Rev.)
216. Mason, David, J.P.
217. Mason, William, J.P., Adams Twp.
218. Mathews, Ephraim, J.P.
219. Matthews, Philo (Rev.), Wesley Twp.
220. Meigs, Return Jonathan, J.P.
221. Mellor, George, J.P.
222. Melvin, Isaac, J.P., Roxbury Twp.
370. Merrick, F. (Rev.)
223. Merwin, Simon, J.P.
224. Middleswart, Jacob, J.P.
225. Miller, Oliver, J.P.
226. Miller, P. L. (Rev.)
227. Miller, William, J.P.
228. Miner, Israel W., J.P.
229. Minor, John W., Rev., Meth. Ch.
230. Minton, Jacob, J.P., Wesley Twp.
231. Montgomery, Charles P., Pas., R.C. Ch.
232. Moore, Thomas (Rev.)
233. Morey, Asa, J.P.
234. Morris, John C. A., J.P.
235. Morris, Jonathan, Min. Ch. of Christ
236. Morris, Joseph (Rev.)
237. Morris, Thomas A., Meth. Min.
238. Munro, Josiah, J.P., Marietta
239. Myers, Benjamin F., Min. Meth. Ch.
240. Needham, Stephen, J.P.
241. Newton, Oren, J.P.
242. Nixon, William, J.P.
243. Nott, Samuel, J.P.
244. Nye, Anselm T., J.P.
245. Oliver, Robert, J.P.

246. Oliver, William, J.P., Deerfield Twp.
247. Otis, Stephen, J.P.
248. Palmer, Ephraim, J.P.
249. Palmer, Joseph, J.P.
250. Parr, Nathan, J.P., Grandview Twp.
251. Parsons, Horace, Min. Bapt. Ch.
252. Patterson, John, J.P.
253. Paulk, E. Cyrus, J.P.
257. Peirce, Isaac, J.C.C.C.P.
254. Petit, John G., J.C.C.C.P.
255. Petty, Ludwell (Rev.)
256. Pewthers, Elias, J.P.
258. Pitkin, John, Pastor Presb. Ch., Waterford and Watertown
259. Poe, Adam, Min. Meth. Ch.
260. Pool, Simeon, J.P., Deerfield Twp.
261. Porter, Amos, J.P., Salem Twp.
262. Porter, John, J.P.
263. Protsman, Daniel, J.P.
264. Putnam, Charles M. (Rev.)
265. Putnam, Edmund B., J.P.
266. Putnam, Edwin, J.P.
267. Putnam, Rufus, J.T.N.W.R.O.
268. Putnam, William Rufus, J.P.
269. Quinn, Isaac, Meth. Min.
270. Quinn, James, Elder
271. Rand, William, J.P.
272. Raymond, Elnathan, Min. M.E. Ch.
273. Read, John, Elder
274. Rector, Enoch, Baptist Min.
275. Reid, James, R.C. Pastor
276. Ridgeway, Thomas, J.P.
277. Riggs, James, J.P.
278. Robbins, Samuel P., Min. Cong. Ch.
279. Robinson, Abel, Min. M.E. Ch.
280. Robinson, John, J.P.
281. Roe, Edward D., Meth. Min.
282. Rogers, James, J.P.
283. Russell, John, J.P., Union Twp.
284. Sadler, L. L., Min. Univ. Ch.
285. Safford, Robert, J.P., Gallipolis
286. Sage, Harlow P., Min. Univ. Ch.
287. Sargent, John, Min. Chr. Ch.
288. Sawyer, T. J. (Rev.)
289. Scott, Obadiah, J.P., Waterford Twp.
290. Scott, Richard, J.P., Ludlow Twp.
291. Sedwick, George C. (Rev.)
292. Seely, Thomas, J.P.
293. Sharp, James, J.P.

294. Sharp, John, J.P.
295. Sheets, Anthony, J.P., Grandview Twp.
296. Shepard, Enoch, J.P.
297. Shields, David, J.P.
298. Shrader, John, J.P.
299. Simmons, William, Min. Meth. Ch.
300. Skinner, James, Elder
301. Skinner, William P., J.P.
302. Smith, George, J.P.
303. Smith, Henry, J.P.
304. Smithers, David, Min. M.E. Ch.
305. Smithson, John, J.P., Aurelius Twp.
306. Sprague, Anson, J.P., Adams Twp.
307. Sprague, Joshua, J.P.
308. Springer, Cornelius, Meth. Min.
309. Stanley, Daniel G., J.P.
310. Stanley, Thomas, J.P.
311. Stedman, Bial, J.P., Belpre Twp.
312. Stedman, Eli, J.P.
313. Stearns, Asa, Elder, Bapt. Ch.
314. Stephens (Stevens), David, J.P.
315. Stone, Derrick, J.P.
316. Stone, Sardine, J.P., Union Twp.
317. Story, Daniel, Clerk C.C.C.P. and Cong. Min.
318. Strickland, Joseph, J.P.
319. Stirckland, William P., Elder, Meth. Ch.
320. Swan, L. R., J.P.
321. Sweet, Alpheus, Min. Univ. Ch.
322. Swormstedt, Leroy, Meth. Min., Marietta
323. Talbot, Benjamin, J.P., Meigsville
324. Taylor, Edward H., Min. Meth. Ch.
325. Taylor, Richard, J.P.
326. Templeton, George, J.P.
327. Thatcher, Tyler (Rev.)
328. Thompson, Enos, Min. Meth. Ch.
329. Townsend, Edward, J.P.
330. True, John, J.P., Salem Twp.
331. Tupper, Benjamin, J.C.C.C.P.
332. Tuttle, Joel, J.P. and Univ. Min.
333. Tuttle, Simeon, J.P.
334. Vandermark, Elias, Min. U.B. Ch.
335. Varnum, Moses, J.P.
336. Vaughn, Ely, J.P.
337. Vincent, Henry E., J.P.
338. Walker, Thomas, J.P.
339. Ward, Nahum, Mayor, Marietta
340. Washburn, Seth, J.P.
341. Wells, Joseph C., J.P.

342. West, William, J.P.
343. Wheat, John T., Rector St. Lukes Epis., Marietta
344. White, David, J.P.
345. White, John H., J.P.
346. White, Peletiah, J.P., Waterford Twp.
347. White, Thomas, J.P., Roxbury Twp.
348. Whiting, James, J.P., Marietta
349. Whitney, James, J.P.
350. Whitney, John (Rev.)
351. Whitney, Nathan, J.P.
352. Wickes, Thomas, Min. Cong. Ch.
353. Williamson, Moses, J.P.
354. Williamson, Samuel, J.P., Newport
355. Wilson, Amos, J.P.
356. Wilson, Johnston, J.P., Roxbury Twp.
369. Wilson, R. G. (Rev.)
357. Wing, Enoch, J.P.
358. Witten, Philip, J.P.
359. Wolf, Reece (Rev.), Wood Co., Va.
360. Wood, Rasellus, J.P.
361. Woodford, Seth, J.P.
362. Woodford, William, J.P., Watertown
363. Woodruff, Isaac, J.P., Barlow Twp.
364. Woodward, Oliver, J.P.
365. Wright, James S., U.B. Min.
366. Young, David, Meth. Min.
367. Young, Jacob, Methodist Min.
368. Young, William, Min. M.E. Ch.
369. Wilson, R.G. (Rev.)
370. Merrick, F. (Rev.)

Abbey, Elijah (Wf); Gates, Ruby (Wf); 31 July 1823; (18); 130
Abbot, Phillip (Ma); Sandburn, Polly (Ma); 1 Feb. 1810; (278); 65
Abbot, Thomas P. (Ma); Dickey, Lucy (Un); 8 Oct. 1825; (27); 156
Abbot, Wm. (Ma); Reece, Nancy Jane (Ma); 6 Feb. 1837; (63); 373
Abbott, John; Biggerstaff, Sarah; 8 Feb. 1803; (151); NW-6
Ackerson, Abram (Ro); Kent, Eleanor (Ro); 18 Sept. 1828; (282); NW-215
Ackerson, Edward (Ro); Jarvis, Jane (Ro); 6 Mar. 1828; (282); 206
Ackerson, Jacob (We); Wilson, Nancy (Wt); 18 Sept. 1831; (66); 270
Adams, George (Wn); Hutchinson, Elizabeth (Wn); 17 Apr. 1822; (75); 123
Adams, George W. (Wn); Clark, Anna (Wn); 19 Jan. 1826; (102); 174
Adams, James (Ro); Bailey, Harriet (Un); 5 Oct. 1813; (147); 78
Adams, Joel; Miller, Love P.; 17 June 1834; (123); 325
Adams, John; Powell, Eliza; 19 Dec. 1839; (290); 444
Adams, Rollin B.; Perkins, Mary; 7 June 1837; (63); 378
Adams, Volney (Wt); Miller, Mary (Wt); 24 Mar. 1831; (24); 263
Adkisson, Wm.; Templeton, Jane; 8 Mar. 1838; (290); 396
Afflick, Wm. (Va); Mitchell, Phebe (La); 27 Dec. 1821; (109); 122
Aikman, Eliab B. (Un); Judd, Amanda (Ma); 28 Apr. 1825; (127); 149
Akins, Robert Jr. (Df); Nash, Elizabeth (Df); 10 Dec. 1818; (237); 105
Alcock, Richard (Ma); Case, Eliza (Ma); 20 Nov. 1806; (340); 53
Alcock, Richard (Ma); Buell, Wealthy (Ma); 30 Dec. 1813; (278); 79
Alcock, Thomas (Ma); Wells, Sally (Ma); 1 May 1813; (197); 77
Alcock, Washington; Hoff, Polly; 8 July 1838; (33); 405
Alcock, William (Ma); Posey, Frances (Ma); 24 Mar. 1811; (197); 69
Alcock, William (Ma); Posey, Sally (Ma); 26 Jan. 1820; (38); 112
Alcock, Wm.; White, Polly; 5 May 1840; (129); M.G. v-3 #22
Alderman, Asabel A.; Biderson, Eliza Ann; 9 Oct. 1838; (219); 414
Alderman, Hezekiah (A.C.); Vincent, Lucinda (Ba); 4 Oct. 1837; (192); 387
Alderman, Julius S. (A.C.); Lumpkins, Lucy A. (Ma); 26 Nov. 1831; (85); 275
Aleehart, Christopher; Nedick, Joanna; 17 Sept. 1840; (216); 468
Alexander, James (Un); Howe, Lucinda (Un); 16 May 1819; (283); 109
Alexander, John (Ad); Sinclair, Polly (Ad); 17 Mar. 1825; (316); 147
Allard, Reuben (Be); Allen, Polly (Be); 13 Dec. 1818; (145); 107
Allard, Samuel (Be); Maxson, Laurana (Fe); 31 May 1819; (309); 109
Allen, Elisha (Ma); Perkins, Elizabeth (Sa); 6 Oct 1808; (197); 59
Allen, Ethan (Ma); Dye, Patience (La); 19 April 1840; (109); 459
Allen, Ethan H.; Benedict, Irene (Be); 27 Aug. 1834; (184); 329
Allen, James (W.C.); McBride, Mary (W.C.); 19 Dec. 1815; (49); 87
Allen, John; Misner, Sally; 28 Dec. 1814; (145); 83M
Allen, Dr. John (Cin); Dana, Charlotte (Wa); 19 April 1835; (195); M.G. v-1 #211

WASHINGTON COUNTY MARRIAGES

Allen, Justus; Devol, Polly (Wf); 23 June 1791; ; NW-5
Allen, Samuel; Glidden, Lydia; 24 Jan. 1818; (309); 100M
Allison, Alexander; Cyphert, Nancy; 25 Nov. 1817; (283); 99M
Allison, Andrew (Ad); Sinclair, Nancy (Un); 4 Apr. 1822; (138); 123
Allison, Charles (Ad); Stutts, Hester (Ad); 24 June 1812; (141); 77
Allison, Charles (Ad); Allison, Sally (Ad); 11 March 1816; (316); 89
Allison, Hugh (Ad); Neel, Patience (Ad); 27 Aug. 1809; (91); 6
Allison, Hugh (Ad); Davis, Drusilla (Ad); 24 May 1827; (316); 188
Allison, Josiah (Wf); Baldwin, Julia (Wf); 22 Mar. 1840; (80); 460
Allison, Robert (Ad); Burch, Mrs. Rhoda (Ad); 25 July 1825; (40); 154
Allison, Stephen (Ad); Kinney, Abigail (Ad); 18 May 1820; (355); 115
Allison, William (W.C.); Kinney, Elizabeth (W.C.); 29 May 1814; (193); 81
Ames, Cyrus (Be); More, Azuba (Be); 3 May 1801; (257); NW-51
Ames, David; Williams, Sarah; 24 May 1838; (311); 410
Ames, Jesse M. (Be); Robbins, Sibul (Be); 3 Aug. 1827; (321); 192
Ames, Joseph; Tilson, Ida; 23 Oct. 1815; (283); 86M
Amlin, Henry S. (Fe); O'Bleniss, Gertrude (La); 30 Dec. 1830; (96); 257
Amlin, Henry T.; Obleness, Maria; 6 Feb. 1838; (33); 399
Amlin, James (W.C.); Campbell, Nancy (W.C.); 2 Jan. 1798; (238); NW-29
Amlin, James M.; Sharp, Eliza; 20 Jan. 1825; (332); 144
Amlin, John Jr. (W.C.); Campbell, Jean (W.C.); 22 Oct. 1799; (310); NW-40
Amlin, Samuel (Sa); Mitchel, Betsey (Sa); 26 June 1806; (197); 52
Amlin, Samuel; Hill, Jane; 30 Mar. 1823; (326); 133
Amlin, Samuel Jr. (Ma); Bowen, Mary Ann (Ma); 22 Dec. 1825; (27); 161
Amos, Benjamin (Jo); Eaton, Susanna (Jo); 29 Oct. 1840; (201); II-1
Amsbury, Otis (Ma); Carver, Mary (Ma); 27 Mar. 1814; (197); 80
Anders, Joseph (Ma); Smith, Adaline (Ma); 29 Apr. 1830; (301); 241
Anders, Moses G. (Ma); Harvey, Elizabeth (Wn); 2 Dec. 1830; (184); 256
Anderson, David B. (Ma); Hall, Eunice (Ma); 3 Sept. 1821; (278); 120
Anderson, Edward (Ma); Calvin, Sally (Ma); 24 July 1804; (64); 43
Anderson, Josiah; Berkinsha, Anna; 10 May 1838; (168); 403
Anderson, Lewis (Ma); Fulton, Elinor (Ma); 11 Feb. 1804; (31); 40
Anderson, Lewis (Ma); Hickman, Martha (Ma); 5 Mar. 1808; (197); 57
Anderson, Lewis Jr.; Hildreth, Louisa (Ma); 15 Apr. 1833; (63); 301
Andrews, Cyrus (Fe); Hait, Jerusha (Fe); 25 Apr. 1824; (162); 134
Andrews, David; McMullen, Betsy; 5 Jan. 1817; (223); 100M
Andrews, Prof. Israel W. (Ma); Clark, Sarah Hayes (Ct); 8 Aug. 1839; M.I.
     v-1 #1
Andrews, John; Jarrett, Sally; 15 June 1815; (249); 85M
Andrews, John; Dutton, Margaret; 14 Sept. 1818; (62); 104M
Andrews, Samuel (Ma); Morris, Elizabeth (Ma); 3 Dec. 1812; (197); 76
Andrews, Samuel (Mg.C.); Evans, Polly (Ro); 30 Nov. 1826; (34); 177
Angle, Peter (Wt); Woodmansee, Mary (Wt); 4 Sept. 1839; (157); 439
Ankram, Jacob (Ma); Porter, Nancy (Ma); 25 Sept. 1806; (197); 51
Ankrom, John; Jolly, Rachel; 27 June 1839; (58); 436
Ankrom, Linsey (W.C.); Franks, Margaret (W.C.); 22 Aug. 1816; (223); 91
Archbold, Rev. Israel; Dana, Frances F. (Np); 25 Sept. 1834; (228); 329
Archer, Joseph (Va); Wells, Sarah (Va); 8 Sept. 1801; (358); NW-48

2

WASHINGTON COUNTY MARRIAGES

Archer, Michael (W.C.); Granden, Rhoda (W.C.); 7 June 1810; (261); 66
Archer, Patrick (Ma); Petty, Lydia (Ma); 13 Mar. 1814; (38); 79
Armintage, George (A.C.); Ward, Maria (Be); 28 Apr. 1825; (311); 151
Armitage, Joshua (Ma); Thornelly, Harriet (Ma); 9 June 1807; (278); 55
Armstrong, Harvey (Ma); Stephenson, Sarah (Ma); 21 Sept. 1824; (38); 138
Armstrong, Lewis (Sa); Broom, Betsy (Sa); 16 Feb. 1832; (44); 278
Armstrong, Wm. (Ma); Byard, Sarah M. (Ma); 4 Sept. 1836; (63); 366
Arnold, Noah (Ma); Chadwick, Nancy (Ma); 20 Nov. 1803; (31); 40
Askins, Edward; Solomon, Mary; 1 Jan. 1839; (209); 425
Atchinson, John (W.C.); Fulton, Elizabeth (W.C.); 24 Apr. 1800; (310); NW-40
Atchinson, Reuben; Seamans, Polly; 20 Jan. 1801; (238); NW-43
Athey, John (Ma); Miller, Ruth H. (A.C.); 17 Nov. 1833; (125); M.G. v-1 #21
Athey, Solomon (Fe); Hill, Lucinda N. (Fe); 24 Sept. 1840; (59); II-10
Athey, Thomas (Fe); Covey, Polly (Un); 22 June 1826; (332); 169
Athey, Walter Jr. (Wf); Johnson, Asenath (Wf); 18 Aug. 1830; (192); 248
Atkinson, John (Ba); Woodruff, Maria (Ba); 15 Mar. 1832; (34); 279
Atkinson, Wm. D.; Arwin, Jean; 29 Aug. 1799; (285); NW-36
Atkisson, James; Templeton, Margaret; 1 Nov. 1838; (290); 415
Avery, John (Np); Roach, Mary Ann (Np); 25 June 1840; (68); 461
Ayles, Elias (Sa); Walker, Mary (Sa); 20 Apr. 1814; (227); 81
Aymes, Cyrus (Be); Rice, Polly (Be); 17 Mar. 1810; (133); 65

Babcock, George C.; Morse, Louisa M.; 26 Oct, 1831; (122); 271
Babcock, Joseph B.; Druse, Melissa; 10 July 1828; (322); 209
Bacon, Martin (Wf); Hurlbut, Mary M. (Wt); 25 Aug. 1829; (66); 230
Bacon, William (Wo); Mellor, Eleanor (Wo); 9 Mar. 1817; (346); 94
Bacon, William (Wf); Vincent, Nancy (Wf); 6 Sept. 1835; (192); 352
Badgley, William L. (Wt); Wilson, Betsey (Wt); 18 Oct. 1832; (360); 288
Bahrenburg, John Henry; Bohling, Barby; Mar. 1840; (319); 461
Bailey, Caleb (Be); James, Anne (Be); 24 July 1791; (331); NW-5
Bailey, Charles P. (Wn); Chapman, Harriet (Fe); 28 Sept. 1837; (184); 385
Bailey, Emery (Fe); Maxson, Sophronia (Fe); 4 Apr. 1827; (332); 189
Bailey, James L.; Amlin, Sarah Ann; 4 Dec. 1834; (87); 336
Bailey, James Willard (Be); Cannon, Rachel (Be); 3 Oct. 1815; (3); 88
Bailey, John (Wn); Chapman, Mary (Fe); 7 Jan. 1836; (184); 357
Bailey, John D.; Hill, Maria; 30 Oct. 1834; (87); 335
Bailey, John Jr. (Mi); Farmer, Sarah (Mi); 29 Jan. 1800; (21); NW-37
Bailey, Martin (Be); Clark, Betsey (Be); 24 Apr. 1809; (81); 62
Bailey, Martin (Wn); Hanley, Mrs. Elizabeth (Ma); 14 May 1836; (85); 364
Bailey, Peter (Wn); Stowell, Mary Ann (Wn); 1 Dec. 1832; (103); 292
Bailey, Seth Jr. (Wn); McCluer, Sarah D. (Wn); 31 Dec. 1833; (184); 316
Bailey, Simon (Ro); Bailey, Louisa (Ro); 27 Nov. 1837; (256); 391
Bailey, Washington (Ma); Buck, Eliza (Ma); 10 Sept. 1820; (27); 116
Bailey, William (Mg.C.); Sanders, Mary A. (W.C.); 5 Oct. 1837; (256); 385
Bailey, William L.; Bailey, Maria N.; 3 May 1840; (29); 457
Bainter, George; Smith, Lucy; 21 Apr. 1830; (306); 239

3

WASHINGTON COUNTY MARRIAGES

Baird, Robert Jr. (Ma); Grigsby, Leah (Ma); 25 Nov. 1810; (197); 69
Baker, Alpheus (Ba); Chapman, Mary (Wt); 12 Jan. 1826; (34); 164
Baker, Barton W. (Ma); Kemple, Lucretia Ann (Ma); 27 Dec. 1833; (259); 318
Baker, Benjamin; Newton, Sarah; 1 Sept. 1791; (331); NW-6
Baker, Benjamin; Shuey, Sophia; 27 July 1836; (13); 366
Baker, Benjamin Jr. (Ba); Gard, Polly (Ba); 1 Jan. 1827; (34); 178
Baker, Darius (Ba); Palmer, Ivah F. (Ba); 7 Apr. 1840; (186); 455
Baker, Isaac (Wf); Dodge, Susanna M. (Wf); 19 Apr, 1804; (93); 41
Baker, Isaac (Mg.C.); Nulton, Mary (Wt); 16 Dec. 1830; (297); 255
Baker, James (Wo); White, Sophia (Wo); 29 June 1817; (183); 96
Baker, James (Wo); Alden, Sarah (Ro); 13 Sept. 1821; (347); 120
Baker, John (Np); Taylor, Elizabeth (Np); 25 Jan. 1838; (109); 393
Baker, Martin (Mn.C.); Farley, Nancy (La); 5 Apr. 1831; (109); 266
Baker, John; Ralston, Sarah; 28 Apr. 1840; (123); 456
Baker, Seth (Wf); VanValey, Phebe (Wf); 14 Oct. 1810; (137); 66
Baker, Samuel Jr. (Wf); Kelly, Margaret (Ma); 16 Dec. 1795; (245); NW-15
Baker, Thomas (Ma); Williams, Elizabeth (Ma); 7 Apr. 1808; (31); 57
Baker, Ulysses (Wt); Riley, Mary A. (Ba); 19 June 1835; (281); 346
Baker, William (Sa); Beiber, Jane (Sa); 19 Feb. 1801; (169); NW-44
Baldwin, Coleman (Wt); Norman, Lucinda (Wt); 7 Sept. 1836; (38); 367
Baldwin, Isaac L. (Ro.); Blackmer, Mary (Ro); 4 Dec. 1817; (347); 98
Baldwin, James P.; Wells, Cynthia; 28 Oct. 1830; (274); 258
Baldwin, Jesse (Sa); Hill, Mary (Sa); 1 Jan. 1805; (90); 47
Baldwin, Stephen P. (Ad); Owens, Azaba (Ad); 18 Mar. 1830; (274); 237
Baley, James (Wo); Allington, Phebe (Ma); 30 Apr. 1816; (293); 89
Ball, Abraham (Be); Fletcher, Sally (Be); 16 Aug. 1818; (3); 106
Ball, Henry; Wyor, Milia; 6 Dec. 1832; (130); 294
Ball, John; Barnes, Loraney; 16 Nov. 1825; (311); 159
Ball, Samuel B. (Be); Shipman, Polly (De); 14 Jan. 1838; (155); 393
Ballantine, Wm. (Ad); Kimberly, Elizabeth (Ad); 1 Nov. 1838; (2); 415
Ballard, Joseph; Doyl, Mary; 14 Sept. 1802; (151); NW-57
Ballard, Z. B.; Cole, Mary Ann; 21 Oct. 1840; (70); 473
Bancroft, Samuel (Grl); Rose, Clarissa (Grl); 28 May 1807; (278); R-76
Barber, Levi (W.C.); Roun, Betsey (W.C.); 15 Feb. 1803; (317); NW-61
Barber, Levi; Kelly, Abigail; 31 Oct. 1837; (33); 392
Barber, Reuben; Norman, Harriet; 2 Nov. 1839; (256); 441
Bardmass, John (La); Snodgrass, Margaret (La); 2 Nov. 1820; (89); 117
Barker, Daniel (Un); Varnum, Mary (Un); 22 Aug. 1813; (316); 77
Barker, Francis A.; Barker, Catherine; 10 Apr. 1827; (322); 185
Barker, George (W.C.); Devol, Emeline (W.C.); 3 May 1831; (22); 289
Barker, Isaac (Mi); Harper, Christina (Mi); 10 Apr. 1804; (135); 41
Barker, Joseph Jr. (Np); Stone, Melissa W. (Be); 11 May 1817; (278); 96
Barker, Joseph Jr. (W.C.); Shipman, Mary Ann (Mrs.) (W.C.); 28 June 1831;
   (22); 289
Barker, Luther D. (Un); Devol, Maria (Un); 6 Mar. 1821; (278); 120
Barker, Michael; Harper, Isabella; 1 Apr. 1801; (151); NW-50
Barkley, Samuel; Burroughs, Nancy; 5 Mar. 1818; (35); 103M
Barnes, Ephraim; Wedge, Mrs. Betsey; 22 Nov. 1827; (311); 382

4

WASHINGTON COUNTY MARRIAGES

Barnes, Jeremiah R.; Webster, Caroline M.; 26 Sept. 1839; (198); 441
Barnett, John; Palmer, Mary; 30 May 1839; (2); 433
Barnhart, Asa, (Lu); Barnhart, Rosanna (Lu); 2 Oct. 1829; (261); 233
Barnhart, Jacob (Gr); Oppe, Sarah (Gr); 16 May 1824; (353); 134
Barns, Lewis; Sloan, Pamela; 15 Aug. 1830; (311); 250
Barns, Samuel (W.C.); Goodale, Cynthia (W.C.); 22 Aug. 1793; (203); NW-7
Barnwell, Matthew (W.C.); Wait, Mrs. Lois (W.C.); 1 Dec. 1821; (38); 122
Baron, Charles (B.C.); Zigler, M. W. F. C. L. F. (Ma); 22 Apr. 1830; (63); 240
Barr, James (Be); Smith, Polly (Be); 3 Aug. 1817; (3); 96
Barr, John (Ba); Fish, Sarah (Ba); 27 Sept. 1838; (337); 410
Barr, Samuel (Be); Pennell, Mrs. Sarah (Be); 22 June 1813; (77); 77
Barr, Samuel (W.C.); Terey, Mary (W.C.); 22 Feb. 1816; (165); 89
Barrett, Henry (Ma); Lincoln, Sarah (Ma); 5 Sept. 1830; (63); 250
Barrett, John H.; Lucas, Mary Ann; 29 June 1834; (224); 325
Barrows, Albert G.; Allen, Clarissa; 23 Nov. 1833; (130); 313
Barrows, Henry (Mi); Hewitt, Bethial (Mi); 28 July 1799; (238); NW-36
Barstow, Albert; Corner, Persis R.; 13 Apr. 1838; (129); 403
Barstow, Henry E.; Woodward, Caroline; 14 Mar. 1839; (87); 460
Barstow, Horace (Np); Richardson, Olive (Np); 7 July 1837; (129); 380
Barstow, Isaac; Rathburn, Frances; 30 Sept. 1824; (194); 138
Barthalow, Thomas; Foster, Mary; 10 July 1836; (224); 364
Bartlett, Amos (Wo); Rardon, Mary (Wo); 16 Sept. 1806; (245); 51
Bartlett, Amos (We); Gerrard, Elizabeth (We); 18 Nov. 1830; (230); 265
Bartlett, Henry (Ma); Taylor, Mary (Ma); 14 June 1832; (38); 281
Bartlett, Daniel (Wo); Chamberlin, Melisa (Wo); 24 Oct. 1824; (362); 140
Bartlett, Jacob; Rubel, Margaret; 20 Apr. 1837; (13); 379
Bartlett, John (Wt); Reeder, Sophia (Wt); 20 Nov. 1827; (106); 202
Bartlett, Levi, Esq. (Un); Dickey, Maria (Un); 26 Oct. 1837; (70); 388
Bartlett, Smith (Un); Willis, Mary (Un); 9 June 1825; (283); 151
Bartlett, Wirum (W.C.); Kinney, Sally D. (W.C.); 3 Feb. 1819; (138); 106
Bartley, David (Ma); Canor, Rachel (Ma); 10 July 1806; (31); 51
Bartmess, Jacob (W.C.); Templeton, Mrs. Eliza (W.C.); 16 Dec. 1824; (109); 142
Bartmess, Samuel (W.C.); Kennedy, Mary (W.C.); 22 Aug. 1822; (53); 126
Bartmess, Septimus (Fe); Palmer, Rebecca (La); 29 June 1830; (109); 245
Barton, Robert C.; Vanduyn, Rachel B.; 6 Apr. 1815; (197); 84M
Bassett, Wm. (We); Swesey, Jane (We); 16 Sept. 1837; (256); 386
Batchelor, Isaac (Ro); Randles, Nancy (Ro); 23 Dec. 1830; (222); 258
Batkin, Charles; White, Experience (W.C.); 28 July 1840; (236); 467
Battelle, Cornelius D.; Greenwood, Elizabeth (Np); 13 July 1829; (212); 227
Battle, Francis (Ma); Welch, Abigail (Ma); 21 May 1801; (268); NW-49
Baughey, Jacob (Ma); Gilpin, Eliza D. (Un); 2 Mar. 1838; (63); 375
Bayard, James W. (A.C.); Scott, Joanna (W.C.); 11 July 1837; (256); 382
Beach, Ebenezer M. (Ky); Whiting, Susan (Be); 23 Nov. 1831; (184); 276
Beach, Hiram (Ma); Mixer, Almonia (Ma); 15 July 1829; (38); 226
Beach, Jesse (Wt); Beswick, Elizabeth (Wt); 8 Apr. 1830; (361); 240
Beach, John; Gushing, Alimira; 11 Jan. 1825; (189); 143
Beach, Rugus; Tompkins, Emily B.; 18 Aug. 1840; (70); 475
Beal, William (Ma); Jones, Mary (Ma); 26 Dec. 1805; (197); 48

5

Beardsley, Phineas (Au); Gevrez, Mary Ann (Au); 26 Feb. 1820; (48); 114
Beaudeau, Francis (Ga); Demier, Jeanette (Ga); 9 Sept. 1791; (254); NW-9
Beaudot, Jean (Ga); Margeret, Margarette (Ga); 4 March 1794; (254); NW-11
Beaver, John (Nt); Baker, Catharine (Nt); 3 Oct. 1799; (303); NW-49
Bebee, Collin; Hall, Sarah; 29 May 1834; (4); 324
Beck, John; Rea, Eliza; 11 Dec. 1838; (255); 416
Beck, Vivian (Gr); Price, Sarah (Gr); 22 Dec. 1836; (114); 375
Beckett, William (Wf); Vincent, Clarinda (Wf); 13 Sept. 1837; (20); 384
Bee, Joseph Jr.; Mosser, Sarah; 19 May 1839; (290); 432
Beebe, Alexander W. (Wt); Brown, Hannah (Wt); 7 Aug. 1828; (361); 214
Beebe, Hopson; Warren, Rebecca; 3 Apr. 1826; (311); 166
Beebe, Richard (Wt); Wolcott, Vilate S. (Wt); 6 Oct. 1839; (70); 447
Beebe, Thomas P. (Wt); Skipton, Catharine (Wt); 8 Mar. 1830; (361); 238
Beebe, William (Be); Loring, Mary (Be); 17 Feb. 1817; (3); 96
Beedle, Benjamin (Hk.C.); Cushing, Bersheba (Wf); 29 Dec. 1818; (271); 106
Beedle, David (Un); McGeehan, Nancy (Un); 27 Feb. 1838; (263); 395
Belknap, Forest (Wf); Bateman, Sarah (Wf); 21 Feb. 1813; (55); 75
Bell, Hiram (Np); McCabe, Margaret (Be); 25 June 1839; (344); 434
Bell, John (Ma); Pool, Nancy (Ma); 20 July 1804; (30); 43
Bell, John R.; Calman, Mary; 2 Apr. 1840; (123); 449
Bell, Johnson (Ma); Francis, Susanna (Ma); 15 Apr. 1804; (31); 41
Bell, Joseph (Np); Williamson, Deborah (Ma); 1 Sept. 1839; (129); M.G.v-2 #40
Bell, Nathan (Ba); Bell, Charlotte (Np); 18 Oct. 1838; (129); 423
Bell, Samuel (Np); Bell, Elizabeth (Ba); 21 Aug. 1828; (258); 215
Bell, Samuel; Wood, Mrs. Lucy; 21 Dec. 1839; (319); 445
Bellows, Benj. (Be); Littleton, Elizabeth (Be); 6 Dec. 1804; (203); 45
Bellows, Elias (Be); Ellenwood, Martha (Be); 28 June 1814; (269); 81
Bellows, Elias; Shukes, Mary; 20 June 1830; (144); 247
Bellows, Elias (Be); Poe, Clarinda (Be); 25 Feb. 1838; (344); 396
Bellows, Ira (Be); Bellows, Maria (Be); 13 Nov. 1834; (144); 332
Benbibber, Jesse (Va); Greenlee, Rachel (Va); 9 July 1799; (285); NW-35
Benjamin, William (Wo); Nott, Rhoda (Wo); 2 Dec. 1819; (47); 111
Bennett, John; Burker, Mary; 9 Jan. 1826; (190); 168
Bennett, Joseph P.; Beebe, Polly; 25 Nov. 1810; (37); 67M
Bensley, James (Wf); Pope, Catharine (Wf); 11 Oct. 1816; (346); 92
Bent, Abner (Be); Williams, Eliza (Ma); 18 Jan. 1802; (317); NW-52
Bent, Abner (Be); Dilley, Betsey (Be); 20 Jan. 1817; (3); 94
Bent, Daniel (Be); Rowland, Betsey (Np); 16 Feb. 1826; (79); 162
Bent, Nahum (Be); Dilly, Susan (Be); 16 Mar. 1810; (37); 65
Bernard, Michel (Ma); Chandevert, Marie M. (Ma); 20 May 1797; (132); NW-27
Best, Henry (Sa); Neushifen, Christiana (Sa); 25 Jan. 1838; (247); 395
Beswick, George (Ha); Biggins, Elizabeth (Wt); 29 June 1837; (207); 379
Beswick, James P. (Wt); Thorniley, Augusta E. (Ma); 10 Dec. 1825; (12); 160
Beswick, Matthew (Ha); Smith, Lydia A. (Ha); 9 Mar. 1840; (70); 447
Beswick, Wm. (Wt); Abbot, Eliza (We); 19 July 1832; (297); 284
Bethel, Edward; Swank, Pemelia; 11 Nov. 1802; (245); NW-60
Bickford, Joshua Jr. (Be); Springer, Abigail (Be); 24 June 1820; (3); 115
Bickfort, Isaac (W.C.); Ellinwood, Lucy (W.C.); 10 Feb. 1823; (308); 128

Biddle, Benj.; Convis, Abigail; 26 Sept. 1791; (331); NW-6
Biddle, Samuel (Gr); Dickenson, Elizabeth (Gr); 14 Aug. 1808; (358); 57
Bierce, Columbus (Be); Curtis, Mary (Be); 17 Nov. 1816; (145); 93
Bigford, John (Be); Haight, Mary (Be); 8 Dec. 1818; (148); 107
Biggerstaff, John (Mi); Lewis, Mary (Mi); 9 Nov. 1802; (21); NW-58
Biggins, John (Wf); Orison, Sarah (Wf); 7 Jan. 1804; (195); 40
Bills, Levi; Wheeler, Maria; 28 Aug. 1817; (278); 99M
Bingham, Joel S. (Vt); Robbin, Jane (Ma); 21 Aug. 1838; (198); 408
Birdsil, Abram; Carolle, Margaret (Wf); 4 Dec. 1828; (66); 216
Bishop, Gilbert Jr. (Ba); Ford, Harriet (Wt); 14 Feb. 1828; (258); 204
Bishop, Isaac N. (Mg.C.); Seely, Lusetta A. M.; 4 Aug. 1830; (192); 248
Bishop, Joshua (Ba); Dunbar, Nancy (Ba); 25 June 1822; (62); 125
Bishop, Nathaniel (Ma); Giles, Elizabeth (Ma); 23 Oct. 1814; (31); 82
Bizer, John (Wn); Finch, Samantha (Be); 9 Nov. 1826; (241); 176
Bizer, John (Ma); Silverton, Elizabeth (Ma); 26 Mar. 1835; (103); 342
Black, Thomas; Johnson, Mrs. Elizabeth; 8 Jan. 1815; (293); 83M
Blackinton, Jason B. (Ky); Cone, Martha S. (Wn); 29 Sept. 1836; (22); M.G.v-2 #47
Blackstone, Ebenezer (Wf); White, Sophia (Wf); 11 Jan. 1810; (197); 64
Blake, Benjamin (Fe); Stanley, Lucy (Fe); 4 Apr. 1813; (73); 75
Blake, Simeon (W.C.); Peck, Lavina (W.C.); 14 Dec. 1797; (238); NW-28
Blancett, David (Ma); Rood, Sylvina (Ma); 8 Nov. 1838; (129); 423
Blanset, Wm. (Ma); Rood, Mrs. Cyrena (Ma); 26 Dec. 1839; (63); 445
Blansett, Wm. (Fe); Nash, Nancy (Fe); 15 May 1824; (162); 134
Blin, Andress; Twitty, Amelia; 29 May 1830; (63); 243
Bliu, Francois (Ga); Davous, Francis (Ga); 8 Nov. 1795; (254); NW-17
Bliss, James (Ma); Byser, Catharine (Ma); 23 Mar. 1823; (38); 128
Blizard, Mason (A.C.); Monroe, Hannah (Be); 31 May 1822; (76); 125
Blizzard, Brooks; Beebe, Mrs. Mary; 27 Mar. 1825; (313); 148
Blough, Jonathan (Be); Dilley, Rebecca (Be); 6 Feb. 1823; (181); 127
Boalt, Eben (Hu.C.); Comstock, Hannah (Wf); 31 Aug. 1820; (271); 116
Bobo, Israel; Graham, Margaret; 2 Apr. 1801; (151); NW-50
Bobo, Martin (Mi); Ross, Sarah (Mi); 2 Aug 1804; (135); 43
Bodkin, Richard (Be); Withington, Betsey (Be); 19 Sept. 1813; (278); 79
Bodkin, Richard (Be); McCullouch, Mrs. Mary (Ma); 25 Feb. 1827; (27); 188
Bodwell, Enoch (W.C.); Bell, Elizabeth (W.C.); 4 Mar. 1817; (165); 94
Boles, Samson (A.C.); Farnham, Lydia (Ro); 13 Dec. 1832; (66); 295
Bond, Alfred G. (Va); Allen, Pamelia (Wf); 10 May 1830; (148); 244
Boomer, Almon; Dempsey, Sarah; 5 May 1831; (63); 264
Boomer, Gilbert; Cromer, Margaret; 4 June 1829; (148); 224
Booth, James M. (Ma); Alcock, Sally (Ma); 1 Mar. 1812; (197); 72
Boothby, Robert (Ma); Chambers, Isabella (Ma); 30 Mar. 1823; (278); 129
Borden, William; Harris, Susanna; 19 July 1815; (171); 85M
Borer, John (Be); Moss, Anna M. W. (Wn); 22 Feb. 1827; (38); 179
Boring, Benjamin (Wn); Skinner, Piety (Un); 4 Jan. 1832; (63); 276
Bosworth, Charles (Ma); Wilson, Betsy (Ma); 23 Sept. 1820; (278); 118
Bosworth, Daniel P.; Dodge, Hannah; 8 Aug. 1824; (194); 136
Bosworth, Sala (Ma); Shipman, Joanna F. (Ma); 17 Oct. 1839; (198); 441

7

Bosworth, Sumner; Chambers, Mary; 11 Oct. 1838; (70); 413, 414
Bosworth, Wm. A.; Agell, Mary; 29 Mar. 1835; (229); 341
Bosworth, Zepheniah (Ma); Burlinggame, Lucy (Ma); 27 Mar. 1817; (278); 96
Boudinot, John (Wf); Williams, Margaret (Wf); 14 Oct. 1817; (252); 98
Bowen, Daniel (Gr); Knight, Elizabeth (Gr); 17 Oct. 1811; (358); 71
Bowen, Dr. George (Wf); Wheeler, Joanna (Ct); 13 Feb. 1837; (159); M.G.v-3 #15
Bowen, James (Wf); Cushing, Betsey (Wf); 23 Sept. 1818; (271); 105
Bowen, James (Wf); Wheeler, Catharine Ann (Wt); 4 Mar. 1834; (96); 320
Bowen, John (Gr); Scott, Eleanor (Gr); 28 July 1811; (358); 70
Bowen, Nathan (W.C.); Nichols, Abigail (W.C.); 8 Dec. 1822; (210); 127
Boyce, Elijah (Va); Stacy, Mary (Un); 8 June 1819; (148); 110
Boyd, James (Wf); Davenport, Mary Ann (Wf); 14 Mar. 1839; (63); 424
Brabham, John P. (Wt); Webster, Doshe E. (Wt); 23 Dec. 1840; (70); 473
Brabham, William A.; Oliver, Amy; 8 Oct. 1840; (157); 468
Brackenridge, John (Wn); Fleming, Agnes (Wn); 7 Dec. 1821; (148); 122
Bradford, Robert; Pond, Louis; 10 Dec. 1812; (138); 76
Bradford, Robert (W.C.); Arnold, Mary L. (W.C.); 10 Nov. 1822; (311); 127
Bradley, Dr. Bun (W.C.); Plummer, Esther W. (W.C.); 4 June 1818; (195); 102
Brady, Charles; Barnes, Polly; 19 Feb. 1815; (295); 84M
Bramel, Thomas; Prunty, Mary; 2 Jan. 1840; (364); 446
Braughton, John; Richardson, Lucy S.; 5 June 1834; (224); 324
Bray, Amaziah (Ct); Wilcox, Rebecca (Ma); 15 Oct. 1812; (148); 71
Brazier, John; Hill, Maria; 27 Feb. 1834; (98); 320
Breakinridge, Hugh; Harvie, Martha; 23 Jan. 1824; (142); 132
Breakenridge, William (Ba); Harvey, Margaret (Wn); 10 Mar. 1831; (184); 262
Breck, John (Sa); Stanley, Nancy (Fe); 15 May 1810; (197); 66
Breckenridge, David (Ba); Harvey, Margaret (Ba); 25 Dec. 1834; (184); 334
Breckenridge, Edward (Wt); Fleming, Jane (Ba); 2 Feb. 1832; (34); 279
Breckenridge, George (Ba); Bell, Jane (Ba); 26 Sept. 1839; (105); 441
Breckenridge, Thomas (Ba); Harvey, Margaret (Wn); 25 Feb. 1836; (184); 359
Bredahl, Hans; McIntosh, Mrs. Deborah (Ma); 3 Apr. 1833; (96); 300
Brewster, Levi (Wo); Waterman, Lydia (Wo); 3 Mar. 1820; (362); 112
Brewster, William (Wn); Fuller, Lucretia (Wn); 10 Jan. 1817; (115); 94
Brewster, William (Wn); Hamlin, Harriet (Wo); 19 May 1822; (25); 126
Bridges, Jacob (Be); Vincent, Eliza (Ba); 24 Mar. 1823; (181); 128
Briggs, Asa B. (W.C.); Nott, Philinda (W.C.); 26 Mar. 1816; (347); 90
Briggs, Dean (Wn); Scott, Sally (Wn); 12 Mar. 1835; (63); 340
Briggs, Marcus D. (Ad); Woodward, Highley C. (Un); 10 Aug. 1820; (316); 116
Briggs, Zara (Ad); Penny, Sally (Ad); 31 July 1817; (316); 97
Britton, Alexander (Fe); Avory, Amanda (Fe); 24 Jan. 1820; (210); 111
Britton, John; Chapman, Maria; 7 Dec. 1837; (59); 389
Britton, Levi (Fe); Kincade, Phebe (Fe); 26 Mar. 1829; (161); 222
Britton, Mark (Fe); Kincade, Sally (Fe); 26 Feb. 1829; (161); 222
Broadhurst, Banks W.; Phillips, Polly W.; 10 Dec. 1837; (364); 394
Broadhurst, John; McGrath, Mary B.; 16 Aug. 1824; (194); 136
Broadhurst, Thomas (Ma); Sears, Mary (Ma); 6 Nov. 1820; (197); 117
Brokaw, Benjamin (A.C.); Ellis, Roxana (Ro); 16 Jan. 1834; (127); 317
Bronn, Selah (Ma); Frazer, Margaret A. (Ma); 8 Jan. 1834; (38); 316

Brooking, Gerrit H.; Weston, Mary; 2 May 1840; (29); 457
Brooks, Abijah (Ky); Brooks, Harriet (W.C.); 27 Feb. 1821; (278) 120
Brooks, Abijah (Un); Woodford, Laura (Wt); 1 Aug. 1827; (258); 195
Brooks, John; Heaney, Delaney; 3 July 1801; (211); NW-50
Brooks, Samuel (W.C.); Dodge, Mary M. (W.C.); 3 July 1831; (22); 289
Broom, Peter (Fe); Davis, Elizabeth (Fe); 3 Dec. 1812; (333); 71
Broom, Thomas (W.C.); Jackson, Elizabeth (W.C.); 24 Apr. 1823; (90); 129
Brophey, William (Ma); Peters, Mariah (Sa); 8 Mar. 1837; (63); 374
Brophy, John (Ma); Smith, Caroline (Ma); 8 June 1823; (38); 129
Brough, Charles H.; Ames, Abigal W.; 25 Apr. 1839; (177); 430
Brough, John (Ma); Garnett, Jane (Ma); 17 Mar. 1808; (197); 57
Brough, John (Ma); Cross, Bridget (Ma); 21 Mar. 1822; (38); 123
Brough, John (Ma); Pruden, Achsah P. (A.C.); 13 Nov. 1832; (369); A.F. &
 M.G.v-16 #49
Brown, Alexander (Df); Riley, Jane (Df); 11 Oct. 1818; (260); 105
Brown, Alpha (Wf); McAtee, Lavina (Wf); 26 Nov. 1835; (2); 356
Brown, Dr. Benjamin; Rayley, Content A.; 23 July 1835; (305); 349
Brown, Benjamin M.; Gard, Maria; 11 May 1826; (230); 167
Brown, Israel (Gr); McCollum, Eleanor (Gr); 18 May 1834; (200); 325
Brown, James (Wf); Oliver, Isabella (Wf); 28 Oct. 1800; (245); NW-51
Brown, James (Ma); Hays, Hannah (Ma); 11 Feb. 1840; (63); 446
Brown, Jesse; Storey, Relief; 1799; (78); E.C.
Brown, John (Ad); Devol, Mrs. Elizabeth (Ad); 28 Mar. 1802; (91); NW-53
Brown, John (A.C.); Philip, Mary (W.F.); 27 Aug. 1810; (90); 66
Brown, John; Fearing, Rebecca; 13 Sept. 1810; (90); 67M
Brown, John (Wf); Beard, Margaret (Wf); 31 Dec. 1815; (143); 88
Brown, John; White, M. Eliza; 4 Feb. 1836; (351); 359
Brown, John (Ba); Green, Susan (Ba); 8 June 1836; (337); 364
Brown, John (Cin); Corvile, Nancy (Be); 9 July 1839; (184); 436
Brown, John W. L. (Fe); White, Mary Ann (Fe); 28 May 1829; (85); 223
Brown, Joseph; Crawford, Eliza (Ma); 30 Dec. 1829; (367); 249
Brown, Michael; Sellers, Christina; 2 July 1840; (216); II-4
Brown, Parley (Wf); Wilson, Celestia (Wt); 14 Feb. 1839; (192); 421
Brown, Parley (Wf); Shaw, Charlott H. (Wf); 1 Sept. 1839; (209); 438
Brown, Samuel, Esq. (We); Jenkins, Sally (We); 23 Sept. 1823; (347); 132
Brown, Samuel S. (Wf); LaGrange, Harriet N.; 8 Feb. 1834; (2); 339
Brown, Silas L.; Witham, Zilpha; 14 May 1835; (247); 344
Brown, William (Mi); Brown, Polly (Wf); 25 Mar. 1800; (78); NW-37
Brown, Wm. (Wo); Wilson, Almedia (Wo); 12 Dec. 1821; (249); 121
Brown, Wm. F.; Lloyd, Maria; 17 June 1838; (33); 405
Brown, Wm. T.; Devol, Nancy; 20 Jan. 1815; (138); 83M
Brown, Zacheus (Va); Uhl, Phebe (W.C.); 24 June 1837; (63); 379
Browning, Bazilia (Fe); Mead, Ann (Fe); 29 May 1814; (73); 81
Browning, Jacob (Ma); Bodwell, Edney (Ma); 5 July 1824; (38); 135
Browning, Thomas (Fe); McKewer, Sally (Fe); 30 Nov. 1809; (262); 64
Browning, Rev. Wesley; Batelle, Phoebe G.; 13 Feb. 1834; (142); 319
Browning, William (Ma); Putnam, Abigail (Ma); 10 Apr. 1791; (267); NW-6
Browning, William Rufus (Be); Barker, Sophia (Un); 27 Oct. 1819; (278); 113

Browning, Wm. (Be); Foster, Mary (Be); 21 Apr. 1805; (203); 47
Bryan, Byrd (Ma); Cole, Diana (Ma); 19 Feb. 1826; (27); 161
Buchanan, Jeffery (Un); Prouty, Rachel (Un); 7 Feb. 1819; (283); 106
Buck, Frederick; Gates, Mary; 14 Apr. 1829; (22); 235
Buck, Titus (Ma); Hart, Betsey (Ma); 2 June 1799; (238); NW-36
Buckingham, Ebenezer (Ma); Putnam, Catharine (Ma); 27 Nov. 1805; (197); 48
Buckingham, Stephen (Be); Cooley, Easter (Be); 13 Jan. 1802; (257); NW-51
Buell, Daniel H. (Ma); Ward, Phebe (Ma); 18 Apr. 1813; (197); 76
Buell, Daniel H.; Hall, Theodocia; 21 Dec. 1829; (22); 235
Buell, Ebenezer D. (Ma); Hildreth, Mary B.; 20 Apr. 1834; (367); M.G.v-1 #44
Buell, Ebenezer D. (Ma); Harris, Irene (Ma); 18 Dec. 1840; (63); 474
Buell, Matthew (G.C.); Hatch, Ida (Wf); 17 Mar. 1814; (197); 80
Buell, Salmon D. (Ad); Buell, Eliza (Ma); 30 Apr. 1817; (278); 96
Buell, Timothy (Ma); Plummer, Clarissa (Ma); 5 Feb. 1812 (197); 72
Buell, Timothy (Ma); Nixon, Laurana (Ro); 25 Aug. 1823; (347); 133
Buell, William Henry (Ma); Rogers, Lavina (Ma); 4 Jan. 1818; (278); 110
Buffington, Wm.; Huges, Sarah; 25 Dec. 1798; (203); NW-39
Bukey, Spencer T. (Ma); Hill, Eliza (Ma); 6 Aug. 1835; (22); M.G.v-1 #39
Bullard, Talbot; Cotton, Susan B. (Ma); 1 Aug. 1839; (19); 436
Bullman, Aaron (Va); Clutter, Rebecca (W.C.); 9 Feb. 1837; (114); 375
Burch, Chester; Davis, Polly; 10 Nov. 1832; (273); 291
Burch, Hiram (Be); Whiting, Nancy (Be); 18 Feb. 1821; (3); 124
Burch, Sherwood R. (Me.C.); Burris, Mary (Np); 27 Mar 1838; (178); 398
Burchett, Benjamin (Wt); Voshel, Susan (We); 17 Sept. 1835; (297); 350
Burchett, George; Gossett, Elizabeth; 7 Jun 1832; (360); 283
Burchett, John (Wt); Ferguson, Mary A. (Wt); 14 Jan. 1834; (297); 185
Burchett, John Jr. (Wt); Wilson, Joan (Wt); 3 Dec. 1826; (362); 157
Burchett, Jonathan (Wt); Pool, Nancy (Wt); 13 Oct. 1825; (362); 305
Burchett, Wm. (Wt); Gossett, Margaret (Wt); 22 May 1833; (297); NW-42
Burford, James (W.C.); Biers, Sally (W.C.); 8 July 1800; (285); 403
Burgess, George D. (A.C.); Temple, Hannah H. (Ma); 23 July 1838; (198); 417
Burk, John; Waters, Margaret; 4 Nov. 1838; (206); 417
Burley, George (Ma); Mixer, Sally (Ma); 9 Apr. 1821; (38); 118
Burlingame, Christopher Jr. (Ma); Bartlett, Elizabeth R. (Ma); 15 Nov. 1826;
   (85); 176
Burlinggame, Edwin (Ma); Evans, Jane (Ma); 14 Mar. 1819; (278); 110
Burnham, Wm.; Oliver, Christian; 27 Aug. 1789; (331); NW-1
Burns, Israel (Ad); Keith, Polly (Ad); 17 Feb. 1820; (138); 112, 114
Burns, James (Mg.C.); Coleman, Hannah (Ro); 7 Apr. 1831; (66); 265
Burns, John S. (Ma); Moore, Nancy (Ma); 30 June 1806; (11); 51
Burns, Thomas M. (A.C.); Bailey, Talitha (Fe); 5 Apr. 1827; (332); 190
Burnside, Ephraim; Shafer, Mrs. Polly Ann; 27 Dec. 1832; (144); 294
Burnside, William (W.C.); VanGordon, Anna (W.C.); 14 Nov. 1822; (311); 127
Burnsides, Alexander; Carpenter, Lydia; 9 Aug. 1838; (326); 412
Burpee, Nathan (We); Cowee, Calista (We); 15 Oct. 1826; (346); 175
Burpee, Pearson (Wo); Bartlett, Cynthia (Wo); 8 Feb. 1822; (47); 123
Burris, James (Wf); Atkinson, Mrs. Harriet (Ba); 16 May 1826; (75); 167
Burris, Stinson; Ellis, Diana; 24 Dec. 1829; (114); 236

WASHINGTON COUNTY MARRIAGES

Burris, Thomas; Bellows, Lucy; 23 Aug. 1832; (144); 285
Burris, Van (Gr); Williamson, Narcissa (Gr); 10 June 1830; (114); 247
Burris, William (Wf); Bellows, Maria (Wt); 7 May 1829; (192); 223
Burroughs, Jarvis (Be); Stone, Susan (Be); 2 Sept. 1821; (278); 120
Burroughs, Wm. (Be); Barkley, Elizabeth (Be); 10 Aug. 1817; (3); 98
Burroughs, Wm. (W.C.); Barkley, Margaret (W.C.); 22 Jul 1824; (82); 136
Burrows, John (Wf); Devol, Electa (Wf); 18 May 1824; (18); 134
Burrows, Robert; Starlin, Orinda; 4 Dec. 1834; (192); 333
Bussard, Samuel (Ba); Jackson, Electra M. (Ba); 4 Nov. 1830; (363); 254
Butler, Isaac (W.C.); Bantham, Nancy (W.C.); 24 June 1802; (45); NW-57
Butts, Aaron W.; Gooding, Zelinda; 11 June 1837; (70); 379
Byard, John D. (Ma); Hoff, Prudence (Ma); 4 June 1836; (63); 363
Byard, Samuel (Np); Freemire, Hannah (Gr); 31 July 1817; (295); 97
Byington, Rev. Cyrus (Ms); Nye, Sophia (Ma); 19 Dec. 1827; (22); 234

Cadwell, James (O.G.); Hamilton, Lucy F. (Ma); 27 Mar. 1826; (65); 166
Cady, William (Mvl); Harris, Elizabeth (Mvl); 12 Feb. 1816; (323); 89
Calder, Alexander; Casey, Seasy; 30 Dec. 1824; (57); 143
Calder, John (Wn); Rathbun, Eley (Be); 25 Oct. 1827; (82); 195
Caldwell, William Jr. (Me.C.); Flake, Elizabeth (Ad); 26 Nov. 1835; (2); 356
Callahan, Rev. James; Burlinggame, Sarah; 24 Sept. 1829; (148); 230
Callahan, John; Hagerman, Maria; 5 Nov. 1826; (189); 177
Callahan, William (Wf); Coffman, Moriah (Wf); 11 Jan. 1818; (183); 101
Cameron, John (Ba); Atkinson, Martha (Ba); 8 Dec. 1825; (230); 161
Camock, John (Ma); Greene, Susanna (Ma); 15 May 1806; (31?); 49
Camp, Edward; Gard, Rowena (Ro); 3 Oct. 1833; (108); 309
Camp, Samuel (W.C.); Corns, Polly E. (W.C.); 24 Sept. 1835; (111); 356
Campbell, Alexander (Ma); Blake, Hannah D. (Ma); 5 Nov. 1811; (91); 70
Campbell, James; Campbell, Margaret (Sa); 9 June 1833; (305); 305
Campbell, James (We); Ray, Mary (We); 28 Dec. 1837; (248); 391
Campbell, John (Au); Driscoll, Lucy (Au); 17 Apr. 1823; (47); 128
Campbell, John; Barr, Sevilla; 17 May 1838; (33); 399
Campbell, Moses (We); Roberts, Eleanor (We); 1 Jan. 1835; (248); 340
Campbell, Oren; Glidden, Mary; 30 July 1815; (185); 85M
Campbell, Patrick; Amlin, Sally D.; 18 Jan. 1818; (134); 100M
Campbell, Robert (We); Davis, Betsey (Sa); 15 Oct, 1826; (69); 174
Campbell, William; Hall, Mary; 29 Nov. 1838; (71); 422
Cannon, John; Parker, Hannah; 15 Aug. 1818; (38); 103M
Carl, William (O.G.); Goodwin, Margaret (O.G.); 22 Dec. 1818; (271); 106
Carlile, Benjamin F. (Un); Chapman, Clarissa (Fe); 30 Nov. 1828; (283); 215
Carmichel, John (Mn.C.); Hupp, Mary (Au); 2 Aug. 1829; (261); 229
Carney, Robert (W.C.); Ryon, Jane (W.C.); 26 Sept. 1822; (53); 126
Carpenter, Jacob; Coss, Barbara; 30 Dec. 1832; (326); 298
Carpenter, Joseph C.; Harper, Mahala; 23 July 1838; (70); 405
Carrel, Andrew (Wf); Gorman, Letitia (Wf); 19 Mar. 1807; (245); 54
Carrel, George (Wf); Ward, Jemima (Wf); 18 Aug. 1803; (245); NW-65

11

Carrell, James S. (Wf); Hull, Rachel (Wf); 13 Mar. 1824; (189); 134
Carter, Dennis; Richards, Diana; 26 Sept. 1840; (129); 467
Carter, Rufus (Wf); Chidester, Sally (Wf); 31 Jan. 1822; (18); 123
Cartner, Nicholas; Saelor, Sophia; 23 Apr. 1839; (13); 432
Cartwright, Reuben (Ma); Protsman, Catherine (Ma); 30 Oct. 1814; (38); 82
Carver, Adonis; Phillips, Anna; 15 May 1834; (224); 323
Carver, Adonis (Np); Phillips, Tabitha (Np); 16 Aug. 1840; (364); 466
Carver, Caleb (Ma); Flagg, Mary (Ma); 7 Aug. 1803; (317); NW-64, 42
Carver, Elizur (Ma); Birth, Katharine (Ma); 24 Sept. 1803; (296); 42
Carver, Elizur (Ma); Walker, Polly (Ma); 4 Nov. 1809; (86); 64
Carver, James F. (Np); Toothaker, Sarah (Fe); 22 Dec. 1833; (332); 317
Carver, Joseph; Luckey, Rachel; 6 Sept. 1832; (224); 286
Case, Augustus (Ma); Curtis, Lucinda (Ma); 31 May 1814; (278); 81
Case, Wm. M. (Ma); Posey, Marian (Ma); 2 Nov. 1809; (197); 63
Case, Wm. M. (Ma); Bryan, Fanny (Ma); 9 May 1824; (27); 137
Caseholt, Jacob (Ch); Porter, Sarah (Ch); 22 Mar. 1838; (63); 396
Casey, Wanton (Ma); Goodale, Elizabeth (Ma); 25 Oct. 1789; (331); NW-1
Cass, George W. (Mu.C.); Lord, Sophia (Ma); 18 May 1809; (278); 63
Cass, Joseph; Briton, Mary; 11 Mar. 1827; (162); 182
Cassady, George; Dye, Hannah; 6 Mar. 1840; (87); 460
Castle, George (Ma); Newton, Alice (Ma); 20 Dec. 1805; (11); 50
Castle, Henry (Mi); Shepard, Rachel (Mi); 29 Mar. 1803; (135); NW-64
Casto, James H. (Bu.C.); Briton, Nancy (W.C.); 22 June 1829; (162); 228
Cawood, Joseph, 2nd (La); Reed, Elizabeth (La); 8 Nov. 1840; (1); 469
Cawood, Wm., 2nd (Fe); Henton, Ann (Fe); 31 Aug. 1837; (59); 383
Caywood, Jonathan (Fe); Henton, Eliza (Fe); 25 Apr. 1833; (162); 305
Caywood, Joseph (Fe); Dye, Hannah (La); 14 Apr. 1822; (205); 124
Caywood, Thomas, 2nd (Fe); Maxson, Harriet (Ma); 20 June 1833; (162); 305
Chad, John; Mills, Wnza; 1809; ; X
Chadwick, Levi (A.C.); Calahan, Mary (Wf); 19 Apr. 1825; (347); 150
Chadwick, Salathiel; Porter, Catharine; 13 Mar. 1834; (92); 321
Chamberlain, Jacob P.; Matthews, Martha; 28 Sept. 1837; (71); 386
Chamberlain, John (Br.C.); Warren, Delia (W.C.); 10 June 1833; (339); 304
Chamberlain, Judah M.; McIntosh, Rhoda Ann; 12 Feb. 1818; (38); 100M
Chamberlain, Lawrance (W.C.); Clark, Laura (W.C.); 24 Apr. 1823; (38); 129
Chamberlain, Lincoln D.; Andrews, Sarah L.; 10 July 1825; (230); 154
Chambers, Greer; Geren, Jane D.; 21 Feb. 1833; (368); 302
Chambers, Hezekiah (Ma); Soul, Hannah C. (Sa); 13 Dec. 1836; (71); 373
Chambers, Hiram; Record, Elizabeth; 9 May 1837; (32); 381
Chambers, John (La); Nixon, Sarah (Ma); 22 May 1828; (85); 210
Chambers, Joseph, Esq. (Wf); Dana, Hannah P. (Wf); 15 Dec. 1825; (258); 164
Chambers, Joseph (Wf); Brooks, Elizabeth (Ma); 6 Apr. 1836; (103); 362
Chambers, Robert (Np); Little, Rebecca (Np); 6 Mar. 1838; (178); 395
Chambers, Thos. (Ma); Hill, Mary G. (La); 31 Mar. 1836; (87); M.G.v-2 #22
Chambers, William Jr. (La); Dye, Emma B. (La); 22 Aug. 1834; (109); 329
Chandivert, Stephen; Brunie, Madalane; 15 Feb. 1796; (285); NW-16
Chandler, Henry (Wo); Humiston, Sally (Wo); 19 May 1821; (138); 119
Chandler, Hiram (Wo); Humiston, Juliana (Wo); 15 Sept. 1822; (307); 126

Chandler, Jesse (Sp); Morris, Henrietta (Ad); 16 Nov. 1809; (197); 63
Chapman, David; McCall, Peggy; 28 Feb. 1799; (121); NW-33
Chapman, Davis (Sa); Davis, Sarah (Sa); 30 May 1822; (90); 125
Chapman, Elisha (Ma); MaGee, Nancy (Ma); 30 Mar. 1810; (197); 65
Chapman, Elisha (Sa); Manahan, Nancy (Sa); 15 Mar. 1832; (44); 278
Chapman, Enos (Fe); Doan, Anna (Fe); 24 Nov. 1825; (332); 159
Chapman, Ezra (W.C.); Jones, Betsey (W.C.); 13 Nov. 1799; (310); NW-40
Chapman, Ezra; Corner, Mary; 15 Dec. 1815; (278); 86M
Chapman, Harvey (Sa); Hill, Ruth (Sa); 5 Nov. 1807; (278); 56
Chapman, Herman Jr. (Ba); Pond, Elida (Ba); 14 Dec. 1826; (34); 178
Chapman, Hezekiah (Sa); Allen, Martha (Ma); 5 Oct. 1808; (197); 59
Chapman, Hiram (W.C.); Lund, Nancy A. (W.C.); 13 May 1830; (32); 289
Chapman, Isaac (Sa); Perkins, Sally (Sa); 7 May 1805; (197); 46
Chapman, Isaac (Mg.C.); Lang, Jane (W.C.); 25 Feb. 1834; (191); 324
Chapman, Isaac (Fe); Payne, Lucy (Sa); 30 Aug. 1840; (96); 465
Chapman, John (W.C.); Newell, Sarah Ann (W.C.); 22 Aug. 1837; (63); 381
Chapman, Nathaniel (Wf); Stephens, Amirila (Wf); 14 Apr. 1808; (292); 57
Chapman, Nicholas P. (Wo); Chamberlain, Anna B. (Wo); 7 May 1820; (183); 114
Chapman, Parley (Sa); Ogle, Polly (Sa); 22 Sept. 1808; (261); 58
Chapman, Samuel (Wo); Clark, Catherine (Ro); 1 Dec. 1816; (147); 93
Chapman, Seldon (Fe); Stanley, Elizabeth (Fe); 28 Dec. 1820; (332); 118
Chapman, Simeon (Fe); Bairdsley, Phebe (Au); 11 Apr. 1822; (48); 124
Chapman, Wheeler; True, Louisa; 20 Apr. 1836; (148); 362
Chappel, James H. (Ma); Bosworth, Amanda (Ma); 11 Sept. 1828; (327); 212
Chappell, Dwight W. (Be); Curtis, Lucy W. (Be); 25 Nov. 1838; (344); 415
Chappell, M. Avery (Be); Putnam, Laura A. (Un); 19 Dec. 1832; (32); 293
Charlot, Calvin G. (Gu.C.); Foster, Hannah G. (Ma); 5 Nov. 1835; (117); 353
Chase, Jedediah Jr. (Ma); Hamilton, Mrs. Barbara (Ma); 12 Mar. 1825; (38); 147
Chase, John (Ma); Dennis, Lydia (Ma); 6 Feb. 1822; (27); 123
Chase, John; Kennedy, Jane; 24 Nov. 1825; (326); 159
Chatick, Richard (Ma); Drown, Mary (Ma); 24 Feb. 1817; (304); 96
Cheadle, Asa (Wf); Hersey, Mercey (Ad); 20 Jan. 1802; (91); NW-52
Cheadle, Asa (Ro); Divens, Sally (Ro); 22 Aug. 1816; (329); 91
Cheadle, Augustus (Mg.C.); Baker, Nancy (Ba); 14 Mar. 1833; (297); 300
Cheadle, Cyrus (Ro); VanClief, Abigail (Wf); 14 Feb. 1808; (51); 56
Chealde, Cutler (Ro); Barnet, Harriet (Ro); 4 Sept. 1834; (127); 328
Cheadle, Gilman (Mg.C.); Rockey, Susanna (Ro); 13 Mar. 1828; (34); 205
Cheadle, John; Sills, Sarah (Ro); 27 Jan. 1810; (51); 64
Cheadle, Peter (We); Welch, Jane (Ro); 12 July 1839; (219); 439
Cheadle, Roswell N.; Farnham, Elizabeth; 24 June 1838; (123); 404
Chedle, Joseph (Ro); Hand, Sarah (Ro); 25 Dec. 1809; (51); 63
Chereau, Auguste (Ga); Duraille, Jeanne F. (Ga); 27 Mar. 1794; (254); NW-11
Cherry, Palmer; Goodwin, Sarah E.; 5 May 1835; (162); 345
Cherry, Richard (Wt); Robinson, Keziah (Be); 12 Apr. 1838; (311); 398
Cherry, William (Fe); Abbott, Rachel (We); 31 Dec. 1835; (337); 361
Chesebro, Amos (Fe); Maxson, Lydia (Fe); 18 Aug. 1819; (349); 109
Chidester, Benj.; Burch, Betsy; 23 Aug. 1818; (349); 104M
Chidester, Richard (Wf); Boudinot, Polly (Wf); 18 July 1822; (18); 125

Childs, Isaac (Wf); Pope, Elizabeth (Wf); 25 Feb. 1821; (272); 118
Childs, Seth C. (Ty.C.); Sheets, Elizabeth (W.C.); 17 May 1838; (178); 403
Chiventon, John (Ma); Patten, Rebeckah (Ma); 6 Apr. 1806; (11); 50
Chivington, John; Dickey, Martha (Ma); 22 Aug. 1809; (266); 62
Churchill, Silas (Np); Gray, Betsy (Un); 8 Feb. 1829; (38); 222
Churchill, Solomon; Pritchard, Mary; 15 Mar. 1818; (316); 100M
Chute, William (We); Varner, Ann (We); 12 Sept. 1822; (63); 126
Cinnamon, Thomas (Ma); Alcock, Aurilla (Ma); 23 July 1835; (63); 347
Clark, Benj. W.; Broadhurst, Marietta; 22 Sept. 1839; (70); 447
Clark, Harvey; Delley, Harriet; 1 Sept. 1831; (311); 272
Clark, Henry (Ma); Herrington, Patty (Ma); 21 July 1816; (38); 91
Clark, John (W.C.); Shepard, Lorena (W.C.); 19 Oct. 1798; (238); NW-31
Clark, John (Be); Chappell, Matilda F. (Wn); 13 Apr. 1825; (311); 149
Clark, John S. (Ma); Peese, Eliza (Ma); 19 June 1811; (197); 69
Clark, Joseph D. (Ba); Moore, Mary (Ba); 28 May 1829; (361); 225
Clark, Levi (Wn); Tilson, Eliza (Wn); 30 Mar. 1825; (349); 149
Clark, Levi W.; Ray, Mary (We); 20 Nov. 1833; (67); 312
Clark, Miller (Be); Corns, Rachel (We); 23 Mar. 1824; (75); 133
Clark, Obadiah (Ma); Ewing, Sally (Ma); 17 July 1804; (203); 42
Clark, Seneca (Wf); Stull, Catharine (Wf); 18 May 1820; (252); 115
Clark, Whipple G. (Ma); McLean, Keziah (Ma); 24 Jan. 1825; (27); 144
Clarke, Isaiah (Wn); Bailey, Nancy (Wn); 21 July 1825; (241); 153
Clarke, Wm. B.; Putnam, Elizabeth A. (Un); 10 Sept. 1840; (26); 467
Clay, Daniel Jr. (Sa); Davis, Martha (Sa); 21 Mar. 1819; (90); 108
Clay, Jonathan (Sa); Lancaster, Betsey (Sa); 7 Apr. 1837; (330); 378
Clayton, Henry W. (Ro); Kidwell, Sarah (We); 9 Nov. 1833; (259); 317
Clayton, James (We); Jarrett, Louisa (We); 20 Sept. 1835; (67); 351
Clayton, John B.; Bishop, Hannah; 21 Mar. 1833; (113); 300
Cline, Conrad (Wd.C.); Crawford, Mary Ann (W.C.); 17 Mar. 1840; (70); 461
Cline, David (Gr); Mills, Sarah (Gr); 29 June (1813); (295); 77
Cline, David (Gr); Brown, Rachel (Gr); 24 July 1814; (295); 81
Cline, George (Gr); Linn, Christiana (Gr); 23 Feb. 1807; (277); 52
Cline, Washington; Groves, Eleanor; 14 Sept. 1837; (180); 384
Cline, William (Gr); Linn, Mary (Gr); 9 Aug. 1803; (354); NW-64
Clissay, John (Fe); Rood, Caroline (Fe); 1 Jan. 1824; (85); 132
Clogston, James; Wood, Cynthia; 23 Aug. 1827; (322); 192
Clogston, John T. (Ma); Wood, Mary Ann (Ma); 20 Mar. 1834; (63); 322
Close, Elnathan M. (W.C.); Evans, Martha (W.C.); 6 Apr. 1837; (71); 380
Close, Theobold; Wagner, Elizabeth; 16 Aug. 1838; (247); 406
Close, Thomas J.; Seevers, Mary Ann; 15 Nov. 1837; (71); 394
Clough, Aaron (Be); Delano, Sarah (Be); 29 Apr. 1804; (203); 42
Cloyne, Samuel; Gray, Phebe; 5 Dec. 1839; (71); 444
Cobern, Phinehas (Wf); Olney, Patience (Wf); 18 July 1796; (245); NW-17
Coburn, Asa (Ad); Baker, Rhoda (Wf); 24 Jan. 1799; (245); NW-32
Coburn, Barzilla (Ro); Cuddington, Anna (Wf); 28 Mar. 1819; (347); 107
Coburn, Phineas (W.C.); Spencer, Polly (W.C.); 1 May 1817; (252); 95
Cochran, Hugh (Ma); Clark, Almira S. (Ma); 14 Dec. 1820; (278); 117
Cochran, William (Gr); Hisum, Sarah (Gr); 31 Oct. 1823; (353); 131

Cockrill, Elijah (A.C.); Barns, Mary (Be); 19 Apr. 1832; (311); 282
Coffee, Lorenzo D. (Mg.C.); Cory, Cynthia; 25 May 1837; (123); 377
Coffman, Jacob (Wf); Harrison, Jane (Wf); 4 June 1833; (192); 308
Coffman, Jacob M. (Wf); Dolin, Polly (Wf); 5 Sept. 1817; (252); 98
Coffman, Thos. C. (Wt); Callahan, Rebecca (Wf); 18 June 1829; (106); 226
Coggshall, Job (Be); Weatherby, Lydia (Be); 9 Nov. 1814; (145); 82
Cogswell, Harry (Ma); McAllister, Polly (Ma); 3 Nov. 1824; (27); 142
Cogswell, Harry (Ma); Carlile, Elizabeth (Un); 15 July 1827; (63); 190
Colburn, Ebenezer (Ma); Smith, Julia A. (Ma); 2 Nov. 1817; (38); 98
Cole, Abisha (Wn); Rathbun, Elsa (Wn); 17 July 1836; (56); 365
Cole, Andrew (Un); Olney, Mary (Un); 30 July 1820; (138); 115
Cole, David; Hall, Jane; 29 July 1824; (311); 136
Cole, Elias (Be); Hollister, Sibel M. (Be); 16 Oct, 1819; (311); 111
Cole, Flavel C.; Dye, Mary; 6 Oct. 1839; (38); 439
Cole, John (Ma); Harden, Nancy (Ma); 23 June 1807; (11); 54
Cole, John Jr. (Wn); Needham, Mary S. (Wn); 12 Jan. 1836; (56); 359
Cole, Joseph (Np); Case, Polly (Np); 13 Nov. 1805; (31); 47
Cole, Levi (Ma); Duncan, Sally (Ma); 27 Mar. 1814; (197); 80
Cole, Malichi (Wn); Harris, Romantha (Wn); 21 Jan. 1816; (293); 88
Cole, Nathan (Wn); Bryan, Levina (Ma); 5 Apr. 1821; (38); 118
Cole, Sampson (Ma); Duncan, Polly (Ma); 28 Jan. 1812; (197); 72
Cole, William (Ma); Patten, Elizabeth B. (Wn); 4 Nov. 1833; (174); 315
Cole, William P. (Wn); Shields, Louisa (Wt); 24 Nov. 1840; (70); 473
Coleman, Daniel (Wf); Nott, Mary (Wf); 2 Aug. 1802; (245); NW-57
Coleman, Elijah; Jennings, Nancy; 5 Aug. 1818; (346); 103M
Coleman, Thomas; Raridin, Jane; 18 Aug. 1800; (203); NW-42
Coler, Henry Wm.; Martin, Nancy; 28 May 1840; (123); 462
Coley, Wm. H. (Ma); Vincent, Mary (Ma); 5 Apr. 1812; (266); 74
Colkings, Eloser (Ma); Westgate, Patty (Fe); 4 Sept. 1808; (101); 59
Collens, Thomas W.; Edwards, Hannah; 25 July 1829; (114); 227
Collins, Elliott W.; Reinard, Elizabeth; 12 Mar. 1835; (118); 344
Collins, John (Gr); Edwards, Rachel (Gr); 3 Feb. 1807; (358); 54
Collins, John (Be); Whaley, Lucetta (Be); 16 Feb. 1838; (344); 396
Collins, Joseph G. (Fe); Bardmas, Mary A. (Fe); 20 Oct. 1834; (85); 336
Collis, Samuel (We); Howe, Betsey Eluira (Ma); 29 June 1828; (63); 209
Collis, William; Howe, Sally Adaline (We); 14 May 1829; (225); 228
Colvin, Samuel (Be); Daly, Sarah (Be); 10 May 1797; (257); NW-21
Compton, Geo.; Dana, Mary P.; 21 Jan. 1830; (79); A.F. & M.G.v-14 #15
Conaway, John (Ad); Brooker, Sibyl (Ad); 17 Feb. 1820; (355); 112
Conkright, Richard (Ba); Manahan, Mrs. Catharine (Ma); 28 Oct. 1828; (363); 214
Conkrite, Richard (Gr); Gardner, Hannah (Gr); 1 Jan. 1817; (304); 96
Connal, Abner (Ma); Shannon, Jane (Ma); 27 Dec. 1804; (151); 44
Converse, Daniel; Munro, Sally; 3 Apr. 1800; (203); NW-39
Converse, James (Wf); Olney, Lois (Wf); 18 Oct. 1795; (245); NW-15
Cook, Adam; Shrum, Catharine; 22 Nov. 1838; (330); 421
Cook, Barker (Wd.C.); McClintick, Polly (Ma); 3 Nov. 1814; (38); 82
Cook, John; Mallecy, R.; 1805; ; X
Cook, John (W.C.); Ackerson, Sarah (W.C.); 5 Feb. 1837; (256); 375

Cook, Johnson T. (Ad); Maxson, Mary (Ad); 19 May 1814; (315); 81
Cook, Capt. Joseph; Cock, Rhoda; 23 Nov. 1817; (35); 100M
Cook, Joseph Jr. (Va); Devol, Clarissa (Un); 29 Nov. 1812; (167); 75
Cook, Orange M. (Ro); Chamberlain, Amanda (Wt); 10 Jan. 1839; (177); 419
Cook, Pardon (Wd.C.); Russell, Polly (Un); 1 Mar. 1819; (316); 107
Cook, Silas (Ma); Mitchell, Sally (Np); 17 Jan. 1811; (197); 69
Cook, Tillinghast (Wd.C.); Russell, Betsey (Un); 9 June 1820; (316); 115
Cook, William; Barton, Nancy; 9 Nov. 1815; (134); 86M
Cooley, William (Ro); Havens, Sophia (Ro); 19 Nov. 1818; (92); 105
Coomes, Henry; Vaughan, Polly; 17 Dec. 1840; (274); II-30
Coon, Isaac (Un); Sargent, Sarah (Sa); 26 June 1823; (90); 130
Cooper, Jacob (Wo); Oakley, Lydia (Wo); 21 Sept. 1820; (47); 117
Cooper, Lemuel (Wn); Druse, Lucy (Wn); 17 Feb. 1822; (205); 124
Cordary, Nathan; Peyton, Drusilla; 25 Dec. 1834; (118); 338
Corey, Ebenezer (Ma); Fenn, Jerusha (Ma); 15 Apr. 1830; (63); 239
Corey, James (La); Wills, Eliza (Sa); 2 Feb. 1826; (332); 165
Corey, John (Ma); McGrew, Hannah (Ma); 3 Oct. 1837; (263); 385
Corey, Thomas; Welles, Nancy; 17 Feb. 1791; (331); NW-4
Cornell, Eli; Dilley, Elizabeth (Be); 23 Dec. 1830; (82); 256
Cornell, Jesse (Be); Wilhelm, Elizabeth (Be); 14 May 1839; (168); 432
Corner, Edwin (Mg.C.); Howe, Rachel (Ma); 19 Nov. 1820; (197); 117
Corner, George (Ma); Burlingame, Susanna (Ma); 29 Nov. 1807; (278); 56
Corner, Matthew (Wf); Ashcroft, Ann (Wf); 4 July 1805; (195); 46
Corner, William (Ma); Maxon, Sarah (Fe); 21 Nov. 1811; (197); 72
Cornes, James (We); Miller, Polly (Wo); 6 Aug. 1811; (141); 70
Cornish, Abraham (Wf); Lawrence, Lydia (Wf); 10 Oct. 1811; (137); 70
Corns, Henry (We); Pugh, Mary (Ba); 30 Jan. 1819; (62); 106
Corns, Henry Jr. (We); Perry, Catharine (We); 10 Aug. 1826; (230); 171
Corns, John (We); Danley, Polly (We); 31 Aug. 1817; (62); 97
Corns, William (We); Haskins, Mrs. Mary (We); 16 Mar. 1826; (230); 163
Corns, William (W.C.); Wilson, Lauranna (W.C.); 23 July 1826; (179); 170
Corns, William (Ro); Pugh, Nancy (Ro); 1 Nov. 1838; (248); 418
Corp, Benj. Jr. (Ma); Thorniley, Mary (Ma); 31 Dec. 1808; (197); 59
Corp, Benj. Jr.; Brady, Nancy; 28 May 1829; (65); 227
Corp, John (Ma); Dodd, Elizabeth (Ma); 27 Aug. 1816; (278); 91, 95
Cory, Charles S. (Ro); White, Anna (Ro); 18 Apr. 1813; (347); 76
Cory, Thomas H. (Wf); Leget, Hannah (Wt); 16 Mar. 1836; (192); 361
Cory, Thomas S. (Ma); Lewis, Lucy Ann (Ma); 21 Aug. 1832; (63); 285
Cory, William (Wf); Evens, Elizabeth (Ro); 10 Apr. 1827; (34); 186
Courtney, Neal (W.C.); McLeane, Polly (W.C.); 22 Nov. 1796; (238); NW-19
Covey, John; Hoff, Margaret; 26 Sept. 1833; (326); 310
Covey, William (W.C.); Douthitt, Nancy Ann (W.C.); 28 June 1838; (71); 402
Cowan, Simeon P. (Ma); Worstell, Mary Ann (Ma); 24 Mar. 1822; (38); 123
Cowee, Jacob (Ro); Ruble, Sarah (Ro); 26 Apr. 1838; (256); 400
Cowee, Seneca (Un); McAtee, Harriet (Wf); 11 Feb. 1830; (274); 236
Cowee, Wm. (Wf); Vanvaley, Hannah (Wf); 25 July 1820; (252); 116
Cozens, Hezekiah (Fe); Graham, Mary (Ma); 29 May 1824; (85); 135
Craft, John (Ro); Cheadle, Patty (Ro); 19 Jan. 1812; (347); 171

WASHINGTON COUNTY MARRIAGES

Craft, Ridgeway (W.C.); Bailey, Esther; 1 Oct. 1815; (293); 87
Craig, Samuel; Johnson, Fanny; 17 Feb. 1801; (285); NW-47
Craigg, Joel; Putnam, Betsey; 7 Dec. 1797; (121); NW-24
Crail, Thomas (Wf); Inbody, Mary M. (Wf); 27 Sept. 1838; (192); 409
Cram, J. A. (Za); Stewart, Elizabeth (Za); 22 Mar. 1836; (72); M.G.v-2 #21
Crandle, Zedekiah (Fe); Widger, Mrs. Margaret (Au); 7 Feb. 1828; (69); 204
Crandol, Zedekiah (Ma); Stillson, Cynthia (Ma); 19 Oct. 1819; (27); 110
Crane, Augustus; Lafield, Mary Ann; 17 Aug. 1835; (224); 348
Crawford, Charles (Ad); Maxson, Sophia (Ad); 4 Dec. 1821; (355); 123
Crawford, John (Ma); Babcock, Martha (Ma); 5 Mar. 1822; (308); 123
Crawford, Robert (Ma); Russell, Lucy (Un); 16 Mar. 1825; (194); 147
Crawford, Wm. (Sa); Wills, Sophrona (Sa); 31 Dec. 1820; (90); 118
Cray, Richard; Knott, Patty; 27 Aug. 1826; (230); 175
Crippen, Henry (Be); Ingles, Elizabeth (Be); 7 Dec. 1815; (3); 88
Crooks, John; Cowre, Tabitha; 12 Nov. 1817; (252); 100M
Cross, Bazel A. (Fe); Bailey, Wealthy (Fe); 20 Dec. 1821; (332); 121
Cross, Lucius (Ma); Stanley, Thirza (Ma); 15 Apr. 1821; (278); 120
Cross, Stephen (Wn); Murphy, Dorcas (Wn); 26 Nov. 1840; (29); 472
Cross, Waid (Ma); Force, Bridgart (Ma); 27 May 1804; (31); 42
Crow, Martin (Fe); Taylor, Phebe (Fe); 19 Nov. 1822; (332); 127
Cubbage, Phillip (Ma); Newton, Betsey (Ma); 18 Dec. 1804; (31); 44
Cuddington, Uriah; Fuller, Theodosia; 14 Dec. 1814; (126); 83M
Culver, Amos (Be); Gates, Phoebe (Be); 4 May 1824; (82); 134
Culver, Horatio N. (Wf); Townsend, Nancy (Wt); 5 Apr. 1832; (66); 280
Cunningham, Ebenezer (Sa); Mogrudge, Sally (Sa); 25 Dec. 1816; (252); 93
Cunningham, George (Wn); Harris, Sally (Wn); 7 Sept. 1826; (362); 175
Cunningham, John O. (Gr); Judge, Mary (Gr); 9 May 1833; (200); 303
Cunningham, Levi; Robinson, Sarah C.; 15 Nov. 1835; (193); 354
Cunningham, Martin; Thomas, Harriet; 21 Oct. 1832; (113); 291
Currier, William (Wf); Hill, Peggy (Ma); 6 Jan. 1814; (278); 79
Curry, George; Mulcher, Betsey Ann (Wt); 5 Apr. 1832; (36); 280
Curtis, Benajah (Ma); Clark, Sally (Ma); 12 May 1813; (197); 77
Curtis, Eleazer (Be); Knowles, Esther (Be); 24 June 1812; (133); 72
Curtis, Horace (Be); Cole, Lydia (Be); 7 Feb. 1819; (145); 107
Curtis, John (Wf); Woodruff, Polly (Wf); 15 Apr. 1804; (93); 41
Curtis, Liberty (Mn.C.); Carmichael, Elizabeth (Au); 26 Dec. 1837; (237); 391
Curtis, Paul B. (Ba); Dilley, Sarah A. (Be); 18 Oct. 1832; (311); 290
Curtis, Tholomiah (Wf); Culver, Avis (Wt); 11 Apr. 1837; (360); 378
Curtis, Walter (Be); Guthrie, Almira (Be); 4 Feb. 1819; (3); 106
Curtiss, Jason R. (Ma); Clark, Polly (Ma); 3 Nov. 1814; (38); 82
Cushing, Gen. Nathan G. (Ga); Merwin, Susan (Ma); 21 Dec. 1819; (278); 113
Cushing, Samuel (Wf); Devol, Bathsheba (Wf); 5 Feb. 1794; (267); NW-9
Cushing, Samuel (Wf); Scott, Almira (Wf); 3 Feb. 1820; (271); 115

Dailey, Charles (Lan); Gates, Sally (W.C.); 5 June 1806; (245); 50
Dailey, John (Gr); Dewees, Mary (Gr); 17 Oct. 1815; (295); 87

17

Dailey, Peter; Bever, Katharine; 14 Feb. 1839; (58); 429
Dale, Jeremiah (Za); Plummer, Nancy B. (Ma); 24 May 1820; (278); 117
Dana, Alfred (Np); Pratt, Anna T. (Ad); 11 Apr. 1831; (79); 264
Dana, Benjamin (Wf); Shaw, Sally (Wf); 17 Apr. 1798; (245); NW-29
Dana, Charles; Churchill, Eunice S.; 1 Sept. 1831; (212); 269
Dana, Edmond B. (Be); Burch, Jerusha (Grl); 27 Nov. 1810; (278); 67M
Dana, George (Be); Fisher, Deborah (Be); 22 Sept. 1816; (278); 95
Dana (?Dains), Levi (W.C.); Dutton, Srah (W.C.); 17 Nov. 1808; (91); 58
Dana, Luther; Stone, Grace; 17 Mar. 1799; (121); NW-33
Dana, Samuel; Thorniley, Louisa; 16 Oct, 1828; (38); 213
Dana, Stephen (Be); Foster, Betsey M. (Be); 14 Apr. 1807; (203); 54
Dana, William (Np); Foster, Polly (Be); 2 May 1802; (257); NW-55
Dana, Wm. (Np); Bent, Dorcas (Be); 4 Feb. 1816; (3); 89
Danford, Phillip (W.C.); Foster, Esther (W.C.); 6 Feb. 1817; (289); 93
Daniels, Abraham (W.C.); Bartlett, Sarah (W.C.); 20 Apr. 1826; (179); 168
Daniels, Hiram; Bartlett, Jane; 22 Aug. 1833; (85); 311
Daniels, John L. (Fe); Cherry, Eliza Ann (Fe); 2 Nov. 1826; (38); 175
Daniels, Stephen (Ma); Warren, Sophia (Ma); 30 Mar. 1823; (27); 129
Danielson, Plyna (Wo); Starlin, Polly (Wo); 25 Apr. 1813; (147); 77
Danley, Joel C. (Ro); Chamberlain, Diana M. (Wt); 28 Aug. 1839; (256); 441
Danley, John (Wt); Brown, Sarah Ann (Ro); 28 Oct. 1830; (297); 253
Danley, John Jr. (We); Pond, Pamela (Ba); 16 Nov. 1826; (34); 177
Danley, Robert Ira (Ro); Perry, Mary (Ro); 4 Nov. 1835; (256); 353
Dare, Jeremiah (Ma); Lyons, Charlotte (Ma); 6 Dec. 1812; (197); 76
Darrough, Archibald (Wo); Witighin, Hannah (Wo); 20 Aug. 1808; (249); 58
Darrough, Russell (Wf); Eveland, Catharine (Wf); 10 Apr. 1806; (245); 49
Daugherty, Joseph (Wf); Rinby, Margaret (Wf); 30 Mar. 1833; (66); 301
Davenport, James C.; Davis, Mary; 29 Oct. 1835; (54); 355
Davenport, William; Bacon, Thirza; 29 June 1837; (54); 580
Davis, Aaron (W.C.); Edwards, Ruth (W.C.); 2 May 1816; (250); 89
Davis, Amsa; Brown, Clarissa; 14 Nov. 1802; (41); NW-59
Davis, Asa (Wf); Olney, Mrs. Joanna (Ma); 25 Mar. 1802; (91); NW-52
Davis, Asa; Hallet, Ruth (Sa); 19 Oct. 1823; (90); 131
Davis, Asa; Lake, Jane; 16 Oct. 1825; (316); 157
Davis, Charles; Ross, Phoebe (Ro); 15 Dec. 1826; (346); 181
Davis, Charles Jr.; Hutchins, Nancy; 16 Nov. 1817; (90); 99M
Davis, Daniel; Olney, Drusilla; 7 Jan. 1795; (220); NW-13
Davis, Daniel (Wf); Olney, Sally (Ma); 14 Feb. 1799; (245); NW-32
Davis, Daniel Jr. (Wf); Foster, Olive (Wf); 14 Nov. 1805; (195); 48
Davis, Daniel (Sa); Dutton, Polly (Sa); 15 Feb. 1819; (92); 108
Davis, David; Bodwell, Elizabeth; 16 Oct. 1814; (345); 83M
Davis, Dudley W. (Ro); Lawrence, Rebecca (Ro); 4 Nov. 1819; (347); 111
Davis, Edward S. (Ma): Alcock, Drusilla (Ma); 20 Nov. 1831; (63); 272
Davis, Elijah; Bodwell, Edith; 20 Nov. 1816; (109); 100M
Davis, Elijah (Fe); Dutton, Nancy (Fe); 24 Oct. 1821; (210); 121
Davis, Elisha (Ad); Allison, Nancy (Ad); 17 Jan. 1805; (195); 45
Davis, Elisha (Ad); Mason, Susanna (Ad); 22 Oct. 1820; (138); 117
Davis, Frederick; Allison, Polly; 9 May 1811; (90); 68M

Davis, Hezekiel (Wf); Coleman, Elizabeth (Wf); 14 Feb. 1799; (245); NW-32
Davis, Hildreth (Fe); Flanders, Ann (Fe); 7 Nov. 1834; (247); 336
Davis, Isaac (Mn.C.); Tice, Mary (Lu); 6 May 1830; (150); 243
Davis, Isaiah; Dickson, Lavina; 21 June 1838; (213); 404
Davis, Jabez (Ma); Learned, Laura (Ma); 13 Feb. 1825; (27); 145
Davis, James (Fe); Hartshorne, Elizabeth (Sa); 4 June 1813; (227); 77
Davis, James (Wo); Stevens, Nancy (Wo); 20 Mar. 1814; (93); 81
Davis, James (Ro); Cheadle, Lecty (Ro); 28 Dec. 1815; (52); 87
Davis, James (Be); Barrows, Atilla L. (Be); 8 Nov. 1840; (344); 474
Davis, James E. (Ma); Matthews, Sally A. (Ma); 21 Dec. 1837; (129); 393, 402
Davis, James M.; McCabe, Patience; 23 Nov. 1828; (148); 217
Davis, Jesse (Wf); Blackmer, Polly (Wf); 15 Aug. 1804; (195); 44
Davis, John (Sa); Barnhart, Dorothy (Sa); 28 Jan. 1823; (90); 128
Davis, John (Ma); Dickey, Pamela (Ma); 26 Aug. 1832; (63); 285
Davis, John (Ad); Cusick, Mary Jane (Ad); 18 Aug. 1840; (2); 465
Davis, Joseph (Ad); Hutchins, Rosanna (Au); 10 June 1819; (90); 109
Davis, Joseph (Wd.C.); Miller, Adaline (Au); 17 July 1834; (204); 327
Davis, Levi (Mg.C.); Chiddester, Rhoda A. (Ro); 3 Aug. 1826; (92); 172
Davis, Levi (Mg.C.); Porter, Hannah (W.C.); 18 Mar. 1830; (66); 240
Davis, Marvel (W.C.); Stull, Anna (W.C.); 18 Aug. 1816; (289); 92
Davis, Nathan; Hurty, Susanna; 13 July 1826; (326); 173
Davis, Nathan Jr. (Fe); Dye, Elisa (Fe); 25 May 1820; (210); 114
Davis, Nehemiah 2nd; Allison, Polly; 1805; ; X
Davis, Russell; Jones, Polly; 3 July 1815; (278); 86M
Davis, Thomas; Snodgrass, Martha; 26 Dec. 1833; (109); 321
Davis, Walter (Ad); Otis, Caroline M. (Un); 27 Aug. 1829; (316); 229
Davis, Williard (Ad); Shepherd, Caroline (Ad); 24 May 1827; (316); 188
Davis (Davies), William (Ad); Ransom, Sarah (Ad); 2 Dec. 1824; (316); 143
Davis, William Jr. (Ad); Porter, Jerusha (Sa); 25 Aug. 1825; (69); 155
Dawes, Henry (Mg.C.); Cutler, Sarah (Wn); 20 Jan. 1829; (22); 234
Day, Noah (Wf); Gates, Bittsa (Wf); 6 Sept. 1799; (245); NW-36
Dazet, Joseph (W.C.); Davrange, Constance (W.C.); 13 July 1800; (285); NW-43
Dean, Lovead T. (A.C.); Scott, Elizabeth (Wn); 10 May 1832; (34); 280
Dearborn, Luther (Ro); Sedlift, Julia (Ro); 24 May 1818; (51); 102
Dearborn, Nathan (Wf); Seely, Sarah (Wf); 6 Feb. 1812; (143); 71
Deary, William (Ma); Hoff, Mary Ann (Ma); 22 Aug. 1836; (63); 365
Decker, Abraham (Np); Rea, Margaret (Np); 11 Nov. 1824; (116); 141
Decker, Elias (Np); Kinzer, Mary (Np); 14 Apr. 1831; (116); 265
Decker, Henry; Lenhart, Catharine; 25 July 1839; (247); 445
Decker, Levi; Ferguson, Grace; 26 Aug. 1835; (326); 350
Delafield, John Jr., Esq.; Wallace, Edith (Cin); 17 June 1833; (19); M.G.v-1 #1
DeLarguillon, Francis (Ga); Harris, Hannah (Ga); 10 July 1796; (285); NW-17
Delano, Amos (Be); Cole, Cynthia (Be); 24 May 1812; (133); 74
Delano, Cornelius (Be); Goodale, Sarah (Be); 8 Aug. 1792; (132); NW-24
Delano, Thomas; Delano, Cynthia; 24 Sept. 1818; (104); 104M
Delong, Henry (Wf); Heit, Sally (Wf); 23 Sept. 1806; (195); 51
Delong, Isaac; Hill, Nancy; 2 Jan. 1815; (293); 83M
Delong, Isaac H.; Lankister, Nancy; 30 Apr. 1826; (261); 169

Delong, Samuel (Sa); Fowler, Jane (Sa); 22 Jan. 1824; (90); 132
Deming, David (Wo); Henry, Ann (Wo); 27 Aug. 1816; (147); 91
Deming, Ezekiel (Wo); Stanley, Abigail (Ma); 25 July 1820; (38); 116
Deming, James H. (Wt); Cole, Diantha (Wn); 25 Jan. 1832; (184); 276
Deming, John T. (Wo); Starlin, Deborah (Wo); 9 Oct. 1812; (147); 73
Deming, Joel (Wt); Humphreys, Mary Ann (Wn); 4 Feb. 1834; (184); 320
Deming, Simeon Jr. (Wt); Ford, Mary A. (Wt); 2 Mar. 1825; (244); 146
Dempsey, Leander (Ma); Waters, Mrs. Rhoda A. (Ma); 13 Nov. 1831; (63); 271
Dennis, Daniel; Eveland, Amy; 16 Apr. 1815; (347); 85M
Dennis, Daniel (Ro); Stump, Cassandra (Ro); 14 Feb. 1819; (347); 107
Dennis, Miles; Root, Lucinda; 10 May 1840; (15); 464
Dennis, Samuel (Ro); Russell, Mary A. (Ro); 18 Oct. 1821; (92); 121
Dennis, Thomas (Ro); Nulton, Susanna (Ro); 30 Dec. 1813; (221); 80
Dennis, Uriah (Ro); Lewis, Jane W. (Ro); 8 Apr. 1824; (92); 134
Denny, John (Ma); Boothby, Sally (Ma); 3 July 1796; (78); NW-27
Densmore, Horace (We); Bishop, Jane (Ba); 7 Aug. 1823; (63); 130
DePu, George (Wf); Coulter, Mary (Wf); 26 Jan. 1801; (78); NW-49
DeSart, Leander B.; Brayton, Nelly S.; 24 Nov. 1838; (70); 426
DeVacht, Joseph Winon (Ga); Parmentier, Jean (Ga); 27 Apr. 1797; (285); NW-21
Devellers, Jules lemane (Ga); Wonsiter, Mrs. Elizabeth (Ga); 6 June 1792;
   (254); NW-9
Devin, Michael; Chambers, Harriet; 7 Oct. 1824; (194); 139
Devin, Thomas; Davis, Lucena; 15 Mar. 1818; (316); 100M
Devol, Abner; Mason, Clerinda; 2 Sept. 1830; (79); 258
Devol, Allen (Wf); Bartley, Rachel (Ad); 1 Jan. 1824; (10); 132
Devol, Allen (Wf); Bartley, Mrs. Rachel (Wf); 14 Mar. 1829; (192); 220
Devol, Allen (W.C.); LaGrange, Edith (W.C.); 31 Aug. 1834; 341; 328
Devol, Alpha (Wf); Champlin, Nancy (Wf); 28 July 1814; (289); 82
Devol, Alpha; Webster, Avis; 24 Oct. 1839; (2); 442
Devol, Arphaxad (Wf); Dye, Mary (Wf); 20 Sept. 1808; (195); 58
Devol, Benj. F.; Cross, Ruth B.; 16 May 1839; (162); 434
Devol, Cook (Wf); Converse, Hannah (Wf); 3 Jan. 1805; (195); 45
Devol, Cook (Wf); Thomas, Mary (Wf); 3 Aug. 1819; (271); 115
Devol, Cook (Wf); Scott, Patience (We); 8 July 1824; (244); 135
Devol, Daniel (Wf); Devol, Sarah (Wf); 6 Jan. 1825; (244); 144
Devol, Francis (Un); Dunbar, Nancy (Un); 12 Apr. 1818; (283); 101
Devol, Gilbert; Cobern, Mary; 25 Mar. 1790; (331); NW-2
Devol, Gilbert (Ma); Peek, Rachel (Ad); 14 July 1803; (91); NW-65
Devol, Gilbert; Hatch, Anna; 4 Apr 1811; (147); 68M
Devol, Helam (Un); Lewis, Betsey M. (Un); 20 Feb. 1833; (63); 297
Devol, Jonathan (Wf); Sherman, Clarissa (Wf); 11 Nov. 1794; (245); NW-3
Devol, Joseph (Wf); Colby, Pamela (Wt); 23 Nov. 1826; (244); 176
Devol, Philip (Wf); Hatch, Hannah P. (Wf); 25 Dec. 1813; (143); 78
Devol, Presburry (Wf); Brownwell, Patience (Wf); 27 Apr. 1800; (78); NW-37
Devol, Richmond; Stacy, Mary L.; 9 Feb. 1834; (98); 319
Devol, Richmond; Mason, Rachel (Ad); 20 Sept. 1840; (2); 471
Devol, Simeon (Wf); Sprague, Ruby (Wf); 10 Jan. 1822; (138); 122
Devol, Stephen; Wilson, Rebecca; 11 Mar. 1815; (232); 83M

WASHINGTON COUNTY MARRIAGES

Devol, Stephen (Wf); Buell, Silena (Wf); 25 Nov. 1818; (252); 106
Devol, William (Wf); Silvey, Sarah (Wf); 24 Feb. 1820; (252); 114
Devol, William; Putnam, Helen P. (Un); 9 Dec. 1829; (22); 235
Devol, Wing; Hart, Clara; 16 Oct. 1800; (238); NW-43
Dewees, Lewis M. (Mg.C.); Hoops, Sarah Ann (W.C.); 9 Apr. 1840; (186); 455
Dickerson, Joseph (Gr); Daley, Sally (Va); 18 Oct. 1807; (277); 55
Dickerson, Vachel (Gr); Jolly, Liddy (Gr); 11 Apr. 1816; (295); 90
Dickerson, Zadok (Mvl); Thorn, Mrs. Mary (Ma); 13 Feb. 1817; (38); 94
Dickey, Soloman (Ma); Welch, Sally (Ma); 17 Feb. 1805; (31); 45
Dickinson, Jordin (Ro); Dodge, Katharine (Wo); 24 Mar. 1808; (245); 57
Dickson, Christopher (Va); Lewis, Francis (Va); 5 Nov. 1800; (358); NW-42
Dickson, Christopher; Snyder, Eliza Ann E.; 6 Sept. 1834; (180); 330
Dickson, John (W.C.); Silva, Elizabeth (W.C.); 1 June 1820; (355); 115
Dill, James; Ice, Ann E.; 27 Jan. 1839; (116); 420
Dilley, James (Be); French, Melissa (Wn); 22 Mar. 1832; (311); 282
Dilly, John (Be); Blow (or Blough), Nancy (Be); 15 Feb. 1810; (81); 64
Dison, Thomas; Myers, Roesey; 25 Dec. 1801; (303); NW-52
Dison, Zepheniah; Williamson, Deborah; 14 Apr. 1811; (358); 68M
Doan, Asahel (Fe); Stanley, Sarah W. (Fe); 12 Dec. 1825; (85); 163
Doan, Curtis (Fe); Chapman, Esther (Fe); 28 Apr. 1825; (332); 150
Doan, Liman (Sa); Campbell, Martha (Sa); 8 Feb. 1833; (44); 299
Doan, Orzilleous (Sa); Chapman, Jerusha (Sa); 16 July 1807; (278); R-76, X
Doane, Charles (Chs); Lund, Abigail S. (Au); 14 Nov. 1833; (22); M.G.v-1 #21
Doane, Philo (Fe); Chapman, Sybil (Sa); 28 Mar. 1839; (330); 427
Dobbins, Anthony; Morris, Mrs. Selina; 18 Sept. 1835; (65); 355
Doctorman, John; Lawrence, Mrs. Elizabeth; 21 May 1826; (356); 170
Dodge, Benjamin L. (Ma); McCulluch, Lavinia (Ma); 20 June 1822; (278); 126
Dodge, Christopher C.; Vinton, Susan G.; 27 May 1839; (209); 435
Dodge, Dr. Israel S. (Cin); Dana, Emily W. (Be); 8 Oct. 1837; (184); 385
Dodge, Joel (Wn); Greene, Sylvina (Wn); 20 July 1816; (170); 91
Dodge, John (Wf); Galand, Katharine (Sa); 10 July 1799; (317); NW-35
Dodge, M. (W.C.); Fisher, Amanda M. (W.C.); 5 Oct. 1836; (174); 367
Dodge, Nathaniel; Sprague, Experience; 29 Apr. 1827; (306); 191
Dodge, Nathaniel Jr.; Burlinggame, Elizabeth P.; 28 Nov. 1824; (194); 141
Dodge, Oliver (W.C.); Manchester, Mrs. Anna (W.C.); 24 July 1800; (317); NW-41
Dodge, Oliver Jr. (W.C.); Wing, Docia (W.C.); 22 Apr. 1813; (316); 76
Dodge, Richard H. (Ad); McCoy, Betsey (Wf); 4 Oct. 1825; (18); 158
Dodge, Sidney (Ma); Hall, Mary (Ma); 8 May 1821; (272); 119
Dodge, William W.; Holden, Harriet; 29 Apr. 1840; (26); 459
Doland, William Jr. (Wf); Calahan, Dorcas (Wf); 3 Sept. 1835; (54); 349
Dolin, James (Wt); Harrison, Nancy (Wt); 3 Nov. 1831; (297); 272
Dolin, John (Wf); Morris, Sarah (Wf); 23 Sept. 1819; (183); 111
Doneker, Jacob (Mu.C.); Potts, Elizabeth (Wo); 7 Apr. 1818; (346); 101
Dor, Edmon (Mi); Farmen, Anna (Mi); 7 Feb. 1799; (21); NW-33
Dotson, Wm. B.; Ankrom, Louiza; 6 Apr. 1840; (58); 451
Doude, Andrew; Carr, Abigail; 19 Apr. 1791; (132); NW-24
Douglas, John (Mi); Sheppart, Nelly (Mi); 15 Jan. 1804; (110); 45
Douglass, John M. (Ma); Davis, Susan (Ma); 15 Oct. 1838; (63); 411

21

WASHINGTON COUNTY MARRIAGES

Douthitt, John (Fe); Littlefield, Phebe (Fe); 30 Sept. 1819; (332); 110
Dow, Benjamin F. (Ma); Dow, Mary Virginia (Ma); 11 Oct. 1838; (63); 410
Dow, Eliphalet (Ma); Ryan, Catharine (Ma); 25 Aug. 1829; (12); 228
Dow, Peter (Lo.C.); Campbell, Sally (Sa); 9 June 1829; (44); 228
Dowling, James (Sa); Perkins, Anna (Sa); 6 May 1824; (90); 135
Dowling, James F.; Perkins, Jane; 15 Feb. 1838; (59); 398
Dowling, John (Fe); Perking, Phebe (Ad); 18 Sept. 1836; (162); 370
Dowling, Lewis; Young, Elizabeth; 3 Nov. 1836; (59); 368
Doyle, John (Pit); Palmer, Mary (Ma); 5 June 1832; (103); 281
Drain, Thomas (Ba); Fullerton, Jennet (Wn); 7 June 1837; (184); 384
Driggs, George; Corwell, Catharine; 12 Jan. 1840; (311); 445
Driskill, Cornelius (Ad); Marriette, Martha (Ad); 22 May 1837; (2); 377
Driskill, Daniel (Sa); Brooker, Laura (Ad); 3 Mar. 1833; (48); 303
Drown, Gilbert G. (Ma); Perkins, Elvira (Fe); 11 Aug. 1825; (162); 153
Drown, John (Ma); Devol, Nancy (Ma); 29 May 1794; (220); NW-8
Drown, John (Ma); Brown, Mary (Ma); 26 Feb. 1807; (197); 52
Drown, Notley (Ma); Hook, Polly (Ma); 11 Apr. 1820; (38); 114
Drum, Jacob; Barth, Catharine; 10 Feb. 1838; (247); 398
Drury, Ambrose (Wf); Vaughan, Betsey (Wf); 15 Dec. 1831; (192); 273
Druse, Riley (Be); Cockshott, Mary (Be); 2 Oct. 1839; (70); 447
Druse, Stephen; Barkley, Sarah M.; 4 May 1837; (70); 377
Dufur, Abel (De); Fairchild, Polly (De); 25 Dec. 1823; (233); 131
Dufur, David; Root, Susan; 21 Jan. 1827; (130); 181
Dufur, Hiram; Gridley, Caroline; 6 Dec. 1827; (130); 200
Dunbar, Daniel; Lake, Mary C.; 20 May 1827; (322); 188
Dunbar, William (We); English, Elizabeth (Wn); 19 Mar. 1817; (78); 94
Dunbar, William (We); Gard, Martha E. (We); 18 Mar. 1818; (62); 101
Dunbarr, James (Ma); Hill, Jane (Ma); 10 Dec. 1840; (129); 472
Duncan, Charles (We); Gard, Charity (We); 20 Jan. 1820; (62); 112
Dunfee, William; Robinson, Anne; 6 Apr. 1837; (144); 376
Dunham, Amos (Ho); Guthrie, Laura M. (Ho); 27 Dec. 1804; (318); 45
Dunham, Daniel (W.C.); Swett, Keziah (W.C.); 23 Mar. 1797; (238); NW-20
Dunlap, John (Wt); Breckenridge, Charlotte (Ba); 20 Nov. 1834; (337); 332
Dunlevy, George (Ma); Devol, Harriet (Ma); 8 July 1812; (197); 76
Dunlevy, George, Esq.; Buell, Mrs. Eliza (Ad); 19 Apr. 1826; (40); 167
Dunn, Samuel (We); Ellis, Lucy (We); 5 Nov. 1840; (219); II-1
Dunsmoor, Daniel; Goddard, Julia; 8 Mar. 1838; (177); 400
Dunsmoor, Lucius (We); Williams, Mahala (We); 29 June 1837; (248); 382
Dunsmore, Hial (We); Mellor, Susannah (Wt); 1 May 1827; (34); 188
Durfee, Alexander (Be); Carlile, Frances M.; 18 Jan. 1835; (103); 337
Durgee, Silas; Williams, Mrs. Eleanor; 26 July 1802; (317); NW-58
Dustin, Mighill (Ba); Dana, Mary B. (Np); 28 Sept. 1837; (87); M.G.v-3 #46
Duthe, Charles Francis (Ga); Caddot, Jean (Ga); 9 Dec. 1796; (285); NW-20
Dutton, David (Cin); Fearing, Mary (Wf); 4 Feb. 1813; (124); 73
Dutton, James (Be); Bailey, Sally (Be); 26 Jan. 1817; (145); 95
Dutton, James (Au); Bayley, Barbara Ann (Au); 5 Mar. 1823; (47); 128
Dyar, Joseph B.; Hall, Amanda; 22 Feb. 1827; (322); 181
Dyar, Joseph B.; Proctor, Abigal; 24 Jan. 1839; (70); 426

Dye, Amos (Mg.C.); Dye, Sophia (La); 22 Dec. 1825; (79); 162
Dye, Amos; Taylor, Maria; 12 Sept. 1826; (326); 173
Dye, Andrew J.; Petty, Maria; 27 Sept. 1838; (255); 411
Dye, Enoch (Gr); Ridgeway, Mary A. (Gr); 9 Apr. 1812; (176); 74
Dye, Ezekiel; Davis, Phebe; 13 Apr. 1815; (109); 85M
Dye, Ezekiel; Dye, Elizabeth; 21 Dec. 1826; (326); 184
Dye, Henry (Ty.C.); Walton, Nancy (Gr); 22 Nov. 1832; (114); 293
Dye, James H.; Jackson, Clarissa; 26 Oct. 1837; (33); 392
Dye, John (Gr); Ridgeway, Priscilla (Gr); 8 Dec. 1811; (176); 71
Dye, John; Robertson, Eunice; 19 Feb. 1824; (261); 133
Dye, John H. (W.C.); Obleness, Elizabeth (W.C.); 5 Dec. 1822; (85); 127
Dye, Jonathan (Np); Cawood, Fanny (Fe); 10 May 1812; (109); 74
Dye, Jonathan (Ma); Weakley, Catharine (Ma); 2 Feb. 1835; (63); 338
Dye, Reuben F. (Gr); Tewel, Polly (Gr); 7 Apr. 1811; (176); 69
Dye, Samuel, 3rd; Cassidy, Didana; 22 Mar. 1838; (290); 396
Dye, Thomas (Be); Hill, Elizabeth (Be); 29 June 1817; (60); 95
Dyer, John (Un); Stone, Rosanna D. (Un); 13 June 1832; (46); 282

Eachus, Rufus H. (Mu.C.); Sullivan, Nancy (Bev); 12 Sept. 1839; (209); 438
Eadie, John (Ma); Davis, Mrs. Mary (Ma); 5 Dec. 1829; (148); 236
Eakman, Joseph; Murphy, Elizabeth; 10 Mar. 1825; (18); 147
Eastman, Timothy R. (Mg.C.); Gould, Elizabeth G. (Sa); 11 Apr. 1832; (96); 279
Eddlebute, William Jr.; Lyons, Charlotte; 11 Oct. 1837; (54); 387
Eddy, Cyrus (Ro); Vincent, Amy (Ba); 29 Aug. 1826; (311); 171
Edgell, William (Np); Dailey, Mary (Gr); 28 Aug. 1834; (85); 328
Edgerton, Giles (Gr); Ross, Dorcas (Gr); 27 Mar. 1821; (353); 119
Edgerton, Luther (Ma); Morgan, Elizabeth (Wa.Pa.); 15 Dec. 1830; (112); A.F.
   & M.G.v-15, #8
Edington, John (Nt); Walls, Malander (Nt); 27 July 1803; (45); 39
Edleston, Jarvis (Ma); Smith, Mary (Ma); 26 Aug. 1830; (301); 252
Edmonds, Edward S.; Camoren, Mary; 28 May 1840; (58); 461
Edmonds, Elias; Oliver, Sarah; 26 July 1838; (58); 404
Edwards, Nathan P.; Medley, Harriet; 9 Aug. 1838; (213); 409
Efaw, Isaac (Jo); Davis, Mary (Jo); 26 Nov. 1840; (201); II-1
Eickleberger, Jacob D. (Ma); Boomer, Amy Ann (Ma); 29 Nov. 1832; (368); 297
Elder, James (W.C.); Rynard, Sarah (W.C.); 27 June 1816; (250); 91
Elenwood, Charles; Bickford, Mahala; 5 Dec. 1839; (320); 445
Elenwood, Daniel; Ingals, Fanny; 18 Mar. 1798; (257); NW-28
Ellenwood, Augustus (Be); Dilley, Sophia (Be); 8 Dec. 1840; (311); II-3
Ellenwood, Daniel (Be); Gilman, Catherine (Be); 9 Feb. 1824; (82); 132
Ellenwood, Isaac (Be); Robbins, Mary E. (Be); 23 Nov. 1840; (286); 471
Ellenwood, John; Wedge, Lucinda; 10 Oct, 1833; (42); 310
Ellenwood, Milton; Needham, Sophronia S.; 23 Sept. 1840; (286); 466
Ellenwood, Morrison; White, Susanna; 1 Nov. 1837; (148); 392
Ellenwood, Sylvester D. (Be); Delano, Lucy A. (Wn); 17 Sept. 1835; (56); 352
Ellinwood, Joseph (W.C.); Williams, Amanda E. (W.C.); 26 Oct. 1822; (311); 127

Ellis, Alfred (Mg.C.); Lane, Sally (Ro); 18 Oct. 1821; (92); 121
Ellis, D. G.; Farris, Lavina; 4 Apr. 1839; (239); 427
Ellis, Isaac (Ro); Eddleblute, Elizabeth (Ro); 29 Nov. 1821; (92); 121
Ellis, Joel (Ro); Wright, Lauria (Un); 16 Mar. 1826; (316); 164
Ellis, John (Ro); Myers, Patty (Ro); 21 Feb. 1822; (51); 123
Ellis, Reuben (We); Ferris, Rebecca (We); 12 Oct. 1837; (85); 391
Ellis, Silas (Gr); Dickerson, Nelly (Gr); 16 Jan. 1817; (304); 96
Ellis, Thomas J. (Ro); Green, Harriet (Ro); 26 Apr. 1832; (36); 280
Ellis, Wesley K. (We); Biddison, Drusilla (Ba); 26 Oct. 1837; (85); 391
Ellis, William M.; Ankrom, Clarissa; 13 Aug. 1840; (58); 465
Elston, George (W.C.); Scott, Martha (W.C.); 5 Apr. 1832; (22); 290
Elston, Samuel; Widger, Mary; 28 Nov. 1839; (247); 445
Emeigh, Jacob (Wf); Johnson, Sarah (Wf); 20 Mar. 1831; (192); 263
Emerson, Asa Jr. (Ro); Olney, Elizabeth (Ro); 26 Jan. 1809; (292); 61
Emerson, Benjamin (Wf); Hinkley, Mary (Wf); 3 Apr. 1817; (289); 94
Emerson, Caleb (Ma); Dana, Mary (Be); 29 July 1810; (278); 65
Emerson, David; Sprague, Nancy; 11 Dec. 1810; (292); 67M
Emerson, David; Smith, Betsy; 24 Jan. 1818; (347); 100M
Emerson, Luke (Ro); Devin, Catharine (Ro); 26 Sept. 1814; (347); 82
Emmons, Jesse (Be); Stanford, Eliza (Be); 2 Nov. 1820; (3); 124
Enocks, Jesse (Sa); Forshey, Betsey (Sa); 2 June 1811; (261); 69
Eoff, Leonard (Gr); Horton, Eliza (Gr); 14 Nov. 1833; (114); 313
Eoff, Leonard; Williamson, Hannah; 20 Sept. 1840; (58); 470
Erwin, John (Ma); Parker, Charity (Ma); 20 July 1817; (346); 97
Evans, John; Lucas, Nancy; 6 July 1818; (92); 104M
Evans, Samuel M. (Ro); White, Polly (Ro); 29 Aug. 1825; (347); 155
Evans, Simeon (Wf); Miller, Elizabeth (Wf); 16 June 1799; (245); NW-35
Evans, Wm. J.; Anders, Cidee; 9 May 1838; (123); 399
Eveland, Frederick (W.C.); Lee, Nancy (W.C.); 16 Mar. 1797; (238); NW-20
Eveland, John (Ro); Newton, Harriet (Ro); 21 Apr. 1818; (51); 102
Eveland, John (Mg.C.); Walbridge, Elvira (W.C.); 2 Nov 1838; (360); 414
Eveland, Nathaniel (Wf); Scott, Cynthia (Wf); 10 Apr. 1806; (245); 49
Evens, Anthony (Gr); Cline, Susannah (Gr); 13 Oct. 1808; (277); 59
Evens, Bazely (Gr); Robenett, Susanna (Gr); 12 Apr. 1807; (277); 54
Everly, Petter; Greathouse, Mary; 6 May 1827; (326); 187
Ewart, Thomas W.; Dana, Grace; 16 Oct. 1838; (87); 460
Ewing, James (Sa); Sutton, Betsey (Sa); 2 Jan. 1812; (261); 72

Failar, Frederick (Un); Roberts, Elizabeth (Un); 11 Aug. 1835; (63); 347
Fairbrother, Henry; Tolman, Urana (Sa); 23 June 1833; (71); 308
Fairchild, Daniel S.; Haynes, Elvira D.; 1 Mar. 1832; (130); 277
Fairchild, David; Fletcher, Clarrissa; 24 June 1832; (130); 284
Fairchild, Erastus (Wt); Gedins, Elizabeth (De); 14 Apr. 1825; (194); 149
Fairchild, Hiram (Be); Stanton, Emily (Wn); 19 Feb. 1818; (346); 101
Fairchild, Levi (Be); Bellows, Emeline (Be); 12 June 1839; (344); 434
Fairlamb, Samuel (Ma); Scott, Esther (Ma); 17 Aug. 1807; (197); 55

Fairlee, Thomas (Wt); Flowers, Mariam (Wt); 2 Oct. 1834; (297); 330
Fall, Aaron (W.C.); Rood, Charity (W.C.); 2 Feb. 1817; (289); 93
Fall, Bryan (Ad); Owen, Sally (Ad); 5 Mar. 1829; (79); 219
Farley, Andrew; Metheny, Rachel; 20 Dec. 1832; (326); 298
Farley, Andrew (Wt); Flowers, Elizabeth (Wn); 28 Mar. 1838; (29); 400
Farley, David (Np); Burns, Mrs. Elizabeth (Np); 26 May 1831(r); (109); 266
Farmer, Thomas D.; Platter, Lucretia C.; 6 Feb. 1831; (98); 260
Farnsworth, James D. (Ma); Knapp, Eliza (Ma); 30 Nov. 1821; (27); 121
Farris, Matthew (Wn); Fraser, Elizabeth (Wn); 27 Dec. 1832; (184); 294
Faulkner, John; Dye, Polly; 25 Sept. 1815; (330); 86M
Fearing, Franklin (Wf); Coolidge, Hannah (Wf); 26 June 1817; (289); 97
Fearing, Henry (Ma); Dana, Eliza (Wf); 12 Feb. 1824; (194); 132
Fearing, Noah; Rhea, Rebecca; 14 Sept. 1790; (331); NW-3
Fearing, Paul, Esq. (Ma); Rouse, Cynthia (Be); 28 Nov. 1795; (132); NW-26
Fearing, Randolph (Wf); Shaw, Betsy (Wf); 26 Jan. 1817; (252); 94
Fearing, Rodolphus; Babcock, Sarah B.; 2 Jan. 1828; (322); 200
Fearing, Russell (Wf); Reed, Sally (Wf); 1 June 1818; (252); 102
Fearing, Silas (Ma); Babcock, Mary B. (Ma); 24 Feb. 1825; (194); 145
Fearing, Urwin; Kincade, Christiana; 15 Aug. 1839; (13); 438
Featherston, John (Wf); Legget, Sarah (Wf); 23 June 1811; (137); 70
Featherstone, Thomas (Ro); Shrader, Jane (We); 21 Apr. 1833; (154); 302
Fen, Jonathan; Tuttle, Mary Ann; 1 Jan. 1839; (247); 417
Fenn, Olonzo (Sa); McDaniel, Elizabeth (Un); 11 Apr. 1833; (48); 303
Fenn, William B. (W.C.); Flanders, Hannah (W.C.); 24 Oct. 1833; (332); 317
Ferguson, David (Ba); Drain, Catharine (Ba); 8 Oct. 1840; (186); 470
Ferguson, James (Np); Flint, Elizabeth (Lu); 22 Nov. 1832; (114); 293
Ferguson, Thomas (Np); Holdren, Grace (Np); 31 Jan. 1805; (141); 47
Ferrard, Peter (Ga); Violet, Margaret (Ga); 22 Mar. 1799; (285); NW-34
Ferry, Hugh (Wd.C.); Brough, Jane (Ma); 6 July 1826; (12); 170
Fetherby, Joseph (Wt); Winchell, Deborah (Wt); 24 Nov. 1831; (297); 273
Figgins, Thomas (Fe); Perry, Betsey (Fe); 2 Mar. 1832; (44); 278
Finch, Alfred (Ha); Williams, Jane (Ha); 17 Nov. 1839; (70); 447
Finch, Calvin (Wn); Cunningham, Mrs. Sarah (Wn); 21 Sept. 1837; (85); 390
Finch, Lewis (Wn); Cole, Ashia (Wn); 30 May 1819; (57); 109
Finch, Ruben (Ma); Wightman, Eliza A. (Ma); 18 Oct. 1835; (103); 351
Fish, Abner (Wf); Featherstone, Sally (Wf); 18 Oct. 1816; (346); 92
Fish, Abner (Ba); Barr, Susan (Ba); 15 Mar. 1838; (248); 401
Fish, John (Wf); Hooks, Nancy (Wf); 8 Oct. 1835; (192); 351
Fish, Robert; Campbell, Mary; 21 June 1838; (33); 405
Fish, William; Rardin, Polly; 8 Sept. 1833; (127); 309
Fish, William; Crosby, Margaret; 13 Oct. 1833; (88); 310
Fisher, Andrew (Ma); Gray, Polly (Wf); 13 July 1806; (245); 50
Fisher, Gustavus (Be); Stanley, Abigail (Ma); 22 Dec. 1822; (278); 129
Fisher, Thomas; Cozens, Mary; 15 Jan. 1835; (305); 340
Flack, Robert; Caven, Jane (Ma); 13 Jan. 1803; (317); NW-61
Flagg, Gershom J.; Cisler, Margaret; 8 May 1838; (33); 399
Flagg, James (Ma); Corner, Sarah (Ad); 4 Dec. 1803; (197); 40
Flagg, Thos. P. (Ma); Corner, Sarah F. (Ma); 6 Apr. 1836; (87); M.G.v-2 #2

Flake, Wm. C.; Hase, Valeriah; 25 Mar. 1830; (79); A.F. & M.G.v-14, #22
Flanders, Ezekiel; Allan, Eliza; 28 Mar. 1839; (255); 428
Flanders, Jacob (Fe); Spears, Sarah (Un); 5 July 1829; (261); 229
Flanders, Samuel (Fe); Twomley, Deborah H. (Fe); 16 Apr. 1829; (161); 222
Flanders, Thomas; Fenn, Sarah; 9 Nov. 1837; (247); 390
Flannaghan, Hugh; Kelly, Nancy; 10 Mar. 1811; (90); 68M
Fleming, Archibald; Adams, Lucy (Ro); 18 Sept. 1828; (243); 214
Fleming, James (Ba); Breckenridge, Mary (Be); 5 Sept. 1833; (184); 308
Fleming, Jesse (Gr); Collens, Nelly (Gr); 16 Aug. 1812; (176); 75
Fleming, Thomas L.; Edwards, Priscilla; 2 Jan. 1840; (213); 448
Fleming, William W.; Medly, Mariah; 7 Aug. 1840; (263); 464
Flemmin, John; Wilson, Pammelia; 9 Apr. 1830; (243); 241
Fletcher, Charles (W.C.); Starks, Susanna (W.C.); 24 Nov. 1822; (311); 127
Fletcher, John V. (Ad); Emmons, Dorcas (Ma); 1 Feb. 1827; (22); 184
Fletcher, Joseph (Ma); Warth, Catherine (Ma); 29 Aug. 1793; (132); NW-26
Fletcher, Peyton; Fletcher, Nancy; 27 Jan. 1836; (217); 359
Fletcher, Sherebiah; Bellows, Mary Ann; 9 Dec. 1832; (311); 297
Flick, Samuel; Cole, Susan; 8 Feb. 1829; (148); 219
Flint, Isaac (Lu); Edwards, Prusha (Lu); 14 Nov. 1833; (114); 312
Flint, Jacob (Lu); Alpin, Eliza (Gr); 21 June 1833; (114); 307
Flint, Luther; Edwards, Mary; 10 Dec. 1835; (119); 357
Flint, Porter (Lu); Beel, Jane (Np); 18 Feb. 1836; (87); M.G.v-2 #22
Flowers, David (Wo); Woodruff, Hannah (Wo); 22 Aug. 1824; (362); 138
Flowers, John (Wo); Taylor, Ellin (Wo); 23 Feb. 1820; (362); 112
Flowers, Moses; Crosby, Telitha; 3 June 1830; (230); 247
Floyd, John (Mn.C.); Harper, Nancy G. (W.C.); 30 Sept. 1840; (198); 466
Fogel, Robert H. (Ma); Tracy, Mary (Ma); 5 Apr. 1840; (129); 449
Folsom, Samuel (Ga); Smith, Catherine (Ga); 27 Nov. 1802; (280); NW-59
Force, William; Matheny, Jane; 18 Apr. 1811; (218); 68M
Ford, Amon (Wt); Parke, Hannah (Un); 27 Dec. 1827; (258); 204
Ford, Ansel B.; Deming, Lucy (Wt); 30 Jan. 1833; (182); 296
Ford, Joseph N. (W.C.); Wheeler, Clarissa (W.C.); 15 Dec. 1824; (362); 150
Ford, Judah (Wo); Deming, Betsy (Wo); 28 June 1811; (141); 70
Ford, Lory (Wf); Russell, Sarah Ann (Wf); 11 Jan. 1829; (106); 217
Ford,. Phenas (Ma); Benjamin, Mary (Va); 5 Apr. 1798; (238); NW-29
Ford, Truman (Wf); McFarland, Hannah (Wf); 1 Nov. 1804; (195); 44
Ford, William (Wf); Ford, Sarah (Wf); 26 Nov. 1798; (245); NW-30
Ford, William (Wf); Beebe, Elizabeth (Ma); Dec. 1803; (317); 42
Ford, William (Wo); Preston, Artymisa (Wf); 26 June 1823; (18); 130
Fordyce, John (Ma); Parker, Fanny (Ma); 30 Apr. 1807; (197); 54
Forenash, Charles (Nt); Richarts, Sarah (Nt); 12 Apr. 1799; (303); NW-49
Forguson, James (Ma); Morse, Elvira (Ma); 22 Sept. 1825; (38); 154
Forguson, William (Wt); Burchett, Sarah (Wt); 19 Mar. 1829; (248); 224
Forrest, Joseph; Hammond, Meribah; 19 Jan. 1801; (238); NW-43
Foster, Charles (Fe); Cherry, Mary Ann (Fe); 25 Dec. 1834; (98); 334
Foster, Ephraim (Ma); Olney, Sarah (Ma); 8 Oct. 1806; (91); 54
Foster, Peregrine P. (Be); Cushing, Betsy (Be); 4 May 1806; (203); 50
Foster, Theodore S. (Be); Barkley, Jane (Be); 28 Mar. 1822; (205); 124

Foster, Uz (Ma); Riley, Mary (Ma); 1 Apr. 1819; (27); 108
Foster, Wm. (Sp.M.); Foster, Matilda W. (Ma); 20 Nov. 1839; (198); 442
Fouch, John (Np); Tyson, Esther (Np); 2 Dec. 1806; (83); 53
Fountain, Chauncey; Ogle, Ruhama; 10 Aug. 1838; (71); 406
Fouts, Andrew; Clark, Polly; 18 Sept. 1818; (323); 104M
Fouts, Caleb M. (Mg.C.); Jett, Maria H. (W.C.); 25 Apr. 1824; (171); 133
Fouts, Lemen (Mg.C.); Jennings, Elizabeth (W.C.); 26 Feb. (1824); (85); 132
Fouty, Frederick (Mi); Bigerstaff, Nancy (Mi); 22 Jan. 1801; (21); NW-45
Fowler, John S. (Fe); Littlefield, Mahitable (Fe); 9 Nov. 1815; (283); 87
Fowler, Thomas (Fe); Perkins, Asenath (Sa); 8 July 1819; (90); 109
Fowler, Willey (Sa); Perkins, Cynthia (Sa); 21 Oct. 1819; (90); 109
Francis, Allen; Hilliard, Amy; 3 Mar. 1839; (116); 430
Francis, Edward Jr. (Np); Hearn, Hetty Ann (Np); 18 Jan. 1838; (116); 393
Francis, Nicholas (A.C.); Rathbun, Mercy (Wn); 16 Jan. 1831; (241); 257
Franks, Owen; Parr, Catharine; 11 Sept. 1833; (114); 311
Fraser, James (Wn); Bell, Margaret (Ba); 30 Dec. 1835; (184); 356
Frazier, Eliphalet (Ms); Lord, Betsey (Ma); 28 Nov. 1809; (278); 63, 65
Frazier, James; Fulcher, Roxanna; 30 Aug. 1838; (70); 413
Freemyer, George (Mn.C.); Bee, Martha (W.C.); 25 Mar. 1819; (353); 107
French, Charles (Wf); Robinet, Sarah (Wf); 10 Apr. 1804; (354); 41
French, Henry (Be); Fulsome, Temperance (Be); 12 June 1835; (144); 349
French, Isaac (Be); Rathbone, Electa (Be); 8 June 1808; (81); 57
French, Mansfield (Ma); Winchell, A. M. (Grl); 28 Aug. 1832; ; A.F. &
    M.G.v-16 #39
French, William (Np); Swearingame, Phoebe (Np); 14 Dec. 1806; (83); 53
Frie, John (Gr); Cline, Cathrine (Gr); 21 Nov. 1808; (277); 59
Frisby, George P.; Byran, Sarah Ann; 19 Mar. 1829; (34); 221
Frost, Stephen; Ellison, Nancy; 18 Dec. 1800; (91); NW-46
Frost, Stephen Jr. (Ad); Fox, Harriet P. (Ad); 11 Nov. 1835; (2); 356
Frye, Joseph (Ad); Coburn, Lucy (Ad); 23 Feb. 1840; (2); 458
Fulcher, John; Stanton, Nancy Olive; 18 Oct. 1838; (70); 414
Fulcher, Joseph (Wn); Fullerton, Elizabeth (Wn); 8 Sept. 1826; (22); 175
Fuller, Asa (Ma); Toothaker, Eliza (Fe); 7 Dec. 1828; (63); 215
Fuller, Charles S. (Ma); Howe, Harriet R. (Ma); 12 May 1836; (38); 364
Fuller, Daniel; Woodruff, Nancy; 8 Sept. 1829; (230); 231
Fuller, Demick (Ma); Livermore, Mary (Ma); 15 Oct. 1838; (63); 411
Fuller, Herman (Ma); Miller, Zipporah (Ma); 4 July 1837; (129); 380
Fuller, Isaac; Guitteau, Eliza Ann; 14 Feb. 1839; (319); 421
Fuller, Jedediah; Nesmith, Nancy; 27 Nov. 1817; (278); 99M
Fuller, Joseph (Ma); Stacy, Susanna (Ma); 13 Apr. 1796; (238); NW-16
Fuller, Joseph (Ad); Davis, Anna (Ad); 15 Mar. 1801; (91); NW-46
Fuller, Lot; Hoff, Lydia N.; 11 Apr. 1839; (326); 435
Fuller, Nathaniel (Wf); Scott, Celestina (Wf); 3 Aug. 1817; (346); 97
Fuller, Resolved (Ad); Nash, Elizabeth (Sa); 3 Apr. 1806; (310); 48
Fuller, Russel G.; Ackley, Abigail; 5 July 1835; (109); 363
Fuller, Samuel (W.C.); Record, Huldah (W.C.); 13 Oct. 1813; (345); 78
Fuller, Samuel H.; Hoff, Angeline; 29 Oct. 1829; (63); 232
Fuller, Seth (Be); Fisher, Hannah (Be); 18 Oct. 1807; (203); 55

Fuller, Solomon (Ma); Howe, Lucy W. (Ma); 6 Nov. 1825; (241); 157
Fuller, Stephen (Ma); Record, Mary (Ma); 9 Feb. 1809; (310); 61
Fullerton, Daniel (Wn); Fleming, Eliza (Wn); 5 Apr. 1838; (184); 397
Fullerton, Hugh S. (Rs.C.); Bois, Dorothy B. (W.C.); 29 Oct. 1830; (22); 289
Fulmer, John; Selers, Phebe; 6 Aug. 1837; (235); 381
Fulson, John (Be); Schonover, Temperance (Be); 8 Feb 1818; (145); 101
Fulton, James (Ma); Leonard, Lydia (Ma); 26 Mar. 1807; (197); 53
Fulton, John; Douthitt, Calista; 20 Feb. 1840; (71); 454
Fulton, Samuel (Sa); Jackson, Ruhanna (Sa); 16 Feb. 1808; (310); 56

Gage, James D. (Mg.C.); Barker, Fanny D. (Un); 1 Jan. 1829; (22); 234
Gage, Joseph H. (W.C.); Cook, Mary A. (W.C.); 8 Nov. 1838; (256); 412
Galbraith, John; Prior, Sally; 12 Apr. 1801; (285); NW-48
Galer, Andrew (Wf); Allen, Ruth (Wf); 17 Dec. 1800; (41); NW-46
Galer, Peter (Wf); Allen, Elizabeth (Wf); 30 June 1801; (245); NW-50
Galland, Abel (Ro); Forby, Amy (Ro); 28 Nov. 1808; (292); 60
Galor, Jacob (Fe); Dutton, Abigal (Fe); 30 Dec. 1808; (101); 59
Gamble, Samul; Knight, Welthy (Ma); 15 Jan. 1809; (265); 60
Gard, Hiram; Dunsmoor, Ataline; 25 Feb. 1830; (34); 237
Gard, John (Ba); Coleman, Angeline (Ba); 30 Aug. 1829; (139); 230
Gard, Ludley (Ro); Broun, Sophia F. (Ro); 10 Nov. 1831; (34); 274
Gard, Mishael (Un); Baker, Clarissa (Un); 21 Jan. 1816; (283); 88
Gard, Robert (Ba); Putnam, Martha W. (Fe); 2 Sept. 1825; (85); 155
Gard, Syrenes (We); Kidwell, Nancy (We); 1 Sept. 1836; (248); 369
Gardiner, James B. (Ma); Pool, Polly (Ma); 5 Oct. 1810; (86); 66
Gardiner, John (Ga); Robinson, Margaret L. (Ga); 14 Feb. 1794; (254); NW-10
Gardner, Amos F.; Cockshott, Elizabeth; 8 Aug. 1838; (70); 405
Gardner, Daniel; Rees, Mary; 31 Oct. 1824; (326); 142
Gardner, John; Hoff, Sophia; 6 Feb. 1827; (322); 179
Garen, Dudley D. (We); Colwell, Mary (We); 7 June 1840; (219); 458
Garoutte, Wm. D.; Dutton, Elizabeth; 16 Apr. 1829; (65); 222
Garrard, John (We); Roberts, Eliza (We); 14 Apr. 1831; (230); 265
Gates, Abel (Wf); Calahan, Anna (Wf); 27 Aug. 1806; (245); 51
Gates, Ebenezer; Stedman, Mary; 25 Feb. 1830; (311); 241
Gates, Jacob W.; Miller, Catharine F.; 23 Jan. 1840; (129); 445, 450
Gates, James (Ma); Taylor, Mary B. (Ma); 19 Sept. 1811; (86); 70
Gates, Jared (De); Lobdille, Rebecca Ann (De); 25 Dec. 1821; (233); 122
Gates, Jasper (Ma); Gellison, Hannah (Ma); 15 June 1807; (197); 55
Gates, John (Be); Druse, Mrs. Anna (Wn); 13 June 1824; (57); 136
Gates, John Jr.; Cram, Clarrissa Ann; 29 June 1818; (232); 103M
Gates, John M. (Wf); Walker, Eleanor (Ro); 28 Feb. 1833; (66); 298
Gates, Nathaniel (Ma); Hally, Anne (Ma); 17 Mar. 1807; (197); 53
Gates, Nathaniel; Cross, Julia Ann; 25 June 1835; (42); 348
Gates, Rufus H. (Wf); Baker, Hester (Wt); 31 May 1832; (66); 283
Gates, Samuel (Wf); Emerson, Susanna (Ro); 20 Apr. 1809; (51); 62(2X)
Gates, Samuel H. (Ma); Wheeler, Mary T. (Ma); 4 Jan. 1827; (22); 183

Gates, Seth (Ro); Farnham, Philena (Ro); 15 Dec. 1831; (66); 274
Gates, Stephen (Df); Mills, Jane (Ma); 10 July 1814; (31); 81
Gates, Thomas (W.C.); Gold, Sarah (W.C.); 25 May 1818; (38); 102
Gates, Timothy (Wf); Hughs, Margaret (Wf); 14 May 1800; (41); NW-42
Gates, Timothy (Wf); Gates, Susanna (Wf); 25 Aug. 1807; (137); 55
Gates, Wilson Lee; Gates, Mary; 7 Sept. 1815; (347); 86M
Gay, Robert; Palmer, Rebe; 1 Mar. 1833; (113); 298
Gaylor, Wm. Garret (Sa); Dutton, Jain (Sa); 26 June 1806; (310); 52
Geddings, James; Lobdell, Annis; 14 Jan. 1827; (322); 178
Geddings, James; Bodkin, Sarepta; 24 Oct. 1833; (130); 313
Geer, Asa; Wood, Sarah; 30 June 1839; (136); 437
Geer, Asa; Richards, Fanny B.; 22 June 1840; (319); 462
Geering, Joseph (Ma); Hill, Nancy (Ma); 30 July 1817; (38); 96
Geering, Samuel Jr. (Ma); Hill, Jane (Ma); 1 Aug. 1811; (265); 69
Geren, Benjamin (W.C.); Skinner, Rebecca (W.C.); 30 Dec. 1823; (194); 131
Geren, Isaac (Wt); Flowers, Margaret (Wt); 10 Feb. 1831; (297); 261
German, Dr. Morris (Ma); Hook, Hannah (Ma); 5 Apr. 1827; (102); 185
Gevrez, Theodore (Ma); Smithson, Jane (Au); 14 Nov. 1833; (103); 311
Gibbs, Jonathan D.; Lund, Katharine; 17 Aug. 1837; (61); 381
Gibson, John (Ma); Pearsons, Anna (Ma); 7 Mar. 1819; (27); 108
Gibson, Robert (Un); Bartlett, Livy (Un); 30 Jan. 1817; (293); 93
Giddings, John; Noland, Mrs. Elizabeth; 9 Dec. 1827; (251); 203
Gifford, Burton (A.C.); Warrell, Rebecca (Ro); 24 Jan. 1833; (222); 295
Gilbert, Amos (Be); Magruder, Sally (Be); 22 Apr. 1810; (37); 65
Gilbert, Eli Jr.; Fairchild, Lucy; 18 Sept. 1828; (15); 213
Gilbert, Dr. George N. (Be); Putnam, Lucy E. (Be); 16 May 1825; (215); 150
Gilbert, Ira (De); Dills, Saloame (Be); 21 Nov. 1830; (321); 253
Gilbert, Stephen (De); Dufur, Sally (De); 18 Mar. 1832; (155); 282
Gilbert, Truman (De); Dilley, Julia (Be); 29 Nov. 1832; (155); 297
Gilkison, Thomas; Delong, Sally; 14 Apr. 1809; (261); 62
Gill, John (Sa); Holburt, Lucy (Sa); 7 May 1807; (310); 55
Gilliland, John (Wn); McAtee, Betsey (Wf); 21 Mar. 1822; (283); 123
Gillis, Samuel; Kimberly, Maria; 2 Aug. 1838; (247); 406
Gilman, Nathaniel C. (Ma); Goodwin, Sarah (Ma); 3 Aug. 1806; (265); 51
Gilmor, George (Wt); Skipton, Mary Ann (Wt); 6 Jan. 1831; (297); 257
Gilmore, David; Mixer, Sally (Ma); 22 Dec. 1808; (278); 60
Gilpin, Benjamin; Hill, Jane; 30 Aug. 1835; (13); 352
Gilpin, Lewis; Stage, Ann E.; 8 June 1837; (63); 378
Gilpin, Matthew; Barnhart, Rosannah; 13 Oct. 1831; (71); 272
Gilpin, Samuel; Davis, Reschal; 26 Jan. 1838; (59); 398
Gitteau, Benj. (Ma); Taylor, Maria (Ma); 16 Apr. 1807; (278); 54
Gittle, Michael (Ma); Malder, Margaret (Ma); 3 Nov. 1836; (63); 368
Gladman, Reason (Ro); Forst, Mahala (Ro); 15 June 1835; (123); 346
Glidden, John; Delong, Matilda; 6 Oct. 1836; (65); 369
Glidden, Jonas Galusha; Protsman, Margaret; 22 Nov. 1836; (33); 373
Glidden, Wm. (Mg.C.); Crawford, Florilla (Au); 14 Nov. 1824; (69); 141
Glines, Joseph (Sa); Hill, Polly (Ma); 15 Jan. 1806; (27); 49
Glines, William (Ma); Truesdale, Eliza (Ma); 1 Jan. 1826; (27); 161

WASHINGTON COUNTY MARRIAGES

Glover, James (Ma); Armstrong, Margaret (Ma); 3 Mar. 1816; (197); 90
Gobin, Samuel; Lucas, Peggy; 7 Aug. 1815; (347); 86M
Goddard, Edward H.; Hilderbrand, Jane (We); 6 Mar. 1834; (248); 324
Goddard, Wm. P. (We); Farris, Jane (We); 12 June 1838; (70); 402
Godfrey, Benjamin (Mg.C.); McCluer, Sarah (W.C.); 25 Nov. 1830; (66), 255
Godfrey, Samuel (Wf); McCluer, Hannah (Wf); 13 Mar. 1831; (192); 262
Godfry, Samuel; Boggs, Sarah; 22 Oct. 1839; (123); 443
Goldsmith, Burfet (W.C.); Smith, Charlotte (W.C.); 16 June 1816; (223); 91
Goldsmith, James; Cherry, Catharine; 23 Nov. 1837; (59); 389
Goldsmith, William (Ma); Walker, Eleanor (Ma); 10 Feb. 1814; (278); 80
Gollaher, Allen; Dickson, Sarah; 7 Dec. 1837; (290); 393
Gooden, Jabez (Wn); Hait, Sarah Ann (Wn); 30 Sept. 1838; (263); 413
Gooding, Frederick; Inman, Deborah; 22 Mar. 1840; (29); 448
Gooding, James (Wn); Parks, Electa (Wn); 25 Feb. 1824; (348); 133
Goodno, Daniel; Cushing, Sally; 15 Apr. 1802; (257); NW-55
Goodno, Daniel H., Esq. (Be); Prentiss, Mary C. (Wd.C.Va.); 3 Dec. 1830; (359); A.F. & M.G.v-15 #6
Goodno, Thaddeus (Wo); Woodruff, Betsey (Ba); 21 Feb. 1820; (164); 112
Goodrich, Timothy; Howe, Minerva; 6 July 1815; (283); 85M
Goodwin, Asa (Ma); Williams, Hannah (Ma); 13 Aug. 1810; (197); 66
Goodwin, Thomas; Rieder, Betsey; 15 Oct. 1840; (320); 469
Goomer, Ezekiel (Ma); Stevens, Melissa (Ma); 4 July 1833; (63); 306
Goosman, John (Gr); Brown, Rachel (Gr); 24 Apr. 1835; (200); 343
Gorham, Benj. E.; Deming, Rebecca; 11 May 1824; (311); 136
Gorman, John (W.C.); Alden, Margaret (W.C.); 29 Mar. 1821; (189); 119
Gorral, Wm.; Birchard, Rebecca; 15 Apr. 1803; (354); NW-63
Goss, Daniel (Ma); Ackley, Lydia (Ma); 13 Aug. 1813; (197); 78
Goss, Solomon Jr. (Fe); Devol, Polly (Ma); 19 Nov. 1812; (366); 73
Gosset, Amos (W.C.); Corns, Louisa (W.C.); 11 Oct. 1838; (248); 418
Gossett, Daniel (W.C.); Riley, Susan (W.C.); 10 Sept. 1817; (38); 97
Gossett, Jacob (Wo); Orison, Mary (Wo); 9 Feb. 1812; (147); 71
Gossett, John (Ba); Burchett, Hannah (Wt); 12 Jan. 1832; (297); 277
Gould, Aaron; Gold, Esther; 19 Nov. 1838; (255); 416
Gould, Daniel (Sa); Sharp, Anna Louisa (Fe); 5 Apr. 1831; (96); 267
Gould, Ephraim (Sa); Porter, Lois (Sa); 6 June 1830; (65); 244
Gould, Stephen L. (Ba); Proctor, Polly (Ba); 12 May 1825; (194); 149
Gould, Stephen L. (Ba); Sayles, Louisa (Ba); 5 July 1838; (337); 407
Grady, Strother; Pilcher, Catharine; 10 July 1828; (311); 212
Graham, John (Mi); Norman, Clexanda (Mi); 21 Feb. 1804; (135); 41
Grandstaff, Lewis (Mu.C.); Taylor, Levina (Sa); 9 Jan. 1831; (44); 259
Grandstaff, Moses (W.C.); Waller, Catherine (W.C.); 18 Sept. 1817; (252); 98
Grant, Wm.; Millard, Mary Ann; 5 Dec. 1839; (319); M.G.v-3 #2
Graves, Elijah; Pattin, Sally; 23 Dec. 1824; (57); 143
Gray, Elijah; Cline, Sarah; 19 Oct. 1837; (71); 386
Gray, George W.; Wiley, Olive; 24 Dec. 1837; (130); 394
Gray, Jesse (Li); Cunningham, Elizabeth (Li); 1 Dec. 1836; (71); 373
Gray, Wm. (Wf); Pugh, Sarah (Ro); 10 Jan. 1833; (36); 299
Greathouse, William; Hook, Lydia B.; 18 Nov. 1830; (170); 255

Green, Charles W. (Wt); Parke, Susan (Un); 1 Jan. 1837; (207); 371
Green, Dudley (Mg.C.); Ogle, Nancy Ann (W.C.); 15 Nov. 1832; (22); 291
Green, Eli; Stewart, Elizabeth; 11 Jan. 1824; (142); 132
Green, Eli (Wn); Moore, Barbary (Wn); 24 May 1832; (85); 284
Green, Ezra (Ad); Dodge, Anna (Ad); 6 Apr. 1820; (138); 116
Green, Greenberry (Ro); Melvin, Louisa (Ro); 12 Apr. 1838; (256); 400
Green, John; Greene, Elisa; 11 Aug. 1824; (194); 136
Green, John, Esq. (Cin); Cram, Mrs. Sally (Ma); 26 Jan. 1826; (22); 163
Green, John 2nd. (W.C.); Devoll, Elizabeth (W.C.); 20 Nov. 1808; (91); 58
Green, Oliver (Mg.C.); Davis, Charlotte (Ad); 21 Jan. 1821; (138); 118
Green, Richard (Np); Brown, Harriet (Ba); 15 Nov. 1831; (34); 274
Green, Robert; Broocaw, Marietta; 13 Aug. 1840; (123); 466
Green, Smith (We); Mellor, Sally (Wo); 21 Nov. 1813; (147); 78
Green, Stephen W. (A.C.); Green, Lucy (Wt); 1 Sept. 1836; (207); 367
Green, Thomas (Ma); Marsh, Sally (Ma); 21 Mar. 1813; (197); 76
Greene, Benjamine; Perry, Susanna; 6 June 1811; (310); 68M
Greene, Caleb (Np); McMasters, Catharine (Ma); 17 Dec. 1812; (197); 76
Greene, Caleb (We); Palmer, Jerusha (We); 31 Mar. 1814; (165); 80
Greene, David; Conkright, Harriet; 18 Apr. 1839; (29); 430
Greene, Duty Jr.; Henry, Polly; 11 Apr. 1811; (141); 68M
Greene, Ezra (Wf); Procter, Sally (Wf); 21 Oct. 1805; (195); 46
Greene, John (Np); Hill, Polly (Np); 22 June 1808; (197); 58
Greene, Richard; Rouse, Bathsheba; 7 July 1794; (257); O.C.
Greene, Richard (Np); Lawton, Rebecca (We); 13 Dec. 1813; (366); 78
Greene, William (Ma); Bartlett, Mary Ann (Ma); 6 Jan. 1831 85); 261
Greenlees, Archibald (Be); Young, Mary (Ma); 6 Feb. 1823; (278); 128
Greenman, Jeremiah Jr. (Wf); McCoy, Latitia (Wf); 26 Nov. 1818; (183); 115
Greenwood, George Jr. (Np); Edgerton, Elizabeth (Np); 26 Mar. 1835; (281); 341
Greenwood, John W. (St.C.); Barstow, Adeline M. (Np); 30 Nov. 1827; (79); 204
Greer, Paul (Gn); Evritt, Maria (Gn); 25 Jan. 1801; (169); NW-44
Greiner, John (Ma); Bennett, Laurinda (A); 4 May 1837; (43); M.G.v-3 #25
Gridley, John (Ma); Athey, Elizabeth (Fe); 17 June 1835; (281); 346
Griffin, Asael (W.C.); Chapman, Betsey (W.C.); 21 Oct. 1800; (317); NW-42
Griffing, Ebenezar (Va); Roberts, Grace (Va); 19 June 1797; (203); NW-21
Griffith, William D.; Smith, Experience; 29 Aug. 1839; (13); 438
Griggs, Erastus (Ma); Corner, Melissa; 25 Oct. 1837; (63); 386
Griggs, Samuel (Ma); Wheeler, Asenath (Ma); 30 Dec. 1832; (22); 294
Griggs, William (Ma); Gibson, Harriet (Ma); 11 Mar. 1839; (63); 424
Grimes, Ephraim; Beck, Fanny; 15 Aug. 1839; (29); 438
Grimes, Hugh (Ma); Smith, Sarah (Ma); 22 July 1837; (330); 411
Grimes, Samuel (Ma); Lett, Susannah (Ma); 4 Nov. 1830; (63); 252
Grover, Daniel (Wt); Calwell, Betsey (Wt); 1 Apr. 1834; (259); 323
Groves, James M.; Flint, Lucy; 8 May 1834; (119); 334
Groves, William (We); Danley, Eliza (We); 7 June 1827; (34); 189
Groves, William; Stanton, Sarah; 13 Oct. 1832; (130); 287
Grubb, Andrew (Wf); Gorman, Jane (Wf); 12 Nov. 1815; (143); 88
Grubb, James; White, Cynthia; 19 Feb. 1815; (9); 84M
Grubb, John (Wo); Wilson, Elizabeth (Wo); 5 July 1820; (47); 116

Grubb, Orra (Wf); Gates, Hester (Wf); 17 Feb. 1826; (346); 164
Grubb, Pelatiah (Wf); Coleman, Betsey (Ro); 19 June 1828; (66); 209
Grubb, Peter (W.C.); Townsend, Betsey (W.C.); 15 Mar. 1821; (47); 118
Guitteau, Francis G.; Fulton, Sarah F.; 28 Dec. 1837; (33); 392
Guitteau, Jonathan (Ma); Lord, Polly (Ma); 18 May 1809; (278); 63
Guitteau, Jonathan (Ma); Mills, Sally (Ma); 12 Sept. 1813; (278); 79
Guitteau, William H. (Fe); Chapman, Anthea (Fe); 6 Dec. 1832; (96); 294
Guthrie, Augustus S.; Knowles, Cynthia Ann; 27 Dec. 1832; (144); 294
Guthrie, Erastus (Be); Palmer, Achsah (Ma); 3 July 1821; (349); 119
Guthrie, James H. (G.C.); Oaks, Charlotte (W.C.); 14 May 1835; (281); 343
Guthrie, Stephen (Be); Palmer, Mrs. Martha (Ma); 10 Aug. 1824; (27); 137
Guthrie, Trueman (W.C.); Stone, Elizabeth (W.C.); 21 July 1796; (132); NW-27
Guthrie, Truman; Knowles, Hannah; 16 Feb. 1826; (190); 171

Hagerman, Aaron; Gates, Elizabeth; 24 Nov. 1825; (189); 160
Hagerman, James (Wf); Robinson, Phoebe (Wf); 7 Jan. 1819; (252); 106
Hagerman,Peter; McCoy, Elizabeth; 26 Jan. 1825; (47); 148
Hagerman, William (Wf); Bingham, Phoebe (Wf); 14 Feb. 1830; (106); 239
Hagermon, John B.; Bingum, Flora; 2 Dec. 1834; (54); 33
Haight, John (Wn); Bridges, Minerva (Wn); 24 Mar. 1840; (29); 448
Haise, Henry; Knowlton, Lucy (Gr); 7 July 1825; (353); 153
Hait, Joseph; Elliot, Sarah; 8 Jan. 1828; (162); 201
Hale, Christian (Sa); Jackson, Margaret (Sa); 24 Mar. 1809; (261); 61
Hale, Josiah; Gibson, Lovina; 9 Nov. 1834; (65); 331
Hale, Samuel; Brady, Frances; 7 Dec. 1837; (33); 392
Haley, Thomas (Ma); Keating, Elizabeth (Ma); 19 Nov. 1806; (197); 52
Hall, Alfred; Ross, Narcissa (Ad); 26 Feb. 1824; (306); 133
Hall, Daniel (Ad); Ireland, Susan (Wf); 31 Dec. 1835; (2); 357
Hall, Dudley; Brown, Rebecca; 28 Oct. 1831; (306); 271
Hall, George (Mi); Jackson, Mary (Mi); 30 Aug. 1798; (203); NW-30
Hall, Isaac (Mn.C.); Knowlton, Eunice (W.C.); 26 July 1827; (150); 191
Hall, James; Bartlett, Polly; 8 Apr. 1830; (311); 241
Hall, James; Burlingame, Maria; 20 Dec. 1840; (157); 472
Hall, Jeremiah (De); Ball, Sally (De); 5 Apr. 1827; (311); 184
Hall, John (Sa); Ayles, Louisa (Sa); 5 May 1818; (160); 102
Hall, John; Ross, Sarah; 29 Jan. 1831; (306); 259
Hall, John P.; Drake, Rhoda Jane; 10 Dec. 1840; (71); 472
Hall, Joseph; Bartlet, Arena; 6 June 1833; (305); 306
Hall, Joseph E.; Roe, Rosanna (Ma); 20 Nov. 1834; (343); 335
Hall, Joseph H.; Allen, Margaret; 5 Dec. 1839; (71); 444
Hall, Mitchel; Dilley, Fanny; 31 Jan. 1828; (311); 207
Hall, Norman; Bell, Betsey; 20 June 1830; (336); 245
Hall, Price (Ad); Coffee, Lina (Ad); 15 Mar. 1840; (2); 459
Hall, Thomas (Ma); Carver, Mary (Ma); 25 Feb. 1827; (38); 179
Hall, Walter (Ad); Patterson, Esther (Ad); 5 Dec. 1818; (355); 106
Hall, Washington (Ad); Hunter, Ruth (Ad); 26 July 1832; (47); 286

WASHINGTON COUNTY MARRIAGES

Hall, William; Sprague, Mary M.; 7 Jan. 1829; (306); 218
Hall, William B. (Wt); Quimby, Elizabeth (Wt); 28 June 1838; (360); 402
Hall, Wyllys (Jr.?) (Ma); Sullivan, Emma (Ma); 23 July 1840; (26); 462
Hallet, Isaiah H. (Sa); Sharp, Marget (Sa); 30 Jan. 1835; (71); 339
Hallet, John; Ingram, Neoma (Ro); 17 July 1834; (127); 327
Hallet, Mitchel; Featherston, Sarah (Ro); 14 Mar. 1833; (67); 303
Hallet, Orlano (Sa); Blake, Lucy (Fe); 27 Jan. 1831; (96); 261
Hallett, Solomon; Parker, Sarah Ann; 30 Apr. 1835; (247); 344
Halsey, David (Wf); Collins, Eunice (Wf); 19 July 1821; (189); 121
Hamilton, Daniel H.; Humiston, Wealthy; 11 Sept. 1814; (9); 84M
Hamilton, Thomas R. (A.C.); Hagerman, Latetia (W.C.); 15 May 1823; (10); 130
Hammond, Michael (W.C.); McDonald, Nancy (W.C.); 19 Dec. 1798; (238); NW-31
Hammond, Zoath (Wf); Shekley, Mary (Wf); 7 Feb. 1804; (357); 39
Hammond, Zoeth; Dye, Abigail; 15 Aug. 1797; (245); NW-22
Hand, Elisha; Cheadle, Sally (Ro); 29 Oct. 1809; (51); 62
Handrahan, James; McGeehan, Mary; 2 Dec. 1838; (206); 417, 418
Hankins, John (Mg.C.); Fairlee, Margaret (Wt); 24 Mar. 1833; (297); 300
Hanlen, Richard; French, Nancy (Gr); 30 Oct. 1817; (250); 98
Hanson, Augustus A. (Ma); Skinner, Letitia (Ma); 22 July 1823; (308); 131
Hanson, Ephraim (W.C.); Waller, Eleanor (W.C.); 18 Sept. 1817; (252); 98
Harden, Enos (Wt); Brabham, Louisa M. (Wt); 24 Dec. 1840; (70); 474
Harden, James; Frizel, Sarah; 17 Aug. 1802; (140); NW-56
Hardin, Samuel; Greene, Harriet; 28 Oct. 1824; (57); 141
Hardy, William (Ma); Cole, Clara (Wn); 25 Jan. 1821; (57); 118
Hargo, Lewis (Mu.C.); Stephens, Catharine (Wt); 2 Aug. 1832; (360); 288
Harris, Asa (Ha); Fulcher, Eliza (Wn); 23 Nov. 1837; (70); 388
Harris, Averill (Wn); Terrill, Laura Ann (Wn); 9 June 1821; (57); 119
Harris, Caleb R. (Fe); Wells, Candace (Fe); 16 Apr. 1820; (332); 114
Harris, David; Hill, Anna; 8 Apr. 1815; (278); 86M
Harris, George (Fe); Gates, Mary (Fe); 28 July 1833; (162); 307
Harris, John (Mi); Bingham, Elizabeth (Mi); 19 Feb. 1801; (21); NW-45
Harris, Joseph (Fe); Price, Nancy (Fe); 12 Oct. 1820; (89); 117
Harris, Joseph G. (Ma); McAllister, Irene (Ma); 18 Nov. 1820; (27); 116
Harris, Luther (Wn); Cunningham, Delilah (Wn); 8 Nov. 1827; (241); 195
Harris, Stephen (Li); Koon, Rhoda (Li); 7 Mar. 1833; (136); 195
Harris, Rev. Timothy (Grl); Linnel, Bethiah (Grl); 4 Sept. 1809; (278); R-77
Harris, Wm. (Za); Burnham, Abigail H. (Wf); 21 Feb. 1822; (25); 123
Harrison, Robert (Ma); Wheeler, Rebekah (Ma); 21 Apr. 1808; (31?); 57
Harrison, Robert (W.C.); Henry, Shabariah (W.C.); 17 Nov. 1813; (116); 78
Harriss, Andrue (Fe); Goold, Alizabeth (Fe); 2 Jan. 1809; (101); 59
Harshberger, Thomas P. (Ma); Edson, Berilla (Ma); 18 Jan. 1839; (198); 418
Hart, Benjamin (Ma); Deming, Honor (Wf); 28 July 1805; (195); 46
Hart, Benjamin (Wt); Miner, Mrs. Esther (Wf); 23 July 1826; (258); 172
Hart, Dr. Josiah (Ma); Moulton, Anna (Ma); 28 Dec. 1797; (238); NW-29
Hart, Josiah M.; Atha, Angeline; 11 June 1829; (148); 224
Hart, Josiah M. (Wf); Gray, Clarissa (Wf); 10 Oct. 1831; (46); 270
Hart, Seth (Wt); Wilson, Mary (Wf); 8 June 1828; (258); 210
Hart, Stephen (IL); Buck, Eliza (W.C.); 5 July 1831; (22); 289

33

Hart, Walter; Potts, Hannah; 31 May 1818; (346); 103M
Hart, William (W.C.); McNeal, Mrs. Mary (W.C.); 10 Aug. 1825; (27); 153
Harte, Rufus E. (Ma); Holden, Julia (Ma); 7 Mar. 1839; (198); 424
Hartshorn, Darius; Bowers, Elizabeth; 20 Sept. 1818; (27); 104M
Hartshorn, Edward; Delong, Lydia; 12 Jan. 1815; (330); 84M
Hartshorn, George; Stewart, Amanda; 18 Oct. 1839; (2); 442
Hartshorn, Jesse (Li); Cunningham, Sarah (Li); 31 Dec. 1840; (156); II-2
Hartshorn, Leonard (Ba); Dustin, Eunice (Ba); 20 Sept. 1837; (337); 385
Hartshorn, Silas (Ba); Havens, Dorcas (Be); 10 Dec. 1826; (311); 180
Hartwell, Benjamin (W.C.); Woodard, Elmira (W.C.); 17 Oct. 1832; (116); 287
Harvey, Amos (W.C.); Jones, Rebecca (W.C.); 28 Sept. 1797; (238); NW-22
Harvey, Amos (Ma); Frazer, Margaret (Ma); 3 May 1807; (197); 54
Harvey, Elijah (Nt); Barrack, Margaret (Nt); 22 Dec. 1800; (45); NW-50
Harvey, James (Ba); Fleming, Mary (Ba); 22 Dec. 1825; (258); 164
Harvey, Samuel (Ba); Fleming, Isabella (Ba); 14 Feb. 1839; (184); 421
Harwood, Charles (Wf); Delong, Polly (Wf); 1 Jan. 1806; (195); 48
Harwood, James; Lyles, Elizabeth; 3 May 1838; (129); 402
Harwood, Leroy B. (Wt); Burch, Elvira (Wt); 23 May 1834; (54); 326
Haskell, Charles (Ma); Dana, Elizabeth H. (Np); 5 Apr. 1826; (79); 168
Haskell, Jonathan; Greene, Phoebe; 8 Apr. 1792; (132); NW-24
Haskins, Wait (W.C.); Mead, Abigail (W.C.); 10 Mar. 1816; (223); 90
Hatch, Isaac Jones; Billard, Sarah Ann; 13 Nov. 1817; (355); 99M
Haught, Peter; Pool, Jane; 30 Jan. 1840; (58); 449
Haught, Tobias Jr. (Gr); Weaver, Lavina (Gr); 9 July 1835; (200); 352
Haughton, John (W.C.); Williams, Maria (W.C.); 1 Mar. 1820; (349); 112
Haut, Jesse J. (Jo); Merrick, Mrs. Sarah (Jo); 22 Oct. 1840; (350); II-17
Havens, Henry (Ro); Hinkley, Lydia (Ro); 19 May 1814; (347); 81
Havens, William; Elliot, Maria; 12 Feb. 1839; (123); 422
Hayes, Adam (Va); Pool, Elizabeth (W.C.); 3 July 1814; (295); 81
Hayes, Adam; Michael, Polly; 22 July 1832; (326); 287
Haynes, Andrew J.; Newell, Eliza (De); 1 Sept. 1836; (4); 366
Haynes, John G.; Fairchild, Monday; 24 June 1836; (130); 361
Hays, James (Ad); Murphy, Providence (Ad); 24 Jan. 1835; (341); 337
Hays, John (Gr); Philips, Peggy (Gr); 11 June 1812; (176); 74
Hays, Oren (We); Beach, Anne (Wt); 10 Mar. 1830; (361); 238
Hays, Thomas; Jones, Abigail; 14 Oct. 1835; (87); 353
Hayward, Edward T. (Wf); Gray, Charlotte (Wf); 28 Mar. 1822; (25); 124
Hayward, Rotheus (Ma); Nye, Panthea (Ma); 29 Jan. 1807; (278); 54
Hayward, Rotheus (Wf); Gray, Rebecca (Wf); 18 Mar. 1822; (25); 124
Hazlerigg, John (Ma); Jemason, Abigail (Ma); 15 Feb. 1810; (31); 64
Heald, Dr. Wm. W. (Sa); Porter, Ruth (Sa); 21 Feb. 1839; (330); 423
Heard, Josiah (Mu.C.); Goodwin, Sarah (Ma); 13 May 1819; (38); 109
Hearn, Daniel Jr.; Elder, Margaret; 16 July 1840; (213); 463
Hearn, Hiram L. (W.C.); Knowlton, Betsey (W.C.); 12 Dec. 1822; (109); 131
Hearn, Josiah; Winget, Rachel; 22 Jan. 1824; (326); 133
Hearn, Nehemiah A.; Medley, Elizabeth; 18 July 1833; (326); 309
Hearsey, Samuel (W.C.); Heirin, Patty (W.C.); 18 Oct. 1818; (27); 105
Heart, Selah (Ma); Watrous (Waters), Sally (Ma); 30 Oct. 1793; (220); NW-8

Hebard, James (Ad); Buell, Maria (Ma); 28 Oct. 1821; (205); 121
Heddlestone, Thomas; Smith, Diadama; 29 Nov. 1838; (350); 429
Hedleston, David (Gr); Gordon, Ann (Gr); 17 Sept. 1812; (176); 73
Heitt, George (Ba); Brown, Apphia H. (Ro); 5 Oct. 1836; (248); 369
Hemphill, John (Wf); Gage, Marion (Wf); 24 Mar. 1835; (281); 341
Henderson, Edward; Lovekin, Sally; 5 May 1791; (331); NW-4
Henderson, Edward (Be); Dilley, Minerva (Be); 26 Jan. 1828; (82); 201
Henderson, Geo. W.; Tomlinson, Elizabeth A. (Wd.C.); 10 Aug. 1826; ; A.F.
    & M.G.v-10 #52
Henderson, Josiah; Hutchinson, Catharine; 31 Dec. 1826; (74); 182
Hening, Mathew (La); Taylor, Mrs. Levina (La); 7 Aug. 1828; (109); 213
Henry, David (Wt); Bellows, Mahala (Be); 24 Oct. 1833; (144); 318
Henry, David (Wt); Starling, Anna (Wt); 2 Apr. 1840; (157); 458
Henry, John (Wn); McNitt, Margaret (Ma); 12 Nov. 1811; (197); 72
Henry, John; Posey, Nancy; 13 June 1815; (109); 85M
Henry, John; Proctor, Phebe; 8 Jan. 1818; (165); 99M
Henry, John; Baker, Elizabeth (Wt); 10 Dec. 1834; (360); 339
Henry, Matthew (A.C.); Procter, Lovina (W.C.); 28 Aug. 1817; (165); 98
Henry, Matthew (Wt); Parke, Mary (Un); 28 Apr. 1825; (316); 150
Henry, Robert (Wf); Henry, Betsy (Wf); 11 Sept. 1804; (195); 44
Henry, Robert (III) (Wo); Gifford, Roxana (Wo); 22 Jan. 1817; (147); 93
Henry, Robert, 4th (Wt); Henry, Hannah (Wt); 2 Dec. 1830; (297); 255
Henry, William (Wo); Gilmore, Rebecca (Wo); 10 Mar. 1825; (306); 147
Hensel, John; Heck, Mary; 18 Mar. 1838; (351); 401
Hensel, Nathaniel (Jo); Dye, Emily (Jo); 30 Dec. 1840; (350); II-17
Heron, John; Hinkley, Betsy; 26 Aug. 1824; (347); 139
Herr, Rev. William; Whitney, Sarah (Ma); 21 Sept. 1830; (148); 251
Herron, Otho M. (Pk.C.); Bennett, Abigail (Ma); 30 Mar. 1828; (22); 234
Herron, Thomas; Rumbold, Mrs. Eleanor; 30 Nov. 1828; (148); 217
Hewit, Moses; Hewit, Sally; 3 June 1790; (331); NW-2
Hewitt, Ethan (Mi); Drigs, Mary (Mi); 9 Nov. 1803; (110); 40
Hewitt, Moses (Be); Robinson, Sylvia (Wn); 22 Oct. 1818; (104); 105
Hiatt, Newton (Gr); Cook, Susanna (Gr); 27 May 1840; (153); 457
Hickman, George (We); Sweasey, Margaret (Ba); 2 Oct. 1839; (248); 439
Hicks, Albert; Rump, Eliza Ann; 6 Oct. 1825; (134); 155
Hiet, Jesse (W.C.); Beals, Sarah (W.C.); 4 Aug. 1800; (285); NW-43
Higgins, Alexander (Mg.C.); Tucker, Eleanor (Wf); 1 Dec. 1840; (209); 472
Higgins, Joseph (Ma); Thompson, Elizabeth (Ma); 20 Feb. 1809; (197); 61
Highbarger, George (W.C.); Lane, Hannah (W.C.); 11 Apr. 1816; (347); 90
Hilar, Benjamin; Menair, Betsy; 27 Jan. 1825; (82); 148
Hilar, Richard (Ro); Barkus, Cassandra (Ro); 24 Nov. 1836; (123); 370
Hildebrand, Joel (Fe); Gilpin, Sally (Fe); 28 Aug. 1832; (38); 285
Hilderbrand, George (We); Perry, Rebecca (We); 27 Mar. 1834; (20); 322
Hilderbrand, Jesse, (Fe); Fowler, Senith (Fe); 20 Apr. 1826; (332); 169
Hilderbrand, John (Wf); Currier, Mary (Ro); 20 Dec. 1831; (67); 273
Hildreth, Calvin; Maxon, Susan Eliza; 20 Dec. 1830; (321); 256
Hildreth, Dr. Charles C. (Za); Swearingen, Sarah A. (Wh); 24 Mar. 1836; (6);
    M.G.v-2 #22

Hildreth, Henry (Ma); Haven, Abigail (Ma); 16 Sept. 1817; (38); 97
Hildreth, Sam'l P. (Be); Cook, Rhoda (Be); 19 Aug. 1807; (203); 55
Hill, Abram; Britton, Mary; 23 Sept. 1830; (79); 258
Hill, Alexander (Ma); Foster, Sarah (Ma); 30 Dec. 1802; (317); NW-60
Hill, Anthony (Un); Lewis, Sally (Un); 4 Apr. 1824; (283); 133
Hill, Dan (Sa); Merriam, Mary (Sa); 30 Mar. 1827; (40); 183
Hill, George (Un); Reed, Harriet; 4 Mar. 1828; (261); 207
Hill, Harry (W.C.); Doan, Jerusha (W.C.); 3 June 1824; (194); 134
Hill, Henry (Np); Nicholls, Elizabeth (Np); 14 Nov. 1811; (116); 71
Hill, Ira (Np); Little, Wealthy (Np); 4 Jan. 1816; (278); 95
Hill, Ira 3rd; Lackey, Desdemona; 25 June 1840; (87); 461
Hill, Isaac (Np); Huff, Polly (Np); 15 Oct. 1807; (310); 55
Hill, James (Fe); Hussay, Phoebe (Sa); 13 Aug. 1818; (309); 105
Hill, James (We); Firman, Hannah (We); 16 May 1822; (302); 125
Hill, John (Np); Ritchey, Patty (Ma); 18 Nov. 1807; (197); 56
Hill, John (Ma); Geering, Hannah (Ma); 15 June 1812; (86); 75
Hill, John (Lu); McIntire, Margaret (Lu); 28 Oct. 1824; (353); 143
Hill, John R.; O'Blenness, Rachel; 31 Jan. 1839; (85); 433
Hill, Joseph; Gibson, Jane; 4 May 1815; (38); 84M
Hill, Joseph; Murdough, Aritia; 21 June 1840; (70); 460
Hill, Richard (Ma); Straight, Sally (Ma); 31 Mar. 1816; (278); 95
Hill, Samuel; Dye, Mary; 6 Oct. 1840; (109); II-5
Hill, Thomas (Un); Reed, Nancy (Sa); 5 Nov. 1826; (261); 177
Hill, William; Rankins, Rachael; 1 Apr. 1801; (285); NW-48
Hill, William (Ma); Hill, Elizabeth (Ma); 6 June 1805; (31?); 46
Hill, William (N?); Twiggs, Sarah (Sa); 23 Feb. 1809; (310); 61
Hill, William (Un); Murphy, Mary (Un); 8 June 1826; (332); 169
Hill, William; Hale, Mrs. Margaret; 17 Mar. 1839; (65); 432
Hill, William; Ackerson, Detty; 8 July 1824; (222); 137
Hill, Wm. (La); Sharp, Eleanor (Fe); 5 Apr. 1832; (96); 279
Hill, Wm. Jr. (La); Amlin, Martha (Ma); 31 Jan. 1822; (278); 122
Hilliard, Samuel; Hinds, Amy; 10 Aug. 1834; (326); 330
Hilton, Otho B. (W.C.); Mixer, Elizabeth (W.C.); 30 Jan. 1828; (38); 200
Hinckley, Nath (Wf); Perry, Sally (Wf); 30 Oct. 1796; (245); NW-18
Hinckley, Nathaniel (Wo); Davis, Elizabeth (Wo); 19 Apr. 1817; (346); 95
Hinkley, Daniel (Ro); Walker, Lucy (Ro); 14 Sept. 1820; (347); 116
Hinkley, Jacob L.; Banister, Eliza; 26 Aug. 1824; (347); 139
Hinkley, Stephen (Ro); Hinkley, Ruth (Ro); 30 Jan. 1819; (347); 107
Hinkley, Thomas (Wo); Prewitt, Rachel (Wo); 4 July 1811; (249); 69
Hodgman, Joseph; McCoy, Ann C.; 26 Oct. 1837; (33); 392
Hoff, Alfred; Fuller, Elizabeth; 10 Sept. 1840; (326); II-24
Hoff, Daniel; Corey, Barbara (Ma); 23 Aug. 1825; (109); 155
Hoff, Eli D. (Ma); Price, Sarah S. (Fe); 15 Sept. 1836; (85); 370
Hoff, Enoch (Ma); Murray, Elizabeth (Ma); 10 Feb. 1829; (63); 218
Hoff, Enoch; Smith, Jemima; 9 May 1830; (63); 242
Hoff, James (Np); Dye, Mary (Np); 23 Sept. 1814; (109); 82
Hoff, James (La); Griggs, Jane (Ma); 4 Mar. 1824; (109); 134
Hoff, James 2nd (La); Chambers, Eleanor (La); 8 May 1828; (109); 210

WASHINGTON COUNTY MARRIAGES

Hoff, Jonathan (Ma); Greene, Louisa (Wn); 12 Oct. 1827; (241); 194
Hoff, Jonathan (La); Covey, Mary Ann (La); 24 Dec. 1829; (109); 236
Hoff, Jonathan; Moon, Susan; 29 Jan. 1839; (70); 426
Hoff, Powell (Ma); Brewster, Martha (Ma); 25 May 1824; (205); 134
Hoisington, Earl (A.C.); Vincent, Maria (Ba); 13 Dec. 1836; (337); 374
Holden, Joseph (Ma); Hanway, Eliza (Ma); 8 July 1807; (197); 55
Holden, Nathaniel (Ma); Buell, Frances S. (Ma); 27 Aug. 1826; (22); 175
Holden, Nathaniel; Shipman, Julia; 21 Jan. 1829; (22); 234
Holden, William (Ma); Greene, Isabella (Ma); 30 Sept. 1840; (26); 467
Holden, Wm. Jr. (W.C.); Flanders, Mary (W.C.); 16 Mar. 1837; (59); 375
Holdren, Coleman (Np); Cotter, Margaret (Np); 7 Jan. 1816; (84); 87
Holdren, John; Rinney, Rosey; 1805; ; X
Holdren, Joseph; Colon, Ruth; 25 Apr. 1803; (354); NW-63
Holland, Horace; Flemming, Cynthia; 24 Dec. 1837; (290); 393
Hollenbuk, Chasper (Wf); Booth, Lucy Sherman (Wf); 2 June 1801; (91); NW-51
Hollister, Albert G.; Delano, Julia Ann; 12 Apr. 1835; (56); 343
Hollister, Richard D.; Dana, Sophia B.; 21 Oct. 1832; (158); 291
Hollister, Serano (Ma); Ryan, Mary Ann (Ma); 23 Feb. 1823; (12); 128
Hollister, Serano; Brooks, Cynthia Ann; 4 Nov. 1838; (70); 413
Holyoke, William (Ma); Greenleaf, Lucy (Ma); 18 May 1817; (278); 96
Hook, Bernard T. (Mg.C.); Corner, Olinda (Wt); 3 Feb. 1834; (259); 322
Hook, Henry (Ma); Bukey, Mary (Ma); 15 June 1823; (27); 130
Hook, John (Nt); McClimans, Esbel (Nt); 14 Dec. 1802; (303); NW-61
Hooper, Samuel (Be); Cole, Phoebe (Be); 6 Feb. 1825; (194); 144
Hopkins, Joline; French, Electa; 26 Aug. 1835; (4); 352
Horn, Paul (De); Place, Hannah (De); 9 May 1822; (233); 125
Hoskinson, Ezekiel Jr.; Riley, Susan (Ma); 26 Mar. 1835; (118); 342
Hoskinson, Geo. W. (Np); Bosworth, Lucy (Ma); 19 Sept. 1833; (22); M.G.v-1 #13
Hough, James (Sa); Dutton, Hannah (Sa); 25 Sept. 1806; (310); 54
Hougland, John (Ba); Proctor, Mary R. (Ba); 10 Mar. 1825; (194); 137
Hovey, Harvey C. (Fe); Stanley, Clarissa (Fe); 13 Nov. 1822; (278); 128
Howard, Jesse (Np); Barstow, Mrs. Frances (Np); 26 Sept. 1834; (87); 329
Howard, Thomas H. (Np); Ramsey, Sarah M. (Np); 18 Dec. 1823; (205); 131
Howe, Aaron (Ma); Thorniley, Mary Ann (Ma); 19 Sept. 1833; (22); M.G.v-1 #13
Howe, Benajah (Ba); Hoit, Sally (Ba); 11 Mar. 1821; (62); 119
Howe, Benajah (Ma); Tyler, Mrs. Abigail (Ma); 1 July 1827; (38); 190
Howe, George (Ma); Whitehouse, Mary (Ma); 7 Sept. 1802; (140); NW-58
Howe, Nehemiah (Ba); Hutchinson, Sally (Ba); 1 Jan. 1822; (62); 123
Howe, Pearley (Ma); Putnam, Persis (Ma); 2 May 1798; (238); NW-30
Howe, Perley (Be); Emerson, Sarah (Ma); 4 Sept. 1827; (22); 233
Howe, Rufus W. (Be); Eastman, Lucy (Be); 23 May 1833; (184); 304
Howe, Rufus W. (Be); Proctor, Polly (Wt); 24 June 1835; (184); 346
Howe, Samuel L. (L.C.); Perrin, Charlotte (Ad); 3 Apr. 1829; (316); 221
Howe, Sylvanus (A.C.); Durfie, Abigail (Un); 6 Dec. 1821; (278); 122
Hoyt, Alvey; Porter, Mrs. Mary; 8 Mar. 1840; (330); 452
Hoyt, Ezra (Ho); Stone, Lydia (Ad); 4 Dec. 1803; (197); 40
Hoyt, John; Palmer, Mrs. Sarah; 11 Jan. 1834; (38); 317
Hubbard, Rowland; Howlet, Charlotte; 31 Aug. 1815; (143); 85M

37

Hudson, Daniel; Marhew, Mary; 9 Jan. 1840; (29); 446
Hudson, Whiting (Wo); Springer, Lucy (Wo); 7 Jan. 1816; (143); 88
Huendeen, Hezekiah; Browning, Anne; 8 Dec. 1817; (278); 49M
Huet, Israel (Mi); Bobo, Betsey (Mi); 19 Feb. 1799; (21); NW-33
Huet, Moses; Cooke, Pheebe; 16 Oct. 1797; (121); NW-24
Hughes, James (Wf); Morey, Julia (Wf); 6 Nov. 1831; (66); 274
Hughs, William (Wf); Lucas, Elizabeth (Wf); 23 Mar. 1800; (245); NW-38
Humiston, Jason (Wo); Shaw, Mrs. Margaret (Wo); 26 Oct. 1820; (349); 117
Humiston, Lynde (Wo); Starlin, Betsey (Wo); 13 Apr. 1820; (199); 114
Humphrey, Benoni; Bowrd, Martha; 26 Nov. 1817; (38); 99M
Humphrey, David (Wf); Abbey, Ruby (Wf); 5 Sept. 1840; (234); 466
Humphrey, Isaac (Be); Ackley, Clarissa (Be); 25 Apr. 1822; (367); 124
Humphrey, Thomas (Be); Patten, Ruth (Be); 20 Mar. 1806; (31); 48
Humphrey, William (Ma); Crane, Lydia (Ma); 10 Oct. 1819; (278); 113
Humphreys, Isaac (A.C.); Speck, Susanna (Be); 13 Feb. 1825; (194); 145
Humphreys, Isaac (Wn); McKinney, Mary S. (Wn); 8 Aug. 1830; (63); 250
Humphry, Jacob (Ho); Spacht, Polly (Be); 4 Apr. 1805; (203); 47
Humphry, Wm. (Be); Bellows, Anna (Be); 25 Sept. 1808; (203); 57
Hungerford, Matthew (Ma); Walker, Nancy (Ma); 18 Oct. 1805; (31); 47
Hunley, Jeremiah; Bens, Pamelia; 25 Jan. 1815; (289); 83M
Hunter, Samuel (Mg.C.); Chapman, Eliza (W.C.); 22 Sept. 1831; (96); 273
Hunter, William B.; Morris, Betsey; 16 June 1825; (306); 152
Huntoon, Joseph C.; Longfellow, Sarah; 15 Oct. 1837; (65); 387
Hupp, Daniel (Au); Smith, Lavina (Au); 31 Dec. 1840; (305); II-2
Hupp, Philip (Mn.C.); Lawson, Hannah (Au); 25 May 1828; (261); 208
Hupp, Dr. John (Sa); Ogle, Margaret (Sa); 1 Aug. 1820; (90); 116
Hurlbut, John (Wf); Miller, Betsy (Wf); 13 May 1806; (245); 49
Hurst, Benedick (Np); Dallorson, Martha (Np); 20 Nov. 1809; (83); 64
Hurst, Dickson (Gr); Scott, Malissa (Gr); 17 Feb. 1814; (295); 79
Hussey, Adna; McFarlin, Lydia; 2 July 1818; (138); 103M
Hussey, Asa; McFarland, Sally; 10 Sept. 1818; (138); 104M
Hussey, William; Doan, Linda; 24 Sept. 1835; (305); 354
Hutcheson, Thomas (Ma); Warren, Nancy (Ma); 31 Oct. 1819; (99); 110
Hutchins, John Jr.; Rowland, Jane; 30 Dec. 1825; (90); 145
Hutchinson, Augustus J.; Gard, Eleanor; 8 Dec. 1825; (362); 160
Hutchinson, George (We); Gard, Lucy (We); 12 Feb. 1818; (165); 102
Hutchinson, George (Be); Keirns, Catherine (Be); 31 Mar. 1822; (311); 124
Hutchinson, George (Ba); Rodgers, Margaret (Wt); 10 Oct. 1832; (182); 292
Hutchinson, Isaac (Ba); Gilpin, Mrs. Eunice (Un); 22 July 1832; (98); 284
Hutchinson, James (Gr); Pool, Charlotte (Gr); 10 May 1812; (176); 74
Hutchinson, Thomas (Ma); Welch, Sally (Ma); 25 Dec. 1792; (245); NW-7
Hutchinson, Thomas (Be); Mash, Lydia (Be); 13 Sept. 1821; (311); 120
Hutchinson, William (We); Kent, Harriet (We); 20 Jan. 1820; (249); 111
Hutchinson, William (Be); Bennett, Prudence (Be); 27 Sept. 1832; (184); 288
Hutchison, John; Wallbridge, Roesea; 1 Nov. 1840; (320); 469
Hutson, John; Smith, Melinda (Ma); 20 July 1828; (63); 209

Iams, Eli (W.C.); Crawford, Catharine (Ma); 12 Oct. 1815; (197); 88
Ingles, John (Be); Rathbun, Mercy (Be); 9 Dec. 1819; (2); 115
Ingram, William K. (Ma); Gill, Elizabeth (Ma); 15 Nov. 1835; (63); 354
Inman, Aaron (Wn); Mayhew, Mehitable (Wn); 25 Aug. 1825; (102); 154, 173
Inman, James (Wn); Cass, Narcissa (Fe); 27 Oct. 1825; (162); 158
Inman, Nathan (Wn); Wood, Rebecca (Wn); 15 Jan. 1832; (170); 283
Irwin, David (G.C.); Fletcher, Mary (W.C.); 1 Aug. 1810; (266); 66
Isham, Russell (W.C.); Nott, Elizabeth (W.C.); 2 Jan. 1797; (238); NW-19 O.C.

Jack, David; Hale, Elizabeth; 14 Sept. 1837; (65); 386
Jackson, Bartlett; Bell, Amanda M.; 21 Apr. 1840; ; M.G.v-3 #20
Jackson, David Jr. (Sa); Bell, Margaret (Sa); 21 Dec. 1820; (90); 118
Jackson, Hugh (Sa); Putnam, Harriet (Sa); 6 Feb. 1816; (49); 89
Jackson, John G. (Va); Meigs, Mary Sophia (Ma); 19 July 1810; (197); 66
James, Benjamin; Talbot, Michel; 1 Jan. 1815; (295); 84M
James, David (Ma); Greene, Nancy (Ma); 18 Nov. 1806; (197); 52
James, Henry; Moore, Mary C. (Np); 2 July 1829; (212); 227
James, John; Brickmore, Eliza; 8 June 1817; (223); 101
Jarrett, Wm. (We); Ferris, Eliza (We); 18 Sept. 1839; (85); II-385
Jarvis, Solomon (W.C.); Jameson, Margaret (W.C.); 1 Aug. 1814; (31); 81
Jarvis, Wm. J.; Hoff, Sarah; 12 Nov. 1837; (33); 392
Jeffords, Sherman; Delong, Olive; 19 Jan. 1826; (189); 166
Jenkens, James H.; Lyons, Elizabeth; 14 Mar. 1803; (354); NW-63
Jenkins, Thomas; Dye, Mary; 6 Oct. 1818; (316); 104M
Jenkins, William (Wo); Napier, Elizabeth (Wo); 16 May 1809; (278); 63
Jennings, Henry; Chambers, Sarah Ann; 23 Dec. 1830; (116); 260
Jennings, Jeniah (Ma); McCabe, Hannah (Ma); 6 Aug. 1820; (38); 116
Jennings, Jonathan (Ma); Record, Susan (Ma); 20 Mar. 1823; (85); 128
Jennings, Junia; Record, Eliza Ann; 1 Apr. 1833; (368); 302
Jett, Owens (Ma); Cole, Mary (Wn); 15 June 1816; (170); 90
Jett, Thomas Jr. (W.C.); Obleness, Phebe P. (W.C.); 5 Dec. 1822; (85); 127
Jewell, John T. (Au); Smithson, Mary Ann (Au); 8 Aug. 1819; (173); 110
Jewell, Joseph (Au); Lewis, Betsey (Au); 7 Nov 1819; (173); 111
Johanning, Lewis (Cin); Harpig, Catherine (Ma); 9 Aug. 1837; (63); 381
Johnenson, William; Rice, Cynthia; 24 Aug. 1837; (123); 382
Johnson, Alderman (La); Low, Polly (Fe); 9 Mar. 1819; (109); 108
Johnson, Alexander; Root, Sarah; 8 May 1833; (130); 305
Johnson, Benjamin; James, Hannah; 29 Oct. 1797; (238); NW-23
Johnson, Chester (Ad); Allison, Sophia (Ad); 4 Feb. 1819; (355); 107
Johnson, Erastus; Root, Rosmer; 1 Apr. 1833; (130); 305
Johnson, Henry; Geddings, Mrs. Hannah; 19 Feb. 1829; (130); 221
Johnson, Isaac (Np); Thomas, Nancy (Np); 11 Oct. 1804; (294); 43
Johnson, Isaac (W.C.); Stanton, Laura A. (W.C.); 6 Dec. 1838; (248); 419
Johnson, Jacob (Wo); Baker, Anna (Wo); 13 Jan. 1820; (47); 111
Johnson, James; Corey, Elizabeth; 1 July 1830; (36); 246
Johnson, James B. (De); Place, Jane (De); 5 Dec. 1839; (298); 443

Johnson, John (Be); Robertson, Hannah (Be); 14 Feb. 1813; (141); 76
Johnson, John; Freemire, Margaret; 10 Feb. 1815; (295); 84M
Johnson, John (Wn); Fulcher, Nancy (Wn); 17 Nov. 1835; (85); 358
Johnson, John; Oliver, Mary; 12 Sept. 1839; (58); 440
Johnson, John T. (Ma); Williams, Mary (Ma); 29 July 1834; (259); 326
Johnson, Joseph (W.C.); Wells, Sarah (W.C.); 9 May 1799; (317); NW-35
Johnson, Levi; Cook, Sally; 16 Oct. 1799; (203); NW-39
Johnson, Lewis (Un); Warren, Lucretia (Un); 2 Apr. 1820; (283); 113
Johnson, Dr. Perley B. (Mg.C.); Dodge, Polly M. (Ad); 6 Dec. 1825; (18); 159
Johnson, Serman (Be); Henderson, Louisa (Be); 8 Oct. 1818; (3); 106
Johnson, Sylvester; Walker, Eleanor; 15 Sept. 1840; (71); 466
Johnson, Thomas (Ro); Fleming, Mary Jane (Ro); 5 Oct. 1837; (123); 385
Johnson, Thomas; French, Leafy; 13 Feb. 1840; (320); 445
Johnson, Wm.; Bodkin, Mary; 27 Jan. 1811; (133); 68M
Johnson, William; Batchelder, Lucy; 12 Dec. 1833; (130); 316
Johnston, Allen (Be); Bartlett, Betsey (Be); 18 Apr. 1822; (76); 125
Johnston, Henry; Pinny, Cordealy; 3 Sept. 1837; (114); 384
Johnston, Joseph (Be); Lobdell, Matilda (Be); 13 Feb. 1818; (145); 101
Johnston, Renseller (Be); Dilly, Eliza (Be); 11 Nov. 1827; (321); 195
Johnston, Thomas (Be); Hull, Mary (Be); 5 Nov. 1817; (145); 101
Jolly, Henry (Gr); Williamson, Christina (Gr); 31 May 1806; (358); 50
Jolly, Kinzi (Gr); Dickerson, Elizabeth (Gr); 6 Mar. 1817; (304); 96
Jolly, William (Gr); Martin, Cynthia (Gr); 4 Dec. 1817; (304); 102
Jones, Edward Wm.; Carter, Mrs. Margaret; 4 Jan. 1837; (59); 371
Jones, Jeremiah C. (Fe); Clark, Hannah (Fe); 11 Mar. 1819; (309); 107
Jones, Joab (Ma); Kelly, Polly (Ma); 1 July 1804; (296); 42, 47
Jones, Joab (Ma); White, Lydia (Wo); 24 Nov. 1815 [Year only but reported
   in A.F. of this date.]; (143); 87
Jones, Samuel B. (Fe); Slaughter, Desdemonia (Ma); 15 Apr. 1819; (38); 108
Jones, Seth (Sa); Chapman, Hessibah (Sa); 16 July 1807; (278); X, R
Jones, Thomas (Va-Oh.C.); Hanes, Mary (Va-Oh.C.); 14 May 1801; (358); NW-48
Jones, Thomas J. (Ma); Holleburt, Lydia (Ma); 14 July 1808; (265?); 57
Jones, William; Pilcher, Maria; 22 Nov. 1832; (311); 297
Jordon, Richard; Devol, Sarah; 12 June 1839; (2); 433
Joy, John (A.C.); Ellis, Mary (W.C.); 13 Nov. 1834; (127); 331
Joy, Thomas; Shepard, Lydia; 25 Oct. 1835; (119); 357
Judd, Alberis; Burch, Mahala; 9 Oct. 1837; (217); 387
Judd, Alberus; Williamson, Mary; 22 July 1836; (217); 367
Judd, Chauncey T. (Ma); Hartshorne, Clarissa (Ma); 26 Aug. 1824; (27); 137
Judd, Chester (W.C.); Burch, Mary (W.C.); 10 Oct. 1837; (2); 390
Judd, John T. (Un); Tucker, Nancy B. (Un); 2 Sept. 1823; (27); 131
Judd, Merrit (Un); Mead, Mina (Sa); 2 Sept. 1823; (27); 131
Judd, Zara I. (Ma); Kidwell, Harriet A. (Un); 7 Nov. 1827; (322); 196

Kafer, Christian (Ma); Miller, Magdelena (Ma); 28 May 1839; (263); 431, 433
Kahler, Silas (Ma); Longellow, Lydia (Ma); 10 Jan. 1841; (299); 474

WASHINGTON COUNTY MARRIAGES

Kanaday, Jacob; Everley, Catharine; 24 Feb. 1826; (326); 167
Kanaday, Thomas; Parker, Polly; 31 Aug. 1823; (326); 133
Kapple, Daniel; Penney, Mary (Wf); 18 July 1836; (17); 364
Kazy, William (W.C.); Harden, Nancy (W.C.); 17 Nov. 1800; (238); NW-41, O.C.
Kearns, Peter (Au); Hupp, Rachel (Au); 1 Mar. 1832; (305); 278
Keating, John (Ma); Beebe, Eunice (Ma); 3 July 1803; (317); NW-63
Keeder, Daniel (Np); Wells, Harriet (Np); 23 Apr. 1840; (153); 457
Keeder, David Franklin; Barnhart, Catharine; 21 Mar. 1830; (71); 242
Keirns, William; Dilley, Lucy; 13 Oct. 1824; (311); 138
Keith, Adam; Shirley, Elizabeth; 8 Aug. 1815; (289); 85M
Keith, Joseph; Hughes, Drusilla; 9 Dec. 1817; (355); 99M
Keith, Peter; Shockley, Betsey; 2 July 1818; (271); 103M
Keller, Isaac (W.C.); Goldsmith, Elizabeth (W.C.); 25 Apr. 1816; (223); 90
Kelley, Arthur (Ma); Neal, Harriet (Pkb); 21 Oct. 1835; (226); M.G.v-1 #51
Kelley, William (Ma); Cady, Fanny (W.C.); 22 Oct. 1813; (38); 78
Kelly, George; Williams, Nancy; 17 Feb. 1801; (285); NW-47
Kelly, James (Ma); Hanson, Nancy (Ma); 7 Feb. 1805; (197); 45
Kelly, James (Mg.C.); Cradlebaugh, Anna (We); 29 Dec. 1831; (222); 276
Kelly, John (Ma); Kelly, Nelly (Ma); 24 Feb. 1805; (296); 47
Kelly, John; Palmer, Sarah; 31 Dec. 1837; (71); 394
Kelly, Joseph (Ma); Flagg, Cynthia (Ma); 17 Jan. 1811; (197); 69
Kelsey, Guy (Rs.C.); Fuller, Minerva C. (Be); 20 Oct. 1830; (82); 251
Kemly, James; Johnson, Nancy T.; 27 Jan. 1801; (285); NW-47
Kemmel, Christopher (Un); Spears, Phebe (Un); 11 May 1837; (247); 381
Kendrick, John; Guitteau, Julia (W.C.); 16 Sept. 1832; (22); 290
Kenion, Robert (Ma); Rily, Betsy (Ma); 3 May 1806; (11); 50
Kenne, Nathan; Willson, Mary; 26 Sept. 1791; (331); NW-6
Kerns, John (Be); Strawsnider, Elizabeth (Be); 26 Jan. 1834; (42); 322
Kerr, Hamilton (Ma); Nyghswonger, Sukey (Ma); 10 Jan. 1793; (132); NW-25
Kerr, Jonathan (Np); Kensor, Betsey (Np); 15 Feb. 1827; (12); 182
Kerr, Samuel (Np); Kinzier, Margaret (Np); 6 May 1827; (208); 191
Ketchum, Henry D. (De); Hahn, Hannah (De); 20 Feb. 1839; (130); 423
Keyes, Phineas C. (Ma); Gould, Mary A. (Ma); 15 Apr. 1822; (278); 126
Kidd, Isaac; Roberts, Kaziah; 28 Aug. 1817; (223); 101
Kidd, Nathaniel (Fe); Hill, Mary (Fe); 30 Jan. 1823; (210); 128
Kidd, Peter; Gray, Mary Ann; 23 July 1840; (65); II-1
Kidd, Thomas (Fe); Hill, Martha (Fe); 4 Feb. 1813; (73); 73
Kidd, William (Wf); Heywood, Anna (Wf); 15 Dec. 1808; (292); 60
Kidder, Gideon (Sa); Spears, Susanna (Sa); 26 Jan. 1819; (90); 106
Kidwell, Alexander; Stevens, Sophia (Ba); 22 Oct. 1840; (186); 470
Kidwell, James; Gard, Margaret (We); 1 June 1836; (186); 365
Kidwell, John (We); Gard, Priscilla (We); 19 Apr. 1831; (23); 265
Kidwell, William (We); Gard, Mahala (Ba); 13 Sept. 1832; (36); 286
Kierns, John (Be); Ellenwood, Mary (Be); 8 Dec. 1818; (148); 107
Kilgor, Matthew L.; Armstrong, Elizabeth; 3 Oct. 1799; (285); NW-36
Kincade, Aaron; Cory, Ruth; 25 July 1839; (13); 438
Kincade, James M. (Fe); Pratt, Parthenia (Fe); 10 Dec. 1829; (162); 235
Kincade, John (Fe); Britton, Elizabeth (Fe); 26 Mar. 1829; (161); 222

41

King, John (We); Jarrett, Elizabeth (We); 30 Apr. 1840; (7); 457
Kingsbury, Rev. Addison (Be); Little, Emma (N.H.); 27 Apr. 1830; (264);
    A.F. & M.G.v-15 #27
Kingsley, Wadsworth (Po.C.); Ulmer, Harriet (Ma); 12 Nov. 1822; (349); 127
Kinley, Wm. M. (Wf); Carl, Ruth (Wf); 3 Mar. 1833; (2); 299
Kinnaird, Alfred M.; Nixon, Julia Ann; 3 Jan. 1839; (319); 418
Kinnimouth, Robert (Wd.C.Va); Hull, Elizabeth (Be); 20 Nov. 1822; (76); 127
Kinsey, David (Gr); Hase, Elizabeth (Gr); 14 Mar. 1822; (353); 124
Kirkpatrick, Alexander; Cole, Cynthia; 21 Feb. 1833; (144); 300
Kirkpatrick, James; Munro, Susanna; 9 Feb. 1801; (238); NW-44
Kitchen, John (Ma); Brewster, Deborah (Ma); 24 Aug. 1832; (22); 290
Kitz, George (Mn.C.); Hall, Louisa (Au); 21 July 1827; (261); 194
Klintworth, Jacob; Balling, Adline; 16 Apr. 1838; (59); 433
Klintworth, Jacob; Boling, Adelheit; 16 Apr. 1838; (59); 397
Knapp, Artemas (Ad); Tucker, Frances (Un); 4 Feb. 1814; (138); 79
Knight, Curtice (Gr); Davis, Hannah (Gr); 12 Apr. 1809; (358); 62
Knowles, Amos (Be); Porter, Mary (Be); 16 Nov. 1811; (133); 70, 74
Knowles, Amos (Be); Miller, Jane (Be); 23 Nov. 1834; (144); 332
Knowles, Richard; Arnold, Harriet; 12 July 1832; (144); 284
Knowles, Ruben C. (Be); Allen, Corinda P. (Be); 6 Oct. 1839; (344); 440
Knowles, Samuel; Curtis, Clarissa; 19 Mar. 1815; (145); 85M
Knowles, William (A.C.); Woodward, Sally (Be); 2 May 1822; (76); 25
Knowlton, Daniel (Np); Holdren, Ruth (Np); 8 Sept, 1808; (83); 58
Knowlton, John; Lucky, Elizabeth; 28 Oct. 1830; (175); 252
Knowlton, William; Freemyer, Elizabeth; 14 Nov. 1839; (213); 444
Knox, John W. (Mg.C.); McKinly, Eliza Ann (Wf); 28 Nov. 1833; (2); 314
Kolb, John H.; Clark, Melinda B.; 16 May 1840; (71); 454
Koon, Anthony; Seivers, Fanny; 1 Dec. 1833; (136); 315
Koon, John; Towell, Margaret; 16 June 1838; (351); 401
Koontz, Henry; Rude, Mariah (Ma); 1 Apr. 1840; (29); 455
Krewson, Burras (Wo); Pain, Lydia (Wo); 28 Feb. 1819; (362); 108
Kyger, Henry; Sims, Elizabeth; 15 Nov. 1827; (114); 199
Kyger, John (Mn.C.); Sheets, Mary (Gr); 7 June 1821; (304); 119

Ladd, Merril (Un); Spears, Damaris D. (Un); 22 Nov 1827; (261); 197
LaFerte, Creatus (Ga); McIntire, Lydia (Ca); 30 Mar. 1794; (254); NW-12
Laflin, Harley; Shields, Anna (Wt); 5 May 1831; (36); 270
Laflin, Lyman (Wo); Chapman, Ruth (Wo); 4 May 1820; (47); 114
Lagor, Peter; Nichols, Sally; 16 Aug. 1818; (27); 104M
Lagore, Enoch (A.C.); Wood, Rebecca (W.C.); 8 Mar. 1840; (7); 448
Lake, Andrew (Ad); Goss, Elizabeth (Ad); 17 May 1798; (238); NW-31
Lake, Cornelious (Be); Castle, Amanda (Be); 28 Dec. 1818; (145); 107
Lake, John (Ad); Matthews, Betsy (Ad); 23 Jan. 1805; (357); 46
Lake, Peter B. (We); Wilson, Caroline (Ad); 23 Mar. 1826; (316); 165
Lake, Peter B. (We); Boomer, Rachel (Un); 21 Oct. 1829; (148); 235
Lake, Peter B.; Kincade, Catharine; 15 Nov. 1838; (219); 414

Laken, Josiah M. (Np); Sweet, Sarah (Np); 12 Mar. 1829; (12); 220
Lalance, Peter (W.C.); Rouse, Catherine (W.C.); 4 Jan. 1799; (238); NW-31
Lamb, Benj. (Ad); Tucker, Mary (Un); 7 Apr. 1816; (283); 89
Lamb, William (Wt); Fraser, Christian (Wn); 11 Oct. 1827; (241); 194
Lancaster, James R.; Gevrez, Felicity; 14 Dec. 1834; (305); 340
Lanckford, Thomas; Hill, Hannah; 1 Aug. 1840; (59); 465
Lane, George M.; Buel, Sally M.; 27 Mar. 1840; (319); 448
Lane, Jacob P.; Stoneman, Elizabeth; 9 Jan. 1833; (100); 295
Lane, Thomas (W.C.); Doubleday, Mary (W.C.); 17 Sept. 1797; (238); NW-22
Langford, Dudley; Staats, Rebecca; 10 Mar. 1799; (203); NW-39
Langly, Wm. M.; Sanders, Sarah; 17 Nov. 1839; (123); 443
Larason, John (Mu.C.); Stump, Mary (W.C.); 9 Apr. 1816; (347); 90
Larken, Amanuel; Ward, Phebe; 1 May 1823; (85); 130
Larne, Union; Hearn, Polly; 11 Aug. 1825; (326); 156
Larrow, Jacob (W.C.); Gardiner, Sally (W.C.); 3 Oct. 1797; (238); NW-23
Lashley, John Johnson (Lu); Farris, Susan (Gr); 19 July 1840; (290); 462
Laurent, James (Ga); Buzelin, Elizabeth (Ga); 3 Jan. 1801; (285); NW-47
Lawrance, Romes (Ro); Gates, Pamela (Wf); 7 Feb. 1822; (10); 123
Lawrence, Almon (Wf); Bridge, Lucy (Wf); 23 Mar. 1826; (306); 165
Lawrence, Dan (Wf); Vaughan, Patty (Wf); 15 Feb. 1821; (347); 118
Lawrence, Gideon (W.C.); Morris, Mary (W.C.); 18 Apr. 1816; (347); 90
Lawrence, Lyman (Ro); Olney, Anna (Ro); 14 Apr. 1821; (347); 119
Lawrence, Lyman (Wf); Olney, Chloe (Wf); 22 Feb. 1827; (258); 183
Lawrence, Moses Jr. (Ro); Walker, Elizabeth (Ro); 4 Feb. 1819; (346); 106
Lawrence, Obadiah; Smith, Sally; 8 Oct. 1826; (346); 175
Lawrence, Orra (Wf); Grubb, Sally (Wf); 11 Mar. 1824; (189); 134
Lawrence, Parker M. C. (Wf); Porter, Mary (Wf); 21 Dec. 1837; (192); 389
Lawrence, Parker M. C.; Barker, Catharine; 1 Nov. 1838; (123); 412
Lawrence, Rufus (W.C.); White, Rebecca (W.C.); 4 Jan. 1821; (47); 118
Lawrence, William (Wf); Grubb, Elizabeth (Wf); 31 Dec. 1818; (346); 206
Lawson, Thomas (Fe); Ayle, Mary (Fe); 16 Nov. 1811; (335); 71
Lawton, James Jr.; Haskell, Eliza W.; 30 Sept. 1824; (194); 138
Lawton, Jesse (Ba); Haskell, Maria (Ma); 6 Nov. 1821; (308); 122
Layhugh, James (A.C.); Dye, Ruth (Ma); 23 July 1830; (63); 246
Leath, John; McKee, Sally; 18 Oct. 1802; (39); NW-58
Leavens, John (Sp); Warner, Patience (Sp); 21 Oct. 1806; (278); R-76
Lecroix, Andrew (Ga); Sarot, Mary Catherine (Ga); 18 Feb. 1797; (285); NW-20
Lee, George (Ma); Bartlett, Susan (Ma); 5 June 1834; (85); 327
Lee, James (We); Dickson, Sarah (We); 19 Mar. 1840; (219); 458
Lee, Joseph C.; Petty, Margaret; 22 Oct. 1840; (364); 474
Lefeevor, George G.; Barns, Mercy; 17 Oct. 1839; (168); 442
Leffingwell, Samuel (Wt); Ford, Farnetta (Wt); 16 Jan. 1840; (186); 447
Leffingwell, Wm. (W.C.); Gossett, Sarah (W.C.); 5 May 1818; (62); 102
Leget, Henry; Wilson, Sarah; 2 June 1825; (189); 154
Leget, Wm. (Wf); Culver, Catherine (Wf); 5 Apr 1824; (189); 134
Legget, James (Wf); Lawrence, Hannah (Wf); 7 July 1811; (137); 70
Legget, Robert (Wf); Featherston, Susanna (Wf); 18 Dec. 1816; (252); 93
Leib, Joseph (Fa.C.); Allen, Clarissa (Wf); 11 July 1828; (258); 210

Lenhart, Jacob; Ortt, Elizabeth; 5 July 1838; (247); 402
Lent, Abraham (W.C.); Matthews, Mary Ann (W.C.); 17 Nov. 1840; (129); 471
Leonard, Horace (Wf); Curtis, Nancy (Wf); 13 July 1836; (360); 370
Leonard, John (Un); Hall, Elizabeth (Un); 30 Mar. 1817; (316); 94
Leonard, Joseph (W.C.); Danley, Betsey (W.C.); 2 June 1831; (131); 267
Leonard, Luther (Wf); Adams, Caroline (Wt); 25 Apr. 1833; (192); 303
Leonard, Sylvester R. (Mu.C.); Rowland, Jane (Np); 15 Sept. 1829; (79); 231
Leonard, William B.; Molton, Lydia; 10 July 1802; (140); NW-56
Leonard, William H. (Ma); Nott, Julia Ann (Ma); 27 Feb. 1838; (87); M.G.v-1 #14
Leonard, Wm.; Nott, Julia; 27 Feb. 1838; (87); 460
Lerue, Jacob; Randols, "Eessbeth"; 6 May 1802; (354); NW-54
LeTalliur, John B. (Ga); LeSunior, Mrs. Marie (Ga); 1 Feb. 1794; (254); NW-10
Lewis, Daniel (Ma); Danker, Anna (Ma); 27 June 1839; (38); 434
Lewis, Hezekiah (Be); Chapin, Milly (Be); 14 Nov. 1813; (278); 79
Lewis, Hezekiah (W.C.); Rose, Ruth (W.C.); 6 Feb. 1816; (109); 89
Lewis, Hezekiah (W.C.); Lakin, Amarillas (W.C.); 30 Oct. 1822; (311); 127
Lewis, James; Jones, Nancy; 8 Mar. 1839; (209); 425
Lewis, John; Gates, Frances; 4 Mar. 1828; (22); 234
Lewis, Loring W. (A.C.); Cole, Caroline (Wn); 26 Mar. 1835; (174); 341
Lewis, Otis A. (W.C.); Wilson, Polly (W.C.); 13 Sept. 1836; (274); 369
Lewis, Valentine (Ro); Grimes, Catharine (Ro); 14 Jan. 1841; (123); 475
Lightfritz, John Jr.; Ackerson, Susanna; 23 May 1839; (13); 432
Lincoln, Joseph; Levins, Frances; 14 Nov. 1790; (331); NW-3
Lincoln, Obediah (W.C.); McCune, Peggy (W.C.); 12 Apr. 1797; (238); NW-22
Lindsly, Stephen (Ma); Saltonstall, Nancy (Ma); 1 May 1806; (195); 49
Linn, Francis (Gr); Little, Nancy (Gr); 23 May 1826; (353); 168
Linn, Henry (Gr); Carmeron, Margaret (Gr); 26 Sept. 1833; (200); 312
Linscott, Israel (A); Nulton, Nancy (Wf); 27 Dec. 1807; (245); 56
Lisk, Samuel P.; Snyder, Jane; 21 Sept. 1838; (351); 410
Little, Charles; Frazier, Mary; 9 Dec. 1817; (278); 99M
Littlefield, George (Sa); Miller, Polly (Sa); 27 June 1822; (330); 125
Littleton, John; Fortner, Betsy; 24 Jan. 1811; ; 68M
Livermore, Andrew (Ma); Fuller, Betsey (Ma); 9 Sept. 1827; (241); 193
Livermore, Jonas (Ma); Wills, Sally (Ma); 2 Sept. 1827; (332); 194
Locker, John (Wd.C.Va.); Locker, Sarah Ann (Ma); 9 Sept. 1819; (278); 110
Lofland, David H. (W.C.); Johnston, Amy (W.C.); 31 Dec. 1822; (308); 128
Long, Wm. (W.C.); Hall, Eliza T. (W.C.); 19 Nov. 1837; (2); 390
Longfellow, George W. (Ad); Judd, Catharine (Ad); 4 July 1830; (274); 246
Longly, George W. (Be); Hilar, Elizabeth (Be); 23 Sept. 1824; (82); 140
Loper, Enoch (Df); Smith, Eliza (Df); 12 Jan. 1814; (128); 79
Loper, Samuel (Wf); Gates, Betsy (Wf); 4 June 1816; (347); 91
Lord, Charles K. B. (K.C.); Shepard, Louisa (Ad); 14 June 1827; (316); 189
Lord, Thomas, Esq. (Ma); Oliver, Elanor (Ma); 28 Apr. 1795; (245); NW-14
Loring, Jesse (Be); Gray, Deborah (Be); 17 Nov. 1821; (25); 121
Loring, Jesse (Be); Durfee, Adaline (Un); 31 July 1835; (194); 152
Loring, Jesse (Be); Fisher, Maria (Be); 22 Apr. 1827; (311); 186
Loring, Oliver R. (Be); Warren, Fanny (Be); 24 Dec. 1820; (278); 117
Loring, Oliver R., Esq. (Be); Howe, Orinda (Be); 9 Oct. 1828; (321); 212

WASHINGTON COUNTY MARRIAGES

Lorrins, Matthew (Un); Wausil, Elizabeth (Un); 12 Jan. 1841; (247); 475
Losey, Jacob (Wn); Risley, Caroline (Wn); 29 Feb. 1820; (57); 113
Lothery, Wm. (W.C.); Gard, Rebecca (W.C.); 8 May 1816; (314); 89
Lott, Jonathan; Penny, Sophia; 18 Jan. 1825; (189); 148
Lound, Ezekiel; Bacon, Sarah; 9 Aug. 1838; (123); 406
Louvat, Daniel; West, Phebe; 1 Jan. 1798; (121); NW-28
Loveland, Jared (W.C.); Hammond, Phila (W.C.); 23 Apr. 1816; (289); 90
Lowe, John (Sa); Ayles, Hannah (Sa); 20 July 1817; (330); 97
Lowery, Wm. (Mi); Hundberry, Mary (Mi); 1 Dec. 1803; (135); 40
Lowry, Melvin (Ky); Cole, Harty (Wn); 24 Feb. 1822; (57); 123
Lowry, Robert; Winters, Rachel; 3 May 1838; (247); 399
Lucas, Albert C.; Fisher, Jane C.; 2 Apr. 1840; (123); 450
Lucas, Charles (Mg.C.); Ward, Tabitha (Be); 28 Nov. 1830; (82); 253
Lucas, Samuel (Ma); Robertson, Elizabeth (Ma); 19 Apr. 1798; (238); NW-30
Lucas, William (Ma); Harris, Peggy (Ma); 11 Apr. 1796; (238); NW-16
Lucas, William (Ma); Madison, Mrs. Experience (Ma); 4 Oct. 1821; (48); 120
Luckey, James (Mi); Speed, Nancy (Mi); 2 June 1803; (135); NW-64
Luckey, Samuel (Ma); Wright, Huldah (Ma); 16 May 1798; (238); NW-30
Luke, Washington; Clark, Emily; 24 Sept. 1840; (305); 469
Lundy, James Jr.; Stewart, Frances; 29 Mar. 1840; (58); 449
Lynn, John (Wf); Cline, Susanna (Wf); 26 Jan. 1804; (354); 40
Lyon, Aaron (Ma); Watkins, Mrs. Elizabeth (Ma); 25 Feb. 1826; (102); 174

Machie, James; Scott, Mary T.; 27 Sept. 1837; (13); 387
Madden, Richard (Lu); Dixon, Mary (Lu); 24 Jan. 1828; (150); 203
Magee, Felix (Sa); Hoff, Eve (Ma); 26 June 1827; (63); 189
Magee, John (Np); Higgins, Mary (Np); 15 May 1810; (242); 65
Magee, Joseph; Williamson, Isabella; 21 Feb. 1839; (88); 422
Magee, Robert (Np); Howell, Maria (Np); 10 Mar. 1807; (197); 53
Mail, John; Bechtold, Mary; 22 Nov. 1838; (247); 417
Main, Jonas (La); Hennan, Eunice (La); 3 Nov. 1816; (109); 92
Maldon, John Lewis (Ga); Berthe, Hannah M. (Ga); 12 Mar. 1797; (285); NW-20
Malster, William (Wo); Baker, Sally (Ba); 12 Dec. 1822; (62); 128
Manby, Samuel (W.C.); Tinsley, Margaret (W.C.); 15 June 1819; (27); 109
Mankins, John; Ellenwood, Elizabeth; 26 Sept. 1833; (56); 310
Mankins, Wm.; Dye, Harriet; 22 Aug. 1839; (240); 439
Mann, James (Nt); Davis, Lucena (Wf); 14 Feb. 1799; (245); NW-32
Mansfield, Edwin J. (Wt); Atkinson, Rosilla (Ba); 28 Feb. 1839; (157); 425
Mansfield, John (Mi); Brachbill, Catherine (Mi); 15 Feb. 1803; (21); NW-61
Mansfield, Martin (Mi); Durham, Margaret (Mi); 7 Mar. 1804; (135); 41
Manwell, James (Ma); Clark, Ruth (Ma); 30 Jan. 1805; (296); 46
Marion, Francois (Ga); Morrel, Mrs. Louise N. (Ga); 18 Feb. 1794; (254); NW-11
Marks, John (Wf); McCoy, Jane B. (Wf); 3 July 1823; (18); 130
Marsh, Emerson (Wh); Stone, Colina (Un); 27 Nov. 1829; (258); 232
Marshall, James (Ma); Sharp, Martha (Ma); 9 Oct. 1837; (63); 385
Martin, Abner (Np); Hoskinson, Sarah (Np); 15 Mar. 1803; (358); NW-62

45

Martin, Abner (Mi); McGee, Elizabeth (Mi); 15 Nov. 1803; (31); 39
Martin, Abner; Jolly, Rebecca; 4 Aug. 1840; (58); 465
Martin, Charles H. (W.C.); Gaylord, Mary (W.C.); 22 Aug. 1797; (238); NW-22
Martin, George (Ro); Emerson, Mary S. (Ro); 23 Aug. 1838; (7); 407
Martin, Hiram (Wt); Woodruff, Caroline (Ba); 22 Oct. 1840; (70); 473
Martin, James (Np); Coon, Mrs. Huldah (Li); 7 Sept. 1838; (136); 410
Martin, William (Ro); Roberts, Maria A. (We); 4 Feb. 1836; (67); 360
Marvin, Picket; Worth, Polly; 21 July 1791; ; NW-5
Marvin, William W. (Ma); Kennedy, Nancy (Ma); 23 Nov. 1834; (281); 333
Mason, Adelphi C. (Ad); Simons, Patience (Ad); 20 May 1836; (2); 369
Mason, Adolphus (Un); Devol, Betsey B. (Wf); 10 Feb. 1830; (274); 236
Mason, Carlo (Ba); Rhodes, Mrs. Lucy (Ba); 7 Mar. 1839; (337); 425
Mason, Elijah (Ad); Pratt, Maria (Ad); 12 Nov. 1828; (79); 219
Mason, James (Ad); Bartley, Judith (Ad); 21 July 1816; (138); 91
Mason, John (Ad); Cook, Rosannah (Ad); 3 Mar. 1831; (48); 263
Mason, John B. (A.C.); Wedge, Eliza (Be); 4 Apr. 1837; (144); 376
Mason, Jonas (Ad); Stacy, Beulah (Un); 24 Jan. 1822; (138); 122
Mason, Joseph; Deaver, Eleanor; 30 May 1815; (316); 85M
Mason, Joseph (Ad); Sprague, Sally (Ad); 12 May 1816; (138); 90
Mason, William; Cobern, Susanna; 14 July 1790; (331); NW-2
Mason, William (Wf); Sprague, Luny (Wf); 22 Apr. 1818; (271); 102
Mason, William (Ad); Shakley, Sally (Ad); 17 June 1819; (355); 109
Mason, William (Ad); Sprague, Nancy (Ad); 1 Jan. 1840; (80); 456
Mason, Wm. Bond (Ad); McDonald, Henrietta (Un); 13 May 1822; (316); 124
Masters, Benjamin; Powell, Meriam; 10 Sept. 1840; (290); 467
Matheny, Nathan; Snodgrass, Barbara; 1 Apr. 1824; (326); 133
Matheny, Nathan Jr.; Farley, Margaret; 4 Oct. 1832; (326); 287
Mathews, Abel (Ad); Woodard, Molly (Ad); 18 June 1806; (218); 50
Matthews, Increase (W.C.); Leavens, Betsey (W.C.); 23 Mar. 1803; (317); NW-62
Matthews, James; Greene, Mary A.; 5 June 1830; (22); 289
Matthews, John (W.C.); Woodbridge, Sally (W.C.); 26 May 1803; (317); NW-62
Matthews, John; Morris, P.; 1805; ; X
Matthews, John; Schofield, Lydia (Sa); 21 July 1836; (71); 367
Matthews, Newman (Gu.C.); Witham, Maria (W.C.); 21 Jan. 1816; (283); 88
Matthews, Philo (Un); Woodward, Eleanor (Un); 13 Mar. 1814; (316); 80
Matthews, William (We); Springer, Mary Ann (Wt); 18 Nov. 1832; ; 295
Maxon, Isaac; Hildreth, Rebecca Ann; 19 Dec. 1830; (321); 256
Maxon, Rufus (Ma); Fuller, Augustina (Ma); 24 Nov. 1833; (163); 314
Maxon, William (La); Hoff, Elizabeth (La); 1 July 1830; (109); 249
Maxson, Henry (Sa); Gaylor, Elizabeth (Sa); 23 Oct. 1807; (310); 55
Maxson, Henry (Fe); Read, Rowena (Fe); 15 Aug. 1824; (85); 137
Maxson, Jacob (Cl.C.); Wells, Electa L. (W.C.); 13 Sept. 1835; (341); 350
Maxson, John (Fe); Tuttle, Sally (Fe); 29 Aug. 1824; (162); 140
Maxson, Thomas; Cawood, Hannah; 31 Aug. 1837; (59); 383
Maxwell, Michael (Low); Kimberly, Mary Jane (Low); 1 Nov. 1838; (2); 415
Mayberry, John P. (Wd.C.); Fearing, Lucy W. (Ma); 15 Aug. 1816; (278); 91
Mayhew, Washington (Wn); Pattin, Mary (Wn); 5 May 1826; (102); 174
Mayo, Daniel; Putnam, Polly; 21 Oct. 1798; (121); NW-31

McAllister, James (Ma); Owens, Susanna (Ma); 10 Mar. 1821; (27); 118
McAllister, John (Ma); Owen, Olive F. (Ma); 3 Aug. 1834; (38); 327
McArty, Hugh (A.C.); Buck, Abigail (A); 27 May 1808; (81); 57
McAtee, Benj. Jr. (Wf); Mason, Eliza (Ad); 24 Sept. 1840; (80); 468
McAtee, Dudley; Allison, Wealthy; 1 Mar. 1840; (88); 451
McAtee, Harrison (Wf); Davis, Eliza (Ad); 14 Sept. 1823; (316); 132
McAtee, Patrick H. (Wf); McAtee, Louisa (Wf); 31 Jan. 1833; (2); 296
McAtee, William (Wf); Mason, Nancy (Ad); 10 Aug. 1820; (355); 116
McBride, Richard (Ma); Hammond, Mrs. Hannah (Wf); 23 Dec. 1802; (357); NW-60
McCabe, Robert (A.C.); Robinson, Sarah C. (Wf); 21 Sept. 1830; (158); 259
McCaig, John (Ba); Harvey, Catharine (Ba); 29 May 1828; (139); 208
McCall, James; Northrup, Jane; 27 May 1802; (45); NW-54
McCallum, Archibald (Ro); Lane, Jamima (Ro); 5 Mar. 1814; (347); 80
McCardil, Philander; McCaig, Margaret; 21 Jan. 1805; (310); 46
McCay, Tiba (Np); Holdren, Betsey (Np); 16 July 1808; (83); 57
McClain, John (Lu); Barrey, Sarah (Lu); 7 Feb. 1820; (97); 115
McClanthan, Lucian C. (Me.C.); Ford, Julia A. (Wt); 17 June 1830; (258); 247
McClarhon, Robert (Wh); Nicoll, Catharine (Ma); 20 June 1826; (38); 169
McClary, Col. Wm. (Mgt.Va.); Hempstead, Esther (Be); 27 Mar. 1806; (197); 48, 49
McClean, Wm. (Va-Oh.C.); Main, Katherine (Gr); 6 Sept. 1810; (176); 66
McClintick, Wm.; Chadwick, Mrs. Mary; 28 June 1838; (33); 405
McClintock, George (Np); Locoe, Rachel (Np); 15 Aug. 1807; (83); 55
McCluer, Andrew (Wf); Allen, Polly (Wf); 11 Nov. 1794; (245); NW-12
McCluer, Austin (Wf); McDonald, Maria (Wf); 31 Jan. 1828; (192); 200
McCluer, Charles (Wf); Webster, Sally (Wf); 12 Oct. 1826; (18); 179
McCluer, Henry (Be); Humiston, Lavina (Wt); 26 Apr. 1827; (258); 191
McCluer, James (Ad); Stacey, Abigail (Ad); 16 Aug. 1808; (91); 57
McCluer, William D. (Be); Steel, Julia Ann (Be); 1 July 1830; (82); 245
McClure, Alexander (Wf); Clark, Fanny (Wf); 20 Aug. 1821; (189); 121
McConnell, Asa (Wn); Cockshott, Ann (Be); 3 Dec. 1834; (42); 333
McCourt, Samuel; Bailey, Angeline; 8 Dec. 1833; (103); 314
McCoy, Alexander (Wf); Beach, Sabrina (Wf); 21 Feb. 1799; (245); NW-33
McCoy, Alexander (Wf); Morey, Elizabeth (Wf); 27 Feb. 1821; (189); 119
McCoy, John; Colwell, Hanna; 18 May 1839; (29); 431
McCoy, John C. (Ma); Olney, Mrs. Apphia (Un); 23 Feb. 1830; (148); 237
McCracken, Dr. John M.; Haskell, Elizabeth H.; 4 Nov. 1834; (87); 335
McCullock, George; Scritchfield, Catharine; 3 Aug. 1802; (45); NW-57
McCullock, Jacob; Inman, Eliza; 12 Aug. 1837; (70); 383
McCullough, Hugh (W.C.); Pratt, Mary (W.C.); 20 Dec. 1822; (210); 127
McCune, James (Np); McCune, Mary (Np); 4 May 1810; (242); 65
McCurdy, Barney (Ad); Roach, Polly (Ad); 15 Feb. 1821; (355); 118
McDaniel, Daniel (Un); Penny, Catherine (Sa); 6 Oct 1816; (49); 92
McDaniel, David; McCarley, Betsey; 5 Mar. 1801; (285); NW-48
McDaniel George (Ma); Grant, Leafy (Ma); 21 Dec. 1819; (27); 112
Mc Donald, Linsey (Wf); Coley, Charlotte (Wf); 12 Apr. 1838; (192); 377
McDonald, Thomas (Wf); McNeal, Susana (Wt); 8 Dec. 1840; (157); 472
McDonald, William (Wf); Vincent, Mary (Wf); 12 Apr. 1838; (192); 397

McDonnald, George (Fe); Broom, Ruth (Fe); 6 Mar. 1823; (332); 129
McDonnald, John (Wo); Walker, Mary (Wo); 12 Dec. 1822; (10); 128
McGarry, David (W.C.); Reed, Anna (W.C.); 11 Oct. 1816; (49); 92
McGarvy, Patrick (Ga); King, Anne (Ga); 20 Mar. 1800; (285); NW-38
McGee, Abner; Riley, Betsey; 27 June 1839; (364); 435
McGee, James; Phillips, Elisabeth; 27 Apr. 1803; (354); NW-63
McGee, William Jr. (Np); Byard, Sarah (Np); 1 Sept. 1822; (27); 126
McGinnes, Edmond (Me.C.); Houghland, Polly (W.C.); 9 June 1821; (279); 119
McGonagle, William (A.C.); Magee, Nancy (Ma); 23 Dec. 1827; (79); 198
McGowan, Rev. Peter M.; Dana, Maria (Np); 19 Nov. 1829; (148); 235
McGrath, Whittington (Ma); Corner, Mary (Ma); 23 Feb. 1806; (197); 48
McGregor, James; Morrison, Eliza Jane; 15 Oct. 1835; (87); 353
McGuire, Felix (Ma); Palmer, Betsey (Ma); 29 Dec. 1831; (22); 289
McGuire, James (Ma); (Murray?), Mary (Ma); 27 Mar. 1814; (197); 80
McGuire, Francis (Bev); Brooks, Mrs. Mary M. (Bev); 12 Mar. 1840; (105); 452
McIntire, Ira J. (Ma); Magee, Electa Ann (Ma); 8 June 1837; (63); 378
McIntosh, Enoch S. (W.C.); Seely, Elizabeth (W.C.); 26 Nov. 1816; (138); 93
McIntosh, Nathan (Ma); Shepard, Rhoda (Ma); 21 June 1792; (132); NW-25
McIntosh, Nathan H.; Foster, Olivia; 29 Aug. 1824; (194); 137
McIntosh, Samuel D. (Ma); Foster, Deborah L. (Ma); 17 Nov. 1825; (241); 159
McIntosh, William W. (Ma); Regnier, Hannah (Au); 21 Dec. 1820; (48); 117
McKartey, Hugh (Mi); McDaniels, Catherine (Mi); 5 July 1804; (135); 44
McKee, John (Gu.C.); Delong, Rachel (W.C.); 15 Aug. 1816; (314); 91
McKee, Robert (Fe); Thurlo, Ruth (Fe); 24 Nov. 1813; (332); 78
McKee, Robert (A.C.); Johnson, Drusilla (Ba); 6 Apr. 1836; (337); 363
McKelfresh, Francis H. (W.C.); Nicholl, Elizabeth (W.C.); 23 Mar. 1831;
    (131); 267
McKewne, Charles (Ma); Fulton, Lydia (Ma); 17 Sept. 1811; (86); 70
McKibben, David; Northorp, Huldah; 21 Jan. 1830; (326); 242
McKibben, David (La); Kerr, Hannah (Np); 23 Sept. 1830; (12); 251
McKibben, David; Cree, Eliza Ann; 11 June 1840; (87); 461
McKibben, John (W.C.); Posey, Polly (W.C.); 10 Oct. 1822; (109); 126
McKibben, Joseph (W.C.); Jennings, Rhoda (W.C.); 1 Aug. 1822; (109); 126
McKibben, Wm. (La); Posey, Louisa (Ma); 13 Aug. 1826; (109); 172
McKibbens, James (W.C.); Posey, Mary A. (W.C.); 1 Aug. 1824; (109); 142
McKinley, Thomas (Un); Gable, Anna (Un); 27 Feb. 1817; (283); 94
McLain, Hugh (Gr); Berry, Jane (Gr); 23 Oct. 1823; (353); 131
McLarty, Edward (Be); Shaw, Catharine (Be); 14 Apr. 1840; (186); 455
McLaughlin, James (Be); Weatherbe, Deborah (Be); 30 Apr. 1817; (145); 95
McLeland, James (Sa); Wilson, Mary (Sa); 25 Sept. 1825; (69); 155
McLellen, James; Stone, Esther C. (Be); 28 May 1830; (82); 243
McMan, Alfred; Day, Nancy; 5 Mar. 1840; (320); 451
McMillan, Thomas (Mtg.C.); Breckenridge, Mary (Be); 28 Apr. 1835; (184); 343
McNeal, David; Willis, Sophrona; 28 Jan. 1836; (54); 358
McNeal, Levi; Beebe, Frances Eliza; 4 Mar. 1830; (361); 238
McNeal, Milton (We); Gregory, Maria (We); 12 Mar. 1824; (36); 133
McNeal, Wm. (Wt); Bellows, Matilda (Be); 20 Mar. 1828; (311); 207
McNeil, Wm.; Corwin, Susanna; 18 Aug. 1818; (38); 103M

WASHINGTON COUNTY MARRIAGES

McQuaid, Henry (Wf); Inbody, Catharine E. (Wf); 7 Jan. 1838; (275); 394
McTaggart, Neil (Be); Lognachan, Catharine; 12 July 1838; (184); 403
McVay, John (Np); Simmons, Betsey (Np); 5 Jan. 1805; (141); 45
McVay, Reuben (Np); Hill, Margaret (Np); 6 Aug. 1813; (295); 77
McVay, William (Gr); Hisem, Catharine (Gr); 18 Nov. 1819; (353); 111
McVey, Jacob; Nicholson, Polly; 9 Feb. 1815; (116); 84M
Mead, William; Harris, Cynthia; 5 Nov. 1815; (134); 86M
Meed, Isaac; Dye, Polly; 29 Dec. 1825; (261); 164
Meek, Lewis; Bebout, Catharine; 30 Apr. 1840; (58); 457
Meeks, Bazel; Williamson, Jane; 10 Nov. 1810; (176); 67M
Meeks, John (Wf); Burden, Jane (Wf); 21 Apr. 1820; (252); 114
Meloy, Andrew; Ballard, Clarissa; 8 Nov. 1840; (15); 474
Mellard, Joseph T. (Un); Pritchard, Betsy (Un); 8 Dec. 1816; (283); 93
Mellor, Samuel (Wf); Jadding, Nancy (Wf); 25 Oct. 1806; (245); 52
Mellor, Samuel (Wf); Young, Margaret (Wf); 31 Aug. 1817; (252); 98
Menerve, Thomas (Wn); Ames, Ida (We); 23 Feb. 1829; (230); 218
Mentel, Auguste Waldmar; Lutere, Victore C.; 15 Apr. 1794; (254); NW-12
Meraben, Bertrand (Ma); Dunbar, Emily (Un); 27 May 1821; (283); 119
Merch, Seth; McMeekon, Margaret; 11 Oct. 1840; (349); II-17
Merriam, Selden N. (Ad); Porter, Lydia (Sa); 13 Nov. 1823; (90); 131
Merritt, James (Sa); Hambelton, Rebecca (Sa); 21 Oct. 1837; (61); 386
Merry, Joseph (Fe); Nicholls, Nancy (Fe); 9 Apr. 1820; (210); 113
Merwin, Elijah B. (Lan); Lincoln, Susan (Ma); 28 Feb. 1811; (278); R-78
Metheny, Elisha; Carpenter, Barbara; 3 Mar. 1836; (326); 360
Metheny, Joseph; Farley, Elizabeth; 2 Aug. 1832; (326); 287
Middleswart, Abraham; Byard, Harriet G.; 29 Mar. 1827; (38); 183
Middleswart, Clark (Np); Barstow, Cynthia W. (Np); 20 Sept. 1827; (12); 193
Middleswart, Jacob (Np); Fulton, Eleanor (Ma); 7 May 1835; (87); 344
Middleswart, Jonathan (Np); Racer, Mary (Ma); 30 May 1830; (12); 243
Middleswart, Tunis (Np); Barstow, Abigail A. (Np); 19 Apr. 1829; (12); 221
Miles, Barzillai (Be); Eastman, Sally (Be); 27 Dec. 1818; (278); 110
Miles, Benj. H. (Be); Burlingame, Persis M. (Ma); 9 Feb. 1810; (278); 65
Miles, David (Low); Davis, Cynthia (Low); 1 Nov. 1838; (2); 415
Miles, Wm. (Be); Eastman, Hannah (Be); 16 Oct. 1814; (145); 82
Millard, Joseph T. (Un); Warren, Larvina (Un); 13 Apr. 1825; (194); 149
Miller, Abel (Mi); Jones, Mary (Mi); 15 Sept. 1803; (135); 40
Miller, Alexander (Gr); Dean, Eleanor (Gr); 17 Nov. 1811; (358); 71
Miller, Amos (Ma); White, Polly (Ma); 16 Oct. 1806; (278); 53
Miller, Amos; Detterly, Louisa; 21 June 1831; (322); 267
Miller, Brice; Hall, Polly; 29 Mar. 1832; (144); 282
Miller, David (We); Tilton, Sarah (Be); 1 May 1834; (248); 324
Miller, Edward (Wf); Nulton, Katherine (Wf); 16 Apr. 1807; (245); 54
Miller, George (Wf); Taylor, Lois (Wf); 25 Oct. 1806; (245); 52
Miller, Isaac (Wn); Vanvaley, Hester (Wt); 1 June 1837; (207); 379
Miller, Jacob (Ma); Hill, Sarah (Ma); 28 Jan. 1808; (310); 56
Miller, Jesse S. (Wt); Kidwell, Mary Ann (We); 22 Mar. 1831; (24); 263
Miller, John (Ma); Wheeler, Betsey (Ma); 19 Oct. 1806; (278); 53
Miller, John (Ma); Taylor, Jane (Ma); 12 May 1808; (197); 58

Miller, John (Ro); Briggs, Abigail (Ro); 24 Dec. 1818; (347); 107
Miller, John (Fe); Taylor, Fanny (Fe); 8 Jan. 1824; (85); 132
Miller, John (Mn.C.); Gray, Elizabeth (Li); 1 Oct. 1835; (330); 354
Miller, John (Ad); Swift, Mary (Ad); 25 Oct. 1840; (87); II-12
Miller, Joseph (Ga); Diggans, Betsy (Ga); 19 June 1797; (285); NW-21
Miller, Joseph; Tharp, Mrs. Hannah; 8 Nov. 1832; (144); 292
Miller, Josiah (Ma); Hill, Matilda (Ma); 17 Sept. 1831; (63); 269
Miller, Oliver Jr. (We); Tilton, Mary (Be); 5 Nov. 1835; (56); 354
Miller, Robert (Ba); Peck, Mrs. Matilda (Ba); 13 Jan. 1825; (75); 144
Miller, Robert T. (Ma); Fuller, Marietta (Ma); 22 Feb. 1838; (87); M.G.v-1 #14
Miller, Samuel (A.C.); Cole, Polly (Be); 8 Mar. 1827; (74); 182
Miller, Samuel (Mg.C.); Bacon, Susanna (W.C.); 26 Jan. 1840; (256); 450
Miller, Thomas (W.C.); Tice, Catharine (W.C.); 5 Feb. 1829; (326); 220
Miller, Wesley (Ba); Burchett, Elizabeth (Ba); 21 Oct. 1830; (297); 253
Miller, William; Close, Eliza Ann; 22 Apr. 1830; (71); 242
Millhouse, James M. (Ma); Worthington, Amy P. (Ma); 1 Oct. 1839; (198); 441
Milligen, Thomas (Ma); Lett, Keziah (Ma); 31 Aug. 1828; (38); 211
Mills, Charles; Nyswonger, Sally; 29 Mar. 1795; (220); NW-13
Mills, Col. John (Ma); Wilson, Deborah S. (Ma); 30 May 1824; (205); 134
Mills, Richard (W.C.); Friend, Mary (W.C.); 6 July 1823; (349); 130
Minair, Peter (Mi); Picket, Elizabeth (Mi); 12 May 1801; (21); NW-50
Miner, Henry (La); Fuller, Experience (Ma); 17 Feb. 1825; (194); 145
Miner, Matthew; Taylor, Catherine; 26 Sept. 1815; (278); 86M
Miner, Richard (Ma); Corner, Ann Maria (Ma); 22 Feb. 1810; (197); 64
Miner, Richard (Wf); Wilson, Esther (Wf); 29 Dec. 1813; (292); 79
Minney, Thomas; Rinard, Cynthia; 23 Dec. 1838; (213); 423
Minton, Joseph; Rarrdon, Rebecca; 4 May 1815; (249); 84M
Misner, Charles D. (Be); Springer, Susannah (Be); 6 Jan. 1825; (311); 146
Misner, Nicholas; Cain, Nancy; 14 Apr. 1829; (311); 226
Mitchell, Edward (Np); Hill, Jane (Fe); 2 Aug. 1810; (197); 66
Mitchell, James (La); O'Blennis, Rachel (La); 12 Nov. 1818; (278); 110
Mitchell, John (Np); Plumer, Ann (Ma); 25 June 1806; (197); 51
Mitchell, Jonathan S.; Hill, Eliza; 26 Sept. 1833; (162); 309
Mitchell, Nathaniel Jr. (Sa); Jackson, Phoebe (Sa); 7 Jan. 1821; (90); 118
Mixer, Lewis (Ma); Bacon, Martha (Wf); 12 Aug. 1832; (192); 288
Moats, Jacob; Young, Elizabeth; 30 May 1840; (263); 458
Molen, Keshe; Little, Jane; 19 Feb. 1811; (116); 68M
Monckton, Isaac (Wo); Haskell, Rebecca (Ma); 2 July 1817; (38); 96
Monett, Isaac; Lake, Sally; 31 July 1838; (33); 405
Monroe, Duncan (Ba); Leineson, Janet (Ba); 11 June 1840; (105); 463
Monroe, William (Mu.C.); Ryder, Mary (W.C.); 13 Aug. 1840; (248); 468
Montgomery, John (W.C.); Johnston, Elizabeth (W.C.); 28 Aug. 1800; (238); NW-41
Montross, Stephen (Ma); Pearson, Mary Ann (Ma); 17 Jan. 1837; (63); 372
Mooney, Wm.; Day, Eliza; 2 Nov. 1837; (123); 388
Moor, John; Wharff, Eliza Ann; 29 Sept. 1839; (71); 444
Moore, Abiram; Moore, Rachael; 12 Oct. 1839; (290); 441
Moore, David (Ba); Stanton, Mary (Ba); 10 Dec. 1829; (362); 233
Moore, Elias (Rs.C.); Rutter, Susan (Wt); 2 Oct. 1833; (191); 316

WASHINGTON COUNTY MARRIAGES

Moore, George (Ma); Sharp, Anna (Ma); 3 Sept. 1835; (63); 349
Moore, John (Be); Rathbon, Elizabeth (Be); 26 Oct. 1823; (142); 130
Moore, John (Wn); Dilley, Nancy (Be); 1 Feb. 1825; (311); 146
Moore, Jonas (W.Fl.); Guitteau, Patience (Ma); 14 Mar. 1813; (278); 79
Moore, John K. (Ma); Smith, Mrs. Katharine (Ma); 25 Feb. 1827; (27); 188
Moore, Samuel S.; Worrell, Eleanor; 28 Mar. 1839; (123); 427
Moore, Wm.; Glover, Priscilla; 26 June 1840; (319); 461
More, John (Be); Dowdell(?), Elizabeth (Be); 24 June 1804; (31); 42
More, Levy; Myers, Mrs. Sarah; 2 Nov. 1837; (136); 390
Moreland, Albert (We); Morris, Rebecca (We); 4 Nov. 1838; (7); 414
Moreland, John; Nichols, Lucinda; 19 Nov. 1837; (85); 391
Moreland, William (We); Pickering, Winnefred (We); 12 Apr. 1838; (7); 401
Morey, Cyrus (Wf); Hagerman, Rebecca (Wf); 15 Oct. 1829; (66); 231
Morfet, John (Wd.C.); Bell, Isabelle (Sa); 6 Jan. 1822; (330); 122
Morgan, Daniel; Doan, Diana; 27 Oct. 1836; (59); 368
Morgan, David T.; Woodbridge, Jane G.; 11 Dec. 1827; (22); 234
Morgan, Josiah (Sa); Chapman, Mary Ann (Fe); 19 Mar. 1835; (281); 341
Morgareidge, Davis; Lewis, Hannah; 28 Dec. 1825; (65); 161
Morgaridge, John (W.C.); Cunningham, Sally (W.C.); 1 Jan. 1817; (49); 93
Morris, Amos; Burch, Gratia; 1 Jan. 1818; (355); 100M
Morris, Daniel D.; Newton, Salena; 26 Feb. 1838; (129); 402
Morris, George (Au); Davis, Mrs. Rhoda (Au); 14 Sept. 1834; (65); 328
Morris, Hugh A. (Ma); Devol, Nancy C. (Wf); 20 Nov. 1840; (209); 471
Morris, James (Au); Hutchins, Louis (Au); 17 Mar. 1822; (173); 124
Morris, John (W.C.); Ellison, Sally (W.C.); 2 May 1816; (355); 90
Morris, John (Ma); Carter, Fortune (Ma); 15 Aug. 1831; (63); 268
Morris, John C. A. (Wf); Vanclief, Elizabeth (Wf); 14 May 1818; (183); 102
Morris, Joseph (Ro); McCullum, Elizabeth (Ro); 3 Sept. 1813; (347); 78
Morris, Joseph; Lapham, Mrs. Polly; 22 July 1827; (22); 233
Morris, Joseph; Ballard, Lucy; 19 Aug. 1840; (319); 465
Morris, Joseph (Ha); Herington, Elizabeth (Ha); 17 Dec. 1840; (70); 473
Morris, Orrin N. (Ad); Sprague, Cynthia (Ad); 10 Aug. 1839; (80); 437
Morris, Richard F. (Ma); Lake, Martha (We); 23 June 1825; (194); 152
Morris, William (Ad); Newell, Hannah (Ma); 1 Dec. 1809; (270); 63
Morris, Wm. 2nd (Ad); Mason, Betsey (Ad); 7 Apr. 1819; (355); 108
Morrison, Alexander; Ranger, Mrs. Mary; 21 July 1838; (33); 405
Morrison, Samuel; Burrell, Nancy; 24 June 1802; (45); NW-57
Morse, Justice (Ma); Hart, Margaret (Wf); 10 Sept. 1809; (137); 63
Morse, Madison R. (Sa); Porter, Mary (Sa); 28 July 1835; (330); 348
Morse, Manley; Shankland, Jane; 22 Dec. 1836; (33); 373
Morse, Manly; Delong, Polly; 1805; ; X
Morse, Marcellus J.; Shanklin, Louisa; 18 Apr. 1833; (368); 302
Morton, Abraham; Reed, Diantha; 17 Feb. 1839; (70); 426
Morton, Elias S.; Ryan, Julia; 12 June 1831; (224); 266
Mosher, Joseph; Akerson, Catharine; 1 Sept. 1825; (224); 153, 157
Moshier, Promise (Ro); Gates, Maria; 28 Feb. 1828; (243); 206
Mulford, Daniel (Mi); Jolly, Mary (Mi); 8 May 1800; (21); NW-37
Muhlen, Jacob (We); Havens, Mary (We); 15 Mar. 1820; (302); 114

WASHINGTON COUNTY MARRIAGES

Mullen, James (Np); Rowland, Sarah (Np); 13 July 1820; (278); 117
Mullen, John (We); Woodruff, Polly (We); 18 June 1817; (62); 97
Mullin, James (Bev); Brady, Jane (Bev); 18 June 1840; (209); 463
Muncton, Isaac Jr.; Colby, Lucy; 10 Jan. 1814; (9); 84M
Muns, Joseph; Foutch, Eliza; 8 Nov. 1828; (230); 215
Munsell, Levi; Oliver, Lucretia; 14 Dec. 1789; (331); NW-1
Munsell, Thomas J. (Ma); Catline, Adelphia (Ma); 26 Jan. 1832; (63); 276
Murdock, Abraham (Mn.C.); Miller, Amanda (W.C.); 26 Nov. 1840; (305); II-1
Murray, William; Tyson, Polly; 15 Jan. 1818; (314); 100M
Murray, William; Hayden, Eleanor (Ma); 28 Mar. 1830; (63); 238

Nash, Chester; Henderson, Lucy; 23 Jan. 1815; (145); 83M
Nash, David; Putnam, Nancy; 4 Jan. 1805; (310); 46
Nash, Oliver; Brayton, Ruth; 29 July 1838; (29); 406
Nash, Uriah (Be); Pewthers, Matilda (Ad); 5 Nov. 1811; (197); 72
Nedecker, William; Mann, Margaret; 26 June 1838; (350); 407
Needham, Stephen (Wn); Hawkins, Margaret (Un); 21 Aug. 1828; (321); 211
Neff, James P.; Cross, Mary; 13 Nov. 1838; (311); 454
Neice, Jacob; Geren, Mary G.; 2 May 1839; (319); 430
Nelson, Jared (Be); Barnes, Elizabeth (Be); 26 Nov. 1840; (311); 471
Nelson, Oliver (Ma); Bohl, Mary Elizabeth (Ma); 1 Apr. 1837; (207); 377
Newbanks, Archibald; Skipton, Susan; 29 May 1828; (306); 208
Newbanks, Jonathan (W.C.); Gearing, Jane (W.C.); 1 Sept. 1822; (308); 126
Newberry, Joseph Jr. (Be); Bennett, Harriet (Be); 10 Feb. 1830; (148); 237
Newbury, Joseph; Withington, Sally (Be); 6 June 1808; (278); 60
Newbury, Joseph (Be); Bennit, Mrs. Margaret (Be); 30 Sept. 1824; (349); 140
Newcomb, George (Mg.C.); Sifers, Elizabeth (Ad); 12 Feb. 1822; (355); 123
Newell, Asa B. (Be); Shettleworth, Eleanor (Be); 12 July 1840; (311); 463
Newell, William (Ma); Seamons, Patty (Ma); 23 Dec. 1792; (132); NW-25
Newland, Jacob (W.C.); Tew (Hee), Sarah (W.C.); 26 Dec. 1817; (250); 93
Newton, John (Ma); Rose, Fanny (Np); 11 Nov. 1812; (86); 75
Newton, John (Ma); Rose, Lydia (Np); 25 Sept. 1814; (109); 82
Newton, John (G.C.); Smith, Sarah (Wn); 13 Sept. 1831; (184); 269
Newton, Nathan (Wf); Keath, Catharine (Wf); 30 Aug. 1814; (292); 82
Newton, Oren (Ma); Fuller, Almira (Ma); 13 Mar. 1810; (310); 64
Newton, Oren (Wn); Fuller, Elizabeth (Wn); 9 Apr. 1822; (349); 125
Newton, Stephen (Wn); Humphrey, Harriet (Wn); 19 Nov. 1835; (184); 355
Nicholls, James; Bailey, Elizabeth; 7 Jan. 1811; (293); 67M
Nichols, Enoch (A.C.); Gates, Susanna (Un); 9 Oct. 1836; (334); 367
Nichols, Henry (Mg.C.); Laughery, Jane (Wf); 17 Mar. 1837; (17); 378
Nichols, James; Benson, Christianna; 6 Aug. 1818; (84); 103M
Nighswonger, Hamilton (Wo); Vandevender, Nancy (Wo); 10 Aug. 1809; (188); 62
Nill, Squire; Sprage, Cynthia Ann; 21 Nov. 1839; (2); 442
Niswanger, John; Coleman, Mrs. Peggy; 19 Nov. 1797; (238); NW-23
Nixon, George (Ma); Jennings, Margaret (Ma); 25 Dec. 1811; (197); 72
Nixon, George; Riheldarfee, Julia A.; 8 Nov. 1837; (33); 392

Nixon, John (Ro); Blackmore, Laurany (Ro); 25 Feb. 1813; (347); 73
Nixon, Jonathan (La); Cisler, Mary (La); 7 Apr. 1836; (87); M.G.v-2 #22
Nixon, William (Ma); Jennings, Eliza (Ma); 23 Dec. 1810; (197); 69
Noel, Philip; McAninch, Nancy L.; 24 Aug. 1826; (189); 172
Nogle, Isaac (W.C.); Patten, Nancy (W.C.); 12 Aug. 1800; (238); NW-40
Noland, Alexander; Giddings, Ann; 13 Dec. 1827; (251); 203
Noland, Alexander; Johnson, Sally; 24 June 1838; (130); 404
Noland, Barnabas (De); Noland, Ann Elizabeth (De); 20 June 1832; (155); 282
Noland, Charles (De); Matthews, Lucy Ann (We); 31 Dec. 1840; (7); 474
Noland, Gregory (Be); Winans, Sally (Be); 7 Aug. 1833; (42); 308
Noland, John; Pilcher, Ann; 15 Aug. 1833; (4); 308
Noland, Philip (De); Ingles, Mrs. Mercy (Be); 12 Dec. 1834; (42); 338
Noland, William (De); Perry, Sally (We); 21 Apr. 1834; (20); 323, 326
Norman, Bazaleel Jr. (Ro); Kenady, Sally (Ro); 13 Sept. 1827; (361); 195
Norman, Grandison; Combs, Ann; 20 Oct. 1809; (31); 61
Norman, Grandison Jr. (W.C.); Cook, Susan (W.C.); 19 Jan. 1837; (256); 375
Norman, James; Stephens, Harriet; 25 Dec. 1816; (62); 100M
Norman, Joseph (W.C.); Keneda, Delilah (W.C.); 15 Dec. 1825; (362); 160
Norman, Quilla (Ma); Fisher, Mary Ann (Ma); 7 Feb. 1828; (38); 201
Northrup, Henry; Painter, Susannah; 27 May 1802; (45); NW-54
Northrup, Thurston (W.C.); Johnson, Huldah (W.C.); 29 Feb. 1816; (109); 89
Norton, Cyrus (Wn); Bigford, Matilda (Wn); 4 Sept. 1828; (241); 211
Norton, Gideon (Be); Ellenwood, Frances (Be); 18 Oct. 1818; (104); 105
Norton, Major (Be); Brooks, Mary (Be); 25 Jan. 1829; (311); 222
Norton, Major C.; Tilton, Lyda; 20 June 1833; (56); 306
Norton, Russell (Wn); Bigford, Harriet (Wn); 6 Dec. 1838; (240); 415
Nott, Benjamin (Va); Tewel, Lavina (Low); 17 Jan. 1839; (247); 428
Nott, Craven R. (W.C.); Lane, Rhoda (W.C.); 1 Jan. 1817; (346); 92
Nott, George (Wf); Hoyt, Cynthia (Wf); 1 Mar. 1814; (292); 79
Nott, James (Wf); Richmond, Phebe (Wf); 13 Aug. 1803; (245); NW-63
Nott, Roswell H. (Ro); Eddleblute, Amanda (Ro); 15 Aug. 1836; (123); 366
Nott, Samuel (Wf); VanClief, Emme (Wf); 15 July 1804; (195); 43
Nott, Samuel B. (Ro); Nulton, Susan (Ro); 30 Jan. 1831; (66); 262
Nott, Simeon P. (Ro); Kent, Sally (Ro); 31 May 1821; (347); 119
Nott, Stewart M. (Ro); Nott, Phebe (Ro); 1 Nov. 1832; (66); 295
Nott, Thadeus (Ro); Kent, Selestia (Wf); 13 Mar. 1828; (243); 206
Nott, Thomas (Wf); Bentley, Jane (Wf); 8 Feb. 1804; (195); 41
Nott, Thomas; Witham, Luceba; 16 Jan. 1834; (123); 321
Nott, Tiffin G. (Ro); Kent, Phebe (Ro); 25 Dec. 1827; (34); 199
Nott, Vandevier (Ro); Edelblute, Polly (Ro); 9 May 1833; (222); 303
Nowell, S. B.; Dana, Amanda F.; 23 July 1839; (87); 460
Noyes, Peter E. (Mg.C.); Cheadle, Lucena (W.C.); 26 Nov. 1840; (123); 475
Nugent, Joseph M.; George, Sarah Ann; 9 Dec. 1838; (70); 426
Nulf, David (Ro); Sanders, Elizabeth (Ro); 5 May 1839; (123); 431
Null, Samuel (Ad); Ames, Anna (Ad); 1 Oct. 1815; (185); 87
Null, Samuel (Wf); Dicks, Mary Ann (Wf); 24 Sept. 1840; (2); 471
Nulton, George (Wf); Corner, Ann (Wf); 18 Mar. 1806; (245); 49
Nulton, Jacob (Mg.C.); Langley, Nancy Ann (W.C.); 9 Aug. 1832; (311); 290

Nulton, John; Scott, Mary Ann; 4 July 1837; (123); 380
Nulton, Luther; Eddlebute, Rebecca; 30 Dec. 1837; (123); 392
Nute, Jonathan (Sa); Walker, Nancy D. (Sa); 22 May 1819; (90); 108
Nye, Anselm T.; Cram, Rebecca D.; 18 Nov. 1828; (22); 234
Nye, Ebenezer (Ad); Gardner, Silence (Ad); 21 Nov. 1802; (91); NW-60
Nye, George (Fe); Gardner, Lydia (Fe); 20 Dec. 1808; (365); 59
Nye, Ichabod (Ma); Beebe, Mrs. Rebecca (Be); 20 Aug. 1839; (184); 437
Nye, Ichabod H.; Wood, Catharine; 5 Feb. 1839; (319); 421
Nye, Nathan (Un); Barker, Rhoda E. (Fe); 21 Mar. 1813; (316); 73
Nye, Theodorus (Un); Varnum, Rebecca (Un); 13 Mar. 1814; (316); 80

Obleness, James R.; Hoff, Hannah; 6 Mar. 1834; (109); 321
O'Bleness, John (La); Hoff, Susanna (La); 29 Oct. 1829; (109); 236
O'Blennis, Henry (La); McKibben, Letty (La); 14 Oct. 1819; (109); 111
Ockerman, William (Un); Judd, Milly (Un); 22 Mar. 1820; (283); 113
Ogle, Elias (Sa); Walker, Mary (Sa); 26 Apr. 1814; (227); 81
Ogle, George (Sa); Shirley, Polly (Wf); 8 Apr. 1813; (333); 75
Ogle, James; Walker, Margaret; 14 Feb. 1809; (261); 61
Ogle, James (Sa); Dixon, Jane (Fe); 20 May 1817; (330); 97
Ogle, John (Sa); Robinson, Elizabeth (Ma); 28 June 1839; (38); 434
Ogle, William (Sa); Perkins, Betsy (Sa); 28 May 1812; (261); 75
Olds, Dr. Benj. S. (Rs.C.); Herron, Theresa S. (Ma); 7 Apr. 1831; (184); 263
Olds, Gilbert (Wf); Kent, Katharine (Wf); 13 Dec. 1827; (243); 197
Oliver, Alexander (Ma); Graham, Betsy (Ma); 22 Nov. 1806; (197); 52
Oliver, Cyrus; McKibbin, Margaret; 14 Jan. 1830; (326); 242
Oliver, David S.; Willis, Jane; 11 Nov. 1838; (29); 413
Oliver, John (Ad); Matthews, Catharine (Ad); 9 Apr. 1801; (317); NW-47
Oliver, John W.; Perdieu, Rebecca; 4 Mar. 1838; (207); 394
Oliver, Lancelot; Akins, Elizabeth; 9 Oct. 1817; (346); 99M
Oliver, Lewis (Gr); Lee, Mary (Gr); 18 Jan. 1833; (200); 301
Oliver, Robert Jr. (Wo); Jordan, Polly (Wo); 13 Jan. 1809; (137); 63
Oliver, Simon (Mg.C.); Mayhew, Minerva (Wn); 22 Nov. 1835; (85); 358
Oliver, William; Oliver, Liza; 19 Mar. 1795; (202); NW-14
Olney, Cogswell (Un); Smith, Matilda P. (Un); 3 Nov. 1816; (91); 92
Olney, Discovery (Wf); Stuck, Sarah (Wf); 23 Apr. 1801; (91); NW-46
Olney, Gilbert (W.C.); Sprague, Abigail (W.C.); 14 Apr. 1813; (316); 76
Olney, Henry (Mg.C.); White, Joanna (W.C.); 29 Dec. 1831; (66); 275
Olney, Nathaniel; Smith, Mary; 12 Mar. 1815; (316); 84M
Olney, Ornan (Ro); Cheadle, Tryphena (Ro); 21 Mar. 1817; (51); 94
Olney, Selvenus (Wf); Stark, Anna (Np); 15 May 1799; (358); NW-33
Olney, Silvanus (Mg.C.); Nixon, Betsey (W.C.); 13 May 1819; (347); 109
Olney, Sylvanius; Cheadle, Tryphena; 13 Aug. 1818; (92); 104M
Olney, Washington (W.C.); Sprague, Cynthia (W.C.); 31 Dec. 1815; (138); 88
Olney, Washington; Cable, Asphia; 27 Aug. 1818; (138); 103M
Olney, William E.; Davenport, Sally; 25 Sept. 1831; (66); 270
Olney, Wm. P. (Ma); Bartlett, Anna (Ma); 2 Sept. 1830; (63); 249

WASHINGTON COUNTY MARRIAGES

Olney, William P. (Be); Bartlett, Miriam (Un); 28 Aug. 1823; (283); 130
O'Neal, Colbert; Dana, Seraph D.; 1 Nov. 1832; (158); 291
O'Neal, Ezra (Be); Ferguson, Matilda (Np); 17 Oct. 1825; (12); 156
O'Neal, Joseph (Be); Cole, Eunice (Wn); 8 Aug. 1828; (327); 211
Ongle, Wm. (Ma); Mitty, Elizabeth (Ma); 27 Mar. 1837; (63); 375
Opp, Jacob (Gr); Johnston, Jane (Gr); 3 June 1824; (353); 135
Opp, Jacob Jr. (Gr); Barnhart, Mary (Gr); 16 May 1824; (353); 135
Ormiston, David; Pond, Eliza; 21 Aug. 1840; (337); 411
Ormiston, James (Ba); Wilmorth, Lucinda (We); 16 Sept. 1834; (20); 331
Ormiston, John (Ro); Benjamin, Dency (Ma); 15 Oct. 1831; (63); 270
Osterhout, Henry; Hoskinson, Delila; 11 July 1838; (70); 405
Otis, Barnabas Jr. (Fe); Bainter, Mary S. (Ma); 28 May 1835; (38); 345
Otis, Stephen (Un); Dyar, Sally (Un); 17 Feb. 1825; (283); 146
Otis, William; Rice, Sabrina; 27 May 1832; (276); 281
Owen, Charles (Ad); McFarlin, Peggy (Ad); 15 Feb. 1816; (138); 88
Owen, Daniel (Ad); Swift, Mrs. Deborah (Ad); 28 Feb. 1828; (40); 203
Owen, James (Ad); Brown, Ajubah (Ad); 27 Apr. 1800; (91); NW-41
Owen, James (Un); Palmer, Polly (Un); 27 Nov. 1823; (316); 131
Owen, James (Ad); Baldwin, Catharine (Ad); 26 Aug. 1830; (274); 248
Owen, Leander (Ad); Crawford, Mary Ann (Ad); 28 May 1836; (274); 362
Owen, Ovid F. (Ma); Jett, Lucena (Ma); 13 Dec. 1838; (38); 416
Owen, Vincent (Ad); Adams, Jane (Wt); 7 June 1833; (2); 299
Owens, Daniel (Ad); Allison, Hannah (Ad); 10 Apr. 1804; (195); 41

Paden, Obediah (Gr); Cline, Christiana (Gr); 18 Feb. 1807; (358); 54
Page, Henry Edwin; Pfaff, Elizabeth; 14 May 1839; (59); 433
Pagett, Hiram (Ad); Simons, Jane (Ad); 10 Apr. 1829; (79); 231
Pain, Charles (Wo); Gregg, Jane (Wo); 21 Sept. 1820; (362); 116
Pain, Truman; Dickeson, Susanna; 6 Mar. 1834; (326); 324
Paine, John (Ma); Bradley, Hannah (Ma); 14 Jan. 1806; (31?); 48
Paine, John (Wt); Stull, Mrs. Frances (Wf); 6 Dec. 1827; (361); 197
Paine, Matthias S. (Ba); Hutchinson, Lucinda (Ba); 12 June 1821; (75); 119
Pallin, Wm. (W.C.); Harden, Mary (W.C.); 17 June 1800; (238); NW-40
Palmer, Benj. F. (We); Houghland, Margaret (We); 27 Nov. 1817; (62); 98
Palmer, Carlton (Np); Humphrey, Mrs. Lydia (Np); 15 June 1828; (79); 208
Palmer, Ephraim (We); Dunsmoor, Mary K. (We); 27 Sept. 1825; (34); 157
Palmer, Harris (Ro); Houghland, Anna (Ba); 3 Apr. 1834; (259); 323
Palmer, Isaac L. (We); Tilton, Persis (Be); 23 May 1822; (62); 124
Palmer, Jabish F. (W.C.); Brown, Lydia G. (W.C.); 4 Mar. 1822; (313); 125
Palmer, James; Tuttle, Polly; 28 May 1826; (162); 170
Palmer, James M.; Gard, Sophia; 4 Nov. 1835; (193); 353
Palmer, Jewett (Fe); Campbell, Rachel (Fe); 30 Mar. 1823; (332); 129
Palmer, John; Ward, Sarah; 15 Sept. 1839; (71); 439
Palmer, Joseph; Ward, Matilda; 24 Aug. 1837; (71); 386
Palmer, Joseph Jr. (Ro); Martin, Sally (Ro); 26 Sept. 1808; (249); 58
Palmer, Waterman (Pkb); Rector, Sallie (Ad); 10 Nov. 1825; (316); 158

Parke, John; Carle, Sabina; 27 Jan. 1831; (306); 259
Parke, Ruel (Un); Beebe, Julia (Wt); 13 Sept. 1827; (258); 195
Parke, Salmon (Un); Mason, Sophonia (Ad); 3 Feb. 1825; (316); 145
Parker, Asher (We); Hallett, Mrs. Margaret (We); 10 May 1824; (67); 134
Parker, John (Np); Coton, Lucy (Np); 2 May 1807; (197); 54
Parker, John S.; Flanders, Maria; 4 July 1837; (59); 380
Parker, Richard (Ma); Chambers, Eleanor (Ma); 17 Mar. 1831; (63); 262
Parker, Sam'l (Un); Hanson, Susanna (Un); 24 Oct. 1813; (316); 78
Parks, John (Un); Shields, Sarah (Wt); 4 June 1837; (248); 382
Parr, Hamilton; Rinard, Margaret (Lu); 22 July 1830; (114); 247
Parr, Isaac (Gr); Sheets, Ruth (Gr); 6 Apr. 1824; (353); 134
Parr, Jesse; Sheets, Balinda; 1 Sept. 1831; (114); 269
Parr, Samuel (Gr); Holdren, Grace (Gr); 24 Oct. 1819; (353); 111
Parr, Samuel (Lu); Cady, Eliza (Np); 7 Aug. 1825; (150); 153
Parr, Samuel (Gr); Judge, Nancy (Gr); 9 May 1833; (200); 302
Parr, Stephen (Gr); Dailey, Nancy (Gr); 16 Nov. 1817; (304); 102
Parr, Vachel (W.C.); Wingett, Cassinda (W.C.); 19 Feb. 1829; (326); 220
Parry, Joshua C.; Pratt, Louisa Jane; 13 July 1834; (341); 327
Parsons, Jefferson; Devol, Harriet; 28 Mar. 1839; (17); 428
Parsons, Rufus (Wt); Chapman, Rhoda (Wt); 15 Nov. 1827; (34); 196
Patchell, Warren alias for Wells, Warren, which see
Patten, Ezekial; Hilderbrand, Sarah (We); 29 Jan. 1839; (256); 429
Patten, Owens; Hopkins, Ann; 9 Jan. 1834; (56); 318
Patten, Richard (Ma); Wier, Sally (Ma); 20 July 1805; (31); 48
Patterson, William (Ad); Herrod, Mary (Ad); 14 June 1804; (357); 43
Pattin, Richard (Wn); Smith, Mary (Wn); 15 Feb. 1831; (241); 260
Pattin, Thomas (Wn); Cole, Nancy (Wn); 13 July 1814; (170); 81
Pattin, Thomas (Wn); Herrin, Susanna (Ma); 11 Nov. 1825; (102); 173
Pattin, Thomas (Wn); Mayhew, Sarah (Wn); 2 Aug. 1832; (85); 285
Patton, Thomas (W.C.); Gill, Lucy (W.C.); (?1822); (109); 126
Patton, Samuel (Fe); Bell, Jane (Sa); 30 Jan. 1824; (48); 134
Patton, Samuel (Fe); Greenlees, Mrs. Mary (Be); 15 Dec. 1826; (162); 178
Payne, Abraham (W.C.); Pixley, Philomela (W.C.); 7 Apr. 1814; (197); 80
Payne, George (Sa); Hill, Julinda (Fe); 16 Dec. 1824; (90); 142
Payne, Joseph (Ba); Quinn, Julian (We); 26 Mar. 1840; (105); 452
Payne, Norman (Sa); Hussay, Lydia (Sa); 13 Aug. 1818; (309); 105
Payne, Rufus (Sa); Perkins, Mary (Sa); 5 Oct. 1814; (232); 82
Payne, Rufus (Sa); Gay, Mrs. Elizabeth (Gu.C.); 24 Sept. 1840; (279); M.I.v-2 #6
Payne, Vincent (Sa); True, Real (Sa); 27 Jan. 1831; (44); 260
Payne, William (Sa); Perkins, Matilda (Sa); 24 May 1832; (96); 285
Payne, William (Ba); Gossett, Sarah Ann (Wt); 7 Sept. 1837; (207); 383
Peaksley, Elijah (Va); Sherwood, Thamur (Va); 4 June 1791; (331); NW-4
Peary, John (Au); Stanley, Martha (Au); 23 Oct. 1824; (172); 131
Peck, Hezekiah (Be); O'Neale, Mary (Be); 4 Apr. 1819; (205); 108
Peck, Hezekiah (W.C.); Dufer, Sally (W.C.); 8 Oct. 1822; (233); 126
Peck, Zachariah (Wo); Gossett, Matilda (Wo); 18 Oct. 1821; (362); 121
Penny, Daniel (W.C.); Taylor, Sally (W.C.); 24 Sept. 1816; (323); 92
People, Nathaniel; Ryan, Mary E.; 2 Apr. 1840; (70); 460

Perkins, Asa (Sa); Twigs, Jemima (Sa); 22 Feb. 1809; (197); 61
Perkins, Calvin (Mn.C.); Tice, Margaret (Lu); 14 Dec. 1834; (180); 338
Perkins, Edward (Sa); Pixley, Cynthia (Sa); 24 Sept. 1818; (90); 105
Perkins, Dr. Eliphaz (Mi); Greene, Catharine (W.C.); 24 Mar. 1802; (140); NW-52
Perkins, John (Sa); Fowler, Miriam (Sa); 2 Oct. 1821 (330); 121
Perkins, Levi (Fe); Hamilton, Mary (Sa); 26 Jan. 1837; (71); 373
Perkins, Samuel (Sa); Ward, Ms. Frances (Sa); 19 Apr. 1827; (261); 187
Perrin, Jesse D.; Davis, Eliza; 5 Apr. 1838; (13); 395
Perry, Allen (Wn); Mayhew, Deborah (Wn); 6 Nov. 1834; (103); 330
Perry, Edmund (A); Mellor, Love P. (Wo); 29 Nov. 1812; (366); 73
Perry, Edmund (Wo); Taylor, Anna (Wo); 5 Dec. 1816; (346); 92
Perry, Ellery (Wf); Lawrence, Olive (Wf); 14 Jan. 1813; (124); 73
Perry, John (Wf); Stevens, Delilah (Wf); 17 Mar. 1803; (41); NW-65
Perry, John; Bailey, Mary Ann; 13 Oct. 1838; (29); 413
Perry, Rowland (Ma); Kelly, Mary (Ma); 15 Apr. 1830; (118); 239
Perry, Seth; Ackeman, Mrs. Mercy; 11 Feb. 1836; (217); 359
Perry, William; Record, Mary Ann; 24 Mar. 1839; (319); 427
Peterson, John; Euitlebus, Mary C.; 7 Oct. 1838; (70); 413
Petit, Allen (Mg.C.); Smith, Betsy (Ro); 23 Sept. 1824; (347); 139
Petit, John G.; Woodbridge, Lucy; 20 Apr. 1795; (202); NW-14
Pettigrue, John; Colman, Rosanna; 18 May 1838; (54); 400
Petty, David; Tollman, Mary M.; 21 Nov. 1839; (5); 444
Petty, Presley; Nixon, Margaret; 23 July 1817; (278); 99M
Pewtherer, Elias; Cooper, Anna F. (We); 7 Dec. 1828; (248); 216
Phelps, Elias; Powel, Aney; 7 Feb. 1839; (116); 420
Phelps, John (Ma); Blake, Sarah (Ma); 23 Aug. 1806; (265); 53
Phelps, Thomas (Ro); Alden, Mary (Ro); 23 Mar. 1820; (347); 112
Philips, Jesse (Lu); Dewees, Sally (Lu); 14 June 1821; (325); 120
Philips, Joseph; Terry, Margaret; 12 Sept. 1830; (63); 250
Philips, Micajah (Wt); Fletcher, Mary (Un); 28 Dec. 1828; (63); 216
Phillipeau, Anthony (Ma); Flagg, Editha (Ma); 20 June 1796; (132); NW-26, O.C.
Phillips, Chad A. (Ma); Morse, Sarah M. (Ma); 13 Jan. 1833; (22); 297
Phillips, Daniel (W.C.); Devol, Cynthia (W.C.); 3 Nov. 1816; (316); 92
Phillips, Ezra (W.C.); Scott, Polly (W.C.); 12 Oct. 1797; (238); NW-23
Pick, Samuel (Wf); Younge, Charity (Wf); 30 Dec. 1804; (151); 44
Pickens, Austin; Wright, Corlinda; 20 Feb. 1838; (129); 402
Pickering, Abner (We); Reynolds, Eliza Ann (We); 6 Dec. 1838; (7); 417
Pier, Ira W. (Be); Bradford, Sally (Be); 21 Oct. 1810; (278); 67M
Pierce, Robert (La); Dye, Susan (La); 2 Dec. 1819; (278); 113
Pierce, Stephen (Ma); Plummer, Hannah R. (Ma); 1 Oct. 1812; (278); 71
Pilcher, Stephen (A.C.); Green, Eliza (W.C.); 30 Dec. 1834; (281); 335
Pixley, Argalus Jr. (Ma); Watkins, Sally (Ma); 14 Nov. 1834; (22); M.G.v-1 (New) #3
Pixley, B. F. (Ma); Corner, Lydia (Be); 26 Dec. 1834; (144); 344
Pixley, Charles H.; Chamberlain, Fidelia; 24 Aug. 1840; (263); 465
Pixley, Freeman (Fe); Penny, Mahala (Fe); 15 Jan. 1826; (332); 165
Pixley, Milton; Perkins, Ann; 2 July 1818; ; 103M
Place, Isaac (De); Taylor, Elizabeth (Be); 30 Dec. 1824; (74); 146

Place, John Jr. (De); Maxson, Phebe (De); 6 Apr. 1823; (233); 129
Place, Joseph; Bridges, Sally; 22 Apr. 1824; (142); 133
Place, Joseph; Noland, Sarah; 1 June 1828; (251); 210
Place, Nathaniel (Be); Allard, Martha (Be); 13 Dec. 1818; (145); 107
Place, Sidney; Dufur, Rhoda; 3 Nov. 1827; (130); 196
Plumer, John M. (Ma); Fulton, Jane H. (Ma); 31 Mar. 1831; (22); 289
Poland, Richard; Place, Lydia; 22 Aug. 1838; (298); 408
Pond, Samuel B. (Ba); Clark, Ethelinde (Be); 27 June 1822; (62); 125
Pool, Dennis (Gr); Ellis, Elizabeth (Gr); 23 Jan. 1814; (295); 79
Pool, Samuel; Yant, Elizabeth; 7 Oct. 1840; (58); 470
Pope, John; VanValey, Iatruda; 4 Jan. 1818; (252); 100M
Pope, Robert; Mutchler, Sylvina (Wt); 26 Apr. 1828; (346); 207
Porter, Almer; Babson, Mary; 24 Mar. 1833; (71); 300
Porter, Amos (Sa); Sutton, Mrs. Sally (Sa); 10 Dec. 1812; (227); 73
Porter, Cummings; Johnson, Eleanor; 3 Mar. 1815; (145); 85M
Porter, Iram (Sa); True, Elizabeth (Sa); 15 Nov. 1836; (330); 370
Porter, John R. (Ro); Stump, Joanna (Ro); 17 July 1814; (347); 81
Porter, Thomas; Still, Polly (Sa); 5 Dec. 1830; (71); 261
Porter, Thos. (Sa); Sutton, Rhoda (Sa); 15 Nov. 1821; (330); 122
Porter, Samuel (Sa); Palmer, Mary (Fe); 4 May 1820; (90); 114
Porter, Simon (Sa); Still, Elizabeth (Sa); 27 Sept. 1804; (90); 43
Porter, Solomon; Bingham, Hannah (Wf); 15 June 1827; (66); 191
Porter, Solomon C. (A.C.); Dodge, Elizabeth (Ma); 20 Apr. 1828; (22); 234
Porter, William (Sa); Sutton, Mary (Sa); 22 Nov. 1818; (90); 105
Porter, William (Sa); Stanley, Mary (Sa); 16 Feb. 1826; (85); 163
Porterfield, Robert G. (Ma); Lyon, Lucy (Ma); 12 Jan. 1823; (27); 128
Posey, Alexander (Ma); Morrison, Mahala (Ma); 5 Feb. 1832; (342); 278
Posey, George; Riley, Mary; 25 Mar. 1838; (364); 396
Posey, Henry (Ma); McKibben, Susan; 19 Sept. 1833; (342); 310
Posey, James (Ma); Racer, Ann (Np); 3 Sept. 1826; (12); 171
Posey, Thomas (Ma); Hoff, Mrs. Lucy (Np); 29 Oct. 1828; (118); 217
Posten, Hugh; French, Delila; 11 Apr. 1833; (56); 301
Potts, Robert; Oliver, Peggy; 3 July 1790; (331); NW-2
Powel, Daniel; Furr, Mary Ann; 6 June 1833; (224); 304
Powers, George (Wf); Drake, Sarah (Ma); 28 Feb. 1822; (278); 125
Powers, Theophilis H. (Wf); Devol, Charlotte (Wf); 16 May 1802; (41); NW-53
Powers, Theophilus H. (Wf); Story, Mary (Wf); 26 Oct. 1812; (55); 73
Powers, William H. (Wf); Gage, Susan H. (Wf); 29 Mar. 1836; (195); 361
Poyser, George F.; Bent, Lucy R.; 27 Mar. 1838; (177); 400
Pratt, Azariah (W.C.); Nye, Sarah (W.C.); 4 May 1797; (238); NW-22
Pratt, Clark (Ma); Mees, Cynthia (Ma); 1 Jan. 1827; (27); 179
Pratt, Elisha (Ma); Morris, Rachel (Ma); 14 Oct. 1803; (317); 39
Pratt, Elisha (Ma); Smith, Lydia B. (Un); 6 Apr. 1826; (316); 166
Pratt, James; VanPelt, Catharine; 4 Dec. 1835; (103); 355
Pratt, Lewis; Britton, Cyrene; 10 June 1839; (59); 433
Prentiss, Genison (Ma); Stone, Eliza (Ma); 12 Feb. 1823; (278); 129
Preston, Horace; Byrum, Angeline; 18 Mar. 1835; (123); 342
Preston, John L. (Ma); Plummer, Sarah (Ma); 1 Mar. 1814; (197); 80

Preston, William H. (Mg.C.); Corp, Harriet (Au); 3 Mar. 1836; (61); 361
Price, Benjamin F.; Bent, Elizabeth; 7 June 1837; (177); 381
Price, Isaiah (Fe); Wells, Elizabeth (Ad); 13 May 1831; (48); 268
Price, John B.; Ballow, Alice Ann; 14 Oct. 1836; (59); 368
Price, Joseph (W.C.); Wood, Catharine A. (W.C.); 6 Oct. 1836; (85); 372
Price, Seth; Little, Catharine; 25 Oct. 1836; (114); 373
Price, William S. (Fe); Briton, Placy (Fe); 15 Sept. 1836; (85); 370
Prier, William (Mn.C.); Hoffman, Louisa (W.C.); 8 Apr. 1838; (237); 400
Priest, Stephen (La); Chambers, Anna (La); 9 June 1838; (178); 403
Pringle, Samuel (Fe); Wolf, Mary (Fe); 19 Aug. 1820; (332); 116
Pritchard, David; Cuddington, Jane; 29 Aug. 1818; (316); 103M
Prior, John (Fe); Gilpin, Anna Maria (Fe); 19 July 1829; (44); 229
Prior, John; Cousins, Elizabeth; 13 June 1839(r); (305); 437
Prior, John P.; Hoffman, Lavina; 5 Mar. 1840; (305); 448
Prior, Nathan; Thomas, Mary; 18 Jan. 1840; (190); 447
Proctor, Daniel (Wt); Longworth, Mary P. (Mg.C.); 23 Mar. 1836; (111);
   M.G.v-2 #21
Proctor, Jacob (Wf); Wells, Elizabeth (Wf); 5 Jan. 1797; (245); NW-18
Proctor, Jacob Jr. (Wt); Eastman, Mary G. (Be); 26 June 1833; (184); 305
Proctor, John M.; Green, Rowena; 25 Nov. 1835; (193); 354
Proctor, William (Gr); Williamson, Elizabeth (Gr); 12 Dec. 1833; (116); 316
Protsman, Wesley H. (Ma); Bailey, Emeline (Ma); 8 July 1834; (259); 325
Province, Levi (Ma); Lyttle, Mary Ann (Ma); 20 Sept. 1839(r); (95); 438
Pugh, Benjamin (Ro); Johnson, Mary (Ro); 28 Feb. 1839; (256); 428
Pugh, Hiram (Ma); Uhl, J. (Wd.C.); 24 Aug. 1837; (274); M.G.v-3 #41
Pugh, Robert (Ba); Payne, Hannah (Ba); 26 Aug. 1835; (248); 355
Pugsley, Joseph (Am); Pugsley, Olive (Am); 4 Apr. 1802; (21); NW-58
Putnam, Aaron Waldo (Be); Loring, Charlotte (Be); 23 June 1791; (267); NW-5
Putnam, Benj. P. (Ma); Dana, Mary (Wf); 14 Aug. 1821; (195); 120
Putnam, Rev. Charles M.; Edgerton, Abby S.; 22 Oct. 1829; (22); 235
Putnam, Douglas (Ma); Hildreth, Mary A. (Ma); 16 Feb. 1831; (22); 289
Putnam, George (Be); Oliver, Lucinda (Ad); 31 Mar. 1799; (12); NW-34
Putnam, George (Ma); Westcott, Susan A. (Ma); 16 Sept. 1840; (352); 467
Putnam, Israel (Un); Wiser, Elizabeth (Un); 24 Aug. 1821; (50); 120
Putnam, Lewis J. P.; Kidwell, Eliza; 15 Mar. 1832; (162); 279
Putnam, Manning (Sp); Haver, Nancy (Sp); 19 Apr. 1812; (278); R-78
Putnam, William R. Esq. (W.C.); Gitteau, Jerusha (W.C.); 4 Feb. 1802; (317);
   NW-52
Putnam, Wm. Pitt (Be); Nye, Rowena (Ma); 4 Feb. 1822; (278); 122

Quick, George (Fe); Avery, Sarah (Fe); 26 Mar. 1820; (210); 113
Quigley, Horace (Wo); Turner, Nancy (Ba); 4 July 1822; (75); 125
Quigley, James; Wilson, Susannah; 1 June 1826; (346); 171
Quigley, William (Wo); Potts, Polly (Wo); 21 Apr. 1808; (245); 57
Quigley, William (Wo); Potts, Mary (Wo) alias Mary Quigley; 24 Nov. 1823;
   (47); 132

Quinby, Dr. Ephraim (Fe); Guitteau, Mrs. Sarah (Fe); 12 July 1825; (194); 152

Racer, Benjamin (Ma); Posey, Sidnah (Ma); 14 Dec. 1828; (12); 216
Racer, Benjamin; Churchill, Abigail; 13 Nov. 1834; (87); 336
Racer, Dennis (Ma); Jett, Rowena (Ma); 25 Dec. 1827; (79); 198
Rake, Abraham; Powell, Nancy; 28 Nov. 1834; (180); 338
Rake, Frederick (Mn.C.); Masters, Eleanor (W.C.); 27 Aug. 1840; (290); 465
Rake, Jacob (Au); Barnhart, Lovice (Au); 25 Sept. 1828; (261); 214
Ralston, Robert; Biggins, Nancy (Wt); 23 Aug. 1838; (157); 409
Randall, John (Ma); Patten, Harriet (Ma); 21 Oct. 1806?; (11); 50
Randals, Alexander; Bartlett, Hannah; 17 Dec. 1829; (34); 237
Randolph, Isaac (Ro); Eddleblute, Hannah (Ro); 28 Oct. 1832; (222); 291
Ranger, Ephraim H.; Ault, Mary Ann; 19 July 1840; (319); 46
Ransom, Theophilus Esq. (Ad); Sheppard, Mrs. Sarah (Ad); 1 Jan. 1822; (283); 121
Ransom, Truman (Ad); Lord, Temperance (Ad); 10 Apr. 1817; (138); 94
Rarden, Samuel (We); Cowee, Sally (We); 30 Oct. 1827; (230); 201, 202
Rarden, William; Vanderventer, Jane; 15 Nov. 1807; (249); 55
Rardin, Henry, Jr.; Cradlebaugh, Catherine; 5 Aug. 1825; (230); 154
Rardin, Jacob; Travis, Samantha (Ro); 26 June 1834; (127); 325
Rardin, James (We); Lewis, Sarah (We); 11 Nov. 1825; (230); 158
Rardin, John (Ro); Emerson, Amazilla G. (Ro); 11 Feb. 1836; (256); 360
Rardin, John N. (W.C.); Ingram, Comfort (W.C.); 19 May 1833; (127); 304
Rardin, Moses (W.C.); Hill, Ruth (W.C.); 17 Oct. 1822; (308); 126
Rardin, Moses (Ro); Burpey, Calista (We); 1 Jan. 1832; (67); 277
Rardin, William (We); Andrews, Elizabeth (We); 2 Apr. 1818; (62); 101
Rardin, William B.; Craft, Sarah; 31 Jan. 1833; (100); 296
Rardon, David (Wo); DeWitt, Margaret (Wo); 22 Jan. 1810; (249); 64
Rardon, Moses; Minton, Rebecca; 4 May 1815; (249); 84M
Raredon, Henry (We); Mullen, Jane (We); 10 Mar. 1812; (165); 74
Raredon, Samuel (We); Harrington, Charity (We); 21 May 1817; (62); 95
Rarredon, Thomas (Mi); Ray, Polly (Mi); 24 Dec. 1800; (21); NW-45
Rasey, Richard; Mason, Harriet; 2 Apr. 1837; (360); 378
Rasor, Benjamin (Np); Holdren, Susanna B. (Np); 28 Mar. 1805; (141); 47
Rasor, Dinnes; Holden, Mary; 28 Jan. 1802; (354); NW-51
Rasor, Jacob; McClimans, Jean; 17 May 1802; (303); NW-55
Rathbone, Deming L. (Col); Putnam, Julia H. (Be); 25 Mar. 1823; (278); 129
Rathbone, Deming L.; Putnam, Catherine; 3 Nov. 1825; (311); 159
Rathbun, David (Wn); Dunlap, Rachel (Ba); 14 Apr. 1840; (186); 454
Rathbun, John; Schoonover, Charlotte; 21 June 1827; (311); 192
Rathbun, Lewis (A.C.); Keirns, Sally (Be); 16 Oct. 1828; (311); 213
Rathbun, William; Stanton, Frances; 7 Apr. 1840; (320); 451
Rathburn, Ebenezer (Be); Hall, Martha (Be); 18 May 1817; (3); 94
Rathburn, Elisha (Be); Richardson, Prudy (Be); 1 Oct. 1808; (203); 60
Ray, James (We); Mullen, Mary (We); 11 Mar. 1812; (249); 74
Rayner, James (La); Mitchell, Nancy (La); 2 Jan. 1820; (109); 112

Rea, Martin; Greene, Phebe H.; 25 Oct. 1838; (255); 412
Rea, William Jr.; Davis, Elizabeth; 2 Apr. 1840; (87); 460
Read, William (Wf); McAtee, Amelia (Wf); 2 Jan. 1823; (307); 127
Reburn, William; Daniel, Jenny; 23 Jan. 1800; (285); NW-36
Reckard, Oliver (Ma); Clark, Hannah (Be); 7 Dec. 1809; (81); 64
Reckard, Salmon (Ma); Stacey, Susan (Un); 9 Aug. 1826; (27); 170
Record, Alvin; Brown, Esther; 18 Oct. 1838; (255); 411
Record, Calvin (Ma); Westgate, Roda (Fe); 1 Jan. 1809; (101); 60
Record, Joseph (Ma); Jennings, Delilah (Ma); 1 Mar. 1816; (197); 90
Rector, Enoch; Ransom, Mindwell; 21 Dec. 1824; (205); 150
Reed, Alexander (Ba); Creighton, Isabella (We); 22 Oct. 1840; (248); 468
Reed, Bantom; Rogers, Eleanor; 7 May 1840; (123); 456
Reed, Benjamin (W.C.); Johnson, Abigail (W.C.); 14 Apr. 1823; (90); 129
Reed, Chauncey (Ma); Cherry, Maria (Ma); 8 Nov. 1834; (63); 330
Reed, David (We); Brackenridge, Elizabeth (Ro); 13 Dec. 1838; (248); 419
Reed, James (W.C.); Noble, Rachel (W.C.); 31 May 1817; (38); 95
Reed, John; Coon, Ann (Sa); 20 Apr. 1827; (69); 186
Reed, Joseph; Jackson, Jane; 2 July 1818; (90); 104M
Reed, Major (W.C.); Barstow, Sylvina; 15 Oct. 1814; (196); 87
Reed, Parkerson (Wd.C.); Crane, Frances E. (Np); 25 Oct. 1832; (342); 288
Reed, Prentis B. (Ad); LaGrange, Elizabeth (Ad); 18 Oct. 1835; (2); 356
Rees, David (Np); Curtiss, Louisa (Np); 19 May 1829; (194); 223
Rees, David; Sprague, Rebecca (Wf); 6 Dec. 1829; (40); 233
Rees, Stephen (Np); Pearl, Hannah (Np); 5 Apr. 1835; (116); 343
Reese, George (Np); Kerr, Margaret (Np); 2 Aug. 1825; (16); 156
Reese, Joseph; Fulmer, Margaret; 17 Dec. 1838; (350); 429
Reeve, Jeremiah (Wo); Quigley, Mary (Wo); 27 Nov. 1808; (245); 60
Reeves, James (Wn); Hancock, Elizabeth (Ba); 2 Nov. 1826; (241); 175
Regnier, Alfred (Au); Rowland, Mary Ann (Au); 27 Dec. 1821; (48); 121
Regnier, Felix (Ma); Barber, Eliza (Ma); 23 Sept. 1835; (343); 351
Reigney, Samuel (Ma); Hill, Mary Jones (Ma); 19 July 1827; (332); 193
Reigney, Samuel (Ma); Tilson, Pamelia (Ma); 31 May 1835; (63); 345
Remel, Michael (Gn); Borrowy, Maria C. (Gn); 8 Nov. 1801; (169); NW-56
Reppert, Jacob (Mad.Io.); Reppert, Ann M. (Wn); 11 Oct. 1839; (184); 439
Reynolds, Caleb F.; Dickerson, Margaret; 9 Jan. 1837; (247); 374
Reynolds, Isaac; Williamson, Maria; 5 Sept. 1825; (353); 157
Reynolds, John; Severs, Margaret; 5 Oct. 1815; (332); 86M
Reynolds, Luke (Be); Barr, Isabella (Be); 28 Mar. 1819; (3); 108
Reynolds, Samuel; Gardner, Lucinda; 8 Jan. 1818; (283); 99M
Reynolds, Samuel H. (A.C.); Green, Pamela (Ba); 23 Apr. 1819; (279); 108
Rice, Adam (Ma); Jett, Eliza B. (Ma); 25 Nov. 1821; (205); 122
Rice, Ezekiel (Ken.C.); Miller, Elizabeth (Ken.C.); 1 Apr. 1800; (285); NW-38
Rice, Isaac (Ma); Devol, Lucy (Ma); 25 Dec. 1816; (38); 92
Rice, Orin (Mich); Gabandan, Josephine (Ma); 25 May 1839; (198); 431
Rice, Thomas (Un); Wilson, Elizabeth (Sa); 28 Sept. 1824; (69); 141
Rich, Joseph R.; Thompson, Esther E.; 28 July 1838; (217); 408
Richard, Luman (Wo); Laflin, Huldah (Wo); 18 Oct. 1824; (362); 140
Richards, Andrew S. (Ba); Cornfield, Betsey (Ba); 29 Sept. 1840; (186); 470

Richards, William (W.C.); Wilson, Sarah (W.C.); 4 Apr. 1816; (223); 90
Richardson, Nathaniel (Mu.C.); Bodkin, Nancy (W.C.); 5 Apr. 1818; (283); 101
Richardson, Silas (W.C.); Flagg, Edna P. (W.C.); 3 May 1832; (122); 279
Richmond, Josiah; Cheadle, Pamela; 29 July 1824; (347); 139
Ridgeway, E. (Gr); Memund, Jane (Gr); 26 Dec. 1822; (353); 128
Ridgeway, Thomas (Un); Dyar, Esther Ann (Un); 16 Feb. 1825; (316); 162
Ridgeway, Thomas; Doan, Sarah A.; 6 Dec. 1838; (319); 415
Riggs, Hazel A.; Rea, Nancy; 11 May 1837; (61); 377
Riggs, Hezekiah (Np); Moreland, Elizabeth (Np); 3 Dec. 1835; (96); 356
Riggs, Jeremiah (W.C.); Keller, Rachel (W.C.); 13 Feb. 1800; (238); NW-40
Riggs, John; Wilson, Sarah; 7 July 1802; (354); NW-57
Riggs, Samuel; Ross, Elizabeth H.; 18 Sept. 1810; (176); 67M
Riggs, Squire D. (Ty.C.); Moreland, Nancy; 3 Sept. 1838; (1); 409
Riggs, William (Ty.C.); Burris, Lavina B. (Gr); 14 Feb. 1828; (353); 206
Rightmire, Samuel (Np); Nixon, Harriet (Ma); 2 July 1835; (281); 347
Riley, George (Wo); Burchett, Patty (Wo); 14 May 1817; (147); 95
Riley, George (Ba); Burchett, Susanna (Wt); 27 Sept. 1836; (186); 368
Riley, James (Ba); Oliver, Elizabeth (Ba); 2 Apr. 1840; (186); 456
Riley, John; Thorniley, Tabitha; 7 Feb. 1833; (342); 296
Riley, Robert; Hoskins, Mary; 12 May 1825; (12); 150
Riley, William (Wo); Gossett, Margaret (Wo); 15 July 1813; (147); 77
Riley, William; Dick, Julia Ann; 19 Oct. 1837; (364); 388
Riley, Wm. (Ba); Oliver, Eliza (Ba); 18 Oct. 1840; (186); 469
Rinard, John; Rea, Nancy (Np); 5 Feb. 1824; (353); 133
Ripley, Joshua (Be); Rouse, Cynthia F. (Be); 18 Aug. 1840; (37); 464
Ritchie, Jeptha (Ma); Browning, Sarah (Ma); 24 Nov. 1812; (278); 71
Rives, Stephen; Baeggs, Mary; 7 Apr. 1803; (303); NW-62
Roach, Daniel (Ad); Stephens, Sally (Ad); 19 Feb. 1817; (138); 94
Roach, John (Ad); Mason, Pamela (Ad); 10 Oct. 1813; (138); 78
Roach, Milton; Mason, Rebecca; 6 Feb. 1840; (88); 446
Roach, Wm. (Ad); Sprague, Lucinda (Ad); 26 Feb. 1816; (138); 89
Roat, Christopher; Bishannts, Louisa; 11 Oct. 1838; (247); 417
Robason, Starling (A.C.); Wilson, Almedia (Wt); 25 Oct. 1832; (360); 292
Robbins, Anderson (Ma); Bartemas, Margaret (Ma); 4 Dec. 1835; (103); 355
Robbins, Joel F. (Be); Newberry, Sally (Be); 5 Jan. 1840; (70); 448
Robbins, Rev. Sam'l P.; Burlingame, Patty; 5 Sept. 1810; (152); 67M
Robbins, Thomas (Ma); Smith, Polly (Ma); 11 Mar. 1827; (107); 181
Roberts, Amos; Taylor, Charlotte; 11 Oct. 1838; (123); 411
Roberts, Levi (Ro); Eveland, Lucy (Ro); 14 May 1812; (128); 74
Robins, William; Haynes, Abigail; 21 Apr. 1839; (177); 430
Robinson, James; Johnston, Molly; 25 Aug. 1807; (245); 55
Robinson, John (Ma); Crandall, Huldah (Fe); 19 Jan. 1826; (332); 165
Robinson, John (Cr.C.); Seeley, Mrs. Margaret (Wf); 23 Sept. 1835; (61); 350
Robinson, Richard P. (Ma); White, Sally Ann (Ma); 10 Dec. 1840; (129); 472
Rodgers, James B.; Noland, Lavina E.; 5 Mar. 1840; (31); 452
Rodgers, Thomas (Wt); Hutchinson, Eleanor (Ba); 17 June 1830; (258); 247
Roe, Philip (Wn); Lamna, Rebecca (Wn); 1 Jan. 1839; (29); 420
Roe, Walten; McCoy, Elizabeth; 10 Dec. 1836; (29); 371

WASHINGTON COUNTY MARRIAGES

Rogers, John (Ma); Capron, Marianne (Ma); 9 July 1789; (331); NW-1
Rogers, Samuel (Gu.C.); Cheadle, Eliza (W.C.); 2 Apr. 1835; (111); 345
Rogers, Thomas (Mg.C.); Bailey, Harriet (W.C.); 22 Aug. 1838; (256); 409
Romig, Abraham (Gn); Borrowy, Johanna (Gn); 18 Apr. 1802; (169); NW-56
Rood, Ira (Wf); Fall, Lydia (Wf); 20 Mar. 1817; (289); 94
Roop, John; Bartlett, Susan (Ma); 14 Feb. 1828; (63); 202
Root, George; Johnson, Matilda; 2 Mar. 1837; (130); 377
Root, Horace (Ma); Mees, Mary (Ma); 29 Dec. 1825; (38); 160
Root, Horace; Totman, Polly; 14 Nov. 1839; (15); 442
Root, Oliver; Buck, Lucretia; 12 Apr. 1838; (130); 397
Root, William; Batchelder, Mrs. Eunice; 21 Sept. 1837; (130); 387
Root, Wm. (De); Place, Lucy (De); 20 Dec. 1821; (233); 122
Rose, Elisha; Fuller, Mrs. Zeppora; 12 Mar. 1811; (197); 69
Rose, Elisha (La); Cook, Rebecca (Fe); 27 Apr. 1817; (109); 95
Rose, Simeon (Wn); Groves, Susanna (Wn); 16 Apr. 1812; (57); 74
Ross, Charles; Burnham, Dolly; 29 Jan. 1818; (223); 101
Ross, Daniel (Ad); Sheldon, Elizabeth (Ad); 20 May 1836; (2); 369
Ross, George (St.L.Mo.); Otis, Rosanna (Un); 4 Apr. 1836; (63); 362
Ross, Gray; Campbell, Rosanna; 15 May 1838; (33); 399
Ross, Isaac Jr. (W.C.); Swift, Phebe (W.C.); 14 Dec. 1820; (347); 120
Ross, John; Burchett, Jemimah; 10 Feb. 1811; (141); 68M
Ross, Jonathan; Sprague, Mrs. Phoebe; 9 May 1825; (306); 151
Ross, Richard (Ro); Corey, Mary (Ro); 6 Apr. 1820; (347); 112
Ross, Simon L.; Mason, Betsy; 4 Jan. 1838; (217); 394
Rossberry, Ambrose (Ma); Emmons, Nelly (Ma); 13 June 1824; (27); 137
Roth, Jacob (Ad); Stroble, Mary (Ad); 24 Sept. 1840; (247); 475
Roth, Jacob (Ad); Bizzants, Margaret (Sa); 10 Jan. 1841; (247); 475
Rouse, Barker (Be); Phillips, Mary (Ma); 6 June 1824; (27); 137
Rouse, Stephen (Be); McClure, Maria T. (Wf); 31 July 1814; (289); 82
Rowe, Vincent (Wn); Harris, Laura Ann (Wn); 20 June 1839; (29); 436
Rowland, Robert; Hayze, Polly (Np); 24 Jan. 1834; (87); 321
Ruggles, Joseph; Fleming, Welthy; 23 Apr. 1836; (109); 363
Rumbold, Charles; Lightfritz, Betsey; 14 Nov. 1839; (13); 441
Rumbold, Henry (Un); Shepard, Mrs. Eleanor (Un); 23 Feb. 1823; (283); 128
Rumbold, Joseph (Ma); Scott, Mary (Wn); 25 Oct. 1827; (102); 195
Runnells, Joseph (Ad); Bysor, Sally (Ad); 28 May 1812; (90); 74
Russell, Charles (Un); Clark, Clarissa J. (Ma); 27 Dec. 1838; (198); 416
Russell, Hiram (W.C.); Stone, Vesta (W.C.); 5 Oct. 1831; (22); 289
Russell, John (Ma); Smith, Betsey (Ma); 2 Apr. 1794; (220); NW-8
Rutter, Benjamin; Leget, Melissa M. (Wt); 21 Aug. 1834; (360); 332
Ryan, Ebenezer (Nt); Barker, Sarah (Nt); 4 July 1803; (303); 39
Ryan, Elisha (La); Parker, Rachel (La); 14 Aug. 1821; (89); 120
Ryan, Ephraim (Ma); Pratt, Mrs. Elizabeth (Ma); 12 Sept. 1824; (27); 139
Ryther, James (W.C.); Peirce, Lois (W.C.); 20 July 1802; (140); NW-56

Safford, Robert, Esq (Ga); Cameron, Catherine (Ga); 15 July 1801 (78); NW-49

WASHINGTON COUNTY MARRIAGES

Sailor, George (Np); Rightmire, Eliza (Np); 25 Feb. 1836; (87); M.G.v-2 #2
St.Clear, Abraham; Griggs, Catherine; 19 Oct. 1834; (109); 363
Salmon, John (Sa); Breck, Mrs. Anna (Sa); 21 Sept. 1818; (309); 105
Sanders, Isaac (Wf); Silvius, Susanna (Wf); 18 Jan. 1817; (252); 93
Sanford, Thomas (Alx.Va.); Leavens, Esther (Ma); 27 Nov. 1803; (317); 40
Sanford, Thos. H. (Ma); Harris, Mary Ann (Ma); 27 Aug. 1835; (118); M.G.v-1 #42
Sanford, William H. (Ma); Dickenson, Harriet (Ma); 18 Sept. 1831; (63); 269
Sargent, John (Me.C.); Seaman, Serena E. (Ad); 14 June 1835; (273); 346
Sargent, Winthrop; Tupper, Rowena; 6 Feb. 1789; (267); *
Schlabach, Peter (Un); Ingle, Catharine (Un); 18 Aug. 1839; (157); 440
Schofield, Henry (Sa); Ward, Mary (Sa); 9 June 1831; (71); 267
Schofield, James; Fowler, Deborah (Sa); 24 Apr. 1836; (71); 363
Schoonover, Henry; Hopkins, Eunice; 7 Apr. 1831; (311); 267
Schoonover, Jacob; Dilley, Susan; 28 Oct. 1830; (321); 252
Schriener, Theodore; Tuttle, Ann Maria (Fe); 11 Jan. 1835; (71); 337
Schwarz, John G. (Ma); Denher, Betsey (Ma); 22 June 1838; (146); 408
Scipton, William (Gr); Bowen, Sarah (Gr); 20 Apr. 1809; (358); 62
Scott, Isaiah; Cole, Sarah Ann; 7 Apr. 1840; (320); 451
Scott, Jesse (Wf); Sherman, Anna (Wf); 1 Jan. 1816; (289); 89
Scott, John (Ad); Roche, Mary (Ad); 18 Feb. 1806; (91); 49
Scott, John (Wf); Beard, Mary (Wf); 28 June 1810; (292); 65
Scott, John; Edwards, Mary; 28 Apr. 1836; (180); 362
Scott, Josiah (Ho); Dickson, Anna (Ho); 15 Feb. 1805; (31); 45
Scott, Leonard; Briggs, Rebecca (We.C.NY.); 21 May 1840; (288); M.I.v-1 #41
Scott, Manassa (Ro); Coleman, Hannah (Ro); 4 July 1838; (256); 403
Scott, Sylvester (Wf); Johnson, Hannah (Wf); 10 Feb. 1820; (271); 115
Scott, Theodore; Booth, Sarah Ann; 29 Mar. 1838; (129); 403
Scott, Thomas (Wd.C.); Keller, Betsey (Wd.C.); 24 Sept. 1799; (238); NW-36
Scott, Thomas; Coley, Sybyl A; 10 Jan. 1838; (192); 392
Scott, Thomas A. (Au); Williams, Elizabeth (Au); 1 Sept. 1833; (305); 310
Scovill, David (Wn); Shears, Rebecca (Wn); 29 Oct. 1838; (70); 414
Scoville, Asahel A. (Tr.C.); Lancaster, Polly (Sa); 10 Apr. 1832; (44); 281
Seamans, Benajah (Ad); Rice, Mrs. Polly (Ad); 26 June 1803; (357); NW-64
Seamans, Preserved (Ad); Patterson, Betsy (Ad); 27 May 1804; (357); 43
Seamans, Samuel (Ad); Law, Sarah (Wf); 28 Nov. 1797; (245); NW-23
Seamons, Gilbert (Ad); Hammon, Anna (Ad); 18 May 1797; (245); NW-21
Seamons, Joseph (W.C.); Neal, Abigil (W.C.); 1 Feb. 1798; (238); NW-29
Seamons, Preserved; Reed, Polly; 25 June 1818; (90); 104M
Seavers, David (Fe); Britton, Hannah (Fe); 4 Mar. 1834; (96); 320
Seavers, Jacob (Sa); Renolds, Margaret (Sa); 29 Nov. 1807; (310); 55
Seavers, John; Devol, Nancy; 21 Aug. 1817; (223); 98
Seeley, Simeon F. (Wf); Curtis, Maria Adelaide (G.C.); 13 Nov. 1833; (166);
   M.G.v-1 #21
Seely, Abijah (Wf); McMillan, Jane (Ro); 16 Apr. 1818; (271); 102
Seevers, Abraham (Fe); Kinzor, Lucinda (Np); 11 Nov. 1830; (332); 254
Selby, Jeremiah; Dyar, Mrs. Rosanna D.; 16 Sept. 1838; (70); 41
Shafer, Abraham (Be); House, Farlana (Be); 1 Mar. 1820; (311); 114
Shanklin, Alexander (Wd.C.); Baker, Sarah Ann (Ma); 19 Feb. 1829; (85); 219

WASHINGTON COUNTY MARRIAGES

Shanks, Frederick S. (W.C.); Hupp, Elizabeth (W.C.); 10 Nov. 1836; (70); 371
Sharp, John (Wf); Cooper, Mrs. Mary (Wf); 13 July 1832; (191); 284
Sharp, Thomas; Merrit, Unity; 24 Mar. 1801; (151); NW-50
Sharp, William (Ma); Gardiner, Sarah (Ma); 27 Jan. 1828; (79); 204
Sharp, Wm.; Eoff, Rachel (W.C.); 10 Aug. 1837; (114); 384
Shaw, Boylston (Wf); Hamlin, Eliza (Wf); 18 Nov. 1819; (271); 115
Shaw, Danil (Wn); Harvie, Mary (Wn); 27 Dec. 1821; (278); 122
Shaw, George (Ro); Brown, Helen M. (Ro); 3 June 1830; (363); 244
Shaw, John; Mills, Caroline; 4 May 1803; (39); NW-63
Shaw, Lincoln C. (Ma); Protzman, Royall (Ma); 16 Feb. 1819; (148); 107
Shawtell, George; Goss, Eliza; 25 Aug. 1830; (367); 249
Sheaklee, Wm. H.; Wilson, Margaret; 16 June 1818; (271); 104M
Shearlock, John (Mg.C.); McDonald, Mary Ann (Un); 8 Oct. 1833; (231); 312
Shears, Samuel; Woodruff, Sarah Ann; 16 Sept. 1838; (70); 413
Sheets, Adam (W.C.); Fosburn, Rachel (W.C.); 5 June 1823; (36); 129
Sheets, Anthony (Gr); Parr, Lucretia W. (Gr); 10 Mar. 1836; (8); 376
Sheets, Henry; Parr, Rebecca; 24 July 1828; (114); 210
Sheets, Jacob (Wf); Bachelor, Margaret (Wf); 18 Jan. 1824; (10); 132
Sheets, Martin; Collans, Sarah (W.C.); 1 Nov. 1803; (354); 40
Shelden, Abiah; Wood, Ruth; 9 July 1801; (211); NW-50
Sheldon, Israel; Sheldon, Mrs. Olive; 15 Sept. 1829; (148); 230
Sheldon, James; Buell, Helen A.; 2 Apr. 1840; (148); 460
Sheldon, William (Mg.C.); Wells, Amanda (W.C.); 23 Feb. 1834; (341); 319
Shepard, Calvin (Ma); Oliver, Mahala (Ad); 1 Jan. 1805; (357); 43
Shepard, Cortland (Un); Lake, Hannah (Un); 3 June 1824; (194); 134
Shepard, Henry (Ma); Shepard, Huldah (Ma); 11 Oct. 1821; (48); 121
Shepard, John (Ad); Burch, Lucy (Ad); 31 Oct. 1817; (38); 98
Shepard, Stephen (Ma); Plumer, Catherine (Ma); 12 Aug. 1805; (197); 47
Shephard, Isiah (Mi); Wadkins, Sarah (Mi); 17 Mar. 1803; (135); NW-65 O.C.
Shepherd, Henry; Miller, Betsy; 6 Dec. 1827; (322); 196
Shepherd, Lewis (Mg.C.); Kidwell, Julia Ann (W.C.); 30 Mar. 1837; (162); 376
Sheppard, Luther; Austin, Sally; 1805; ; X
Sherber, Jacob; Male, Margaret (Sa); 25 Jan. 1838; (247); 395
Sheredain, James (Un); Murphey, Mrs. Nancy (Un); 4 Nov. 1819; (283); 110
Sherman, Abel (Wd.C.); Wells, Louisa (Ad); 17 Nov. 1819; (316); 110
Sherman, Abel (Wf); Brown, Margaret (Wf); 1 June 1820; (252); 115
Sherman, Curtis; Caddington, Lydia; 7 Jan. 1815; (292); 83M
Sherman, Eli (Wf); Findley, Margaret (Wf); 27 Oct. 1804; (195); 44
Sherman, Heman (Wf); Vaughn, Catherine (Wf); 4 May 1820; (252); 115
Sherman, John; Lawrence, Mrs. Pamela (Wf); 8 Nov. 1827; (66); 199
Sherman, Josiah (Wf); Brown, Polly (Wf); 30 Apr. 1798; (245); NW-29
Sherman, Lyman (Wf); Sherman, Mira (Wf); 25 Feb. 1829; (192); 220
Sherman, Uri (Wf); Scott, Mary (Wf); 24 May 1832; (66); 283
Sherman, Wakeman; Walker, Corrine; 17 Oct. 1824; (189); 143
Sherman, William (Wf); Delong, Rebeckah (Wf); 3 July 1810; (292); 66
Sherman, Wm. (Ad); Olney, Huldah (Ad); 28 Dec. 1804; (357); 43
Sherwood, Wm. (W.C.); More, Betsy (W.C.); 28 Nov. 1820; (3); 124
Sheue, Simon P. (Un); Atkinson, Caroline (Ba); 27 Mar. 1840; (2); 459

65

Shewey, Martin; Dunbar, Anna; 2 Nov. 1815; (283); 86M
Shewey, Simon (Un); Willis, Betsey (Un); 26 Dec. 1822; (283); 127
Shewey, Solomon (W.C.); Willis, Eleanor (W.C.); 22 May 1823; (283); 129
Shidler, Jacob (Mi); Bobo, Letty (Mi); 21 June 1803; (151); 39
Shields, Elisha (Wt); Corns, Matilda (We); 17 Mar. 1836; (248); 369
Shields, Wm. (Wt); Nulton, Catharine (Wt); 13 Apr. 1826; (346); A.F. &
    M.G.v-10 #33
Shilling, David; Carmichel, Sarah; 19 Apr. 1838; (65); 401
Shilling, Phillip; Hupp, Elizabeth; 28 Sept. 1837; (247); 390
Shinn, David (Ro); Nash, Malinda (Ro); 16 Dec. 1837; (256); 391
Shipman, Charles (Ma); Dana, Frances (Be); 12 Nov. 1811; (197); 72
Shipman, Frederick (Ma); Bailey, Maria (Wn); 18 Mar. 1830; (148); 244
Shipman, Joshua (Ma); Edgerton, Eunice (Ma); 14 Apr. 1825; (215); 150
Shipman, Samuel (Ma); Bingham, Lucina (Ma); 22 Jan. 1833; (22); 298
Shipman, Wm. Henry (Ma); Edgerton, Mary Ann (Ma); 15 Feb. 1821; (278); 120
Shirley, John; Shanklen, Catherine; 14 May 1811; (292); 68M
Shirley, Joseph; Keath, Elizabeth; 6 Dec. 1814; (292); 83M
Shlobohm, John; Bowles, Martha; 4 Aug. 1838; (33); 405
Shockey, Jacob; Haynes, Minerva; 14 Apr. 1838; (116); 399
Shoeman, John Conrad (Wf); Shereman, Lucy (Wf); 3 Sept. 1795; (245); NW-15
Shook, Rev. Isaac (Ala); Shipman, Maria (Ma); 6 Aug. 1835; (22); M.G.v-1 #39
Short, Elijah (Ad); Palmer, Julia Ann (Ma); 10 July 1834; (343); 335
Shrader, John (We); Melvin, Eliza Ann (Ro); 10 Apr. 1828; (34); 207
Shrader, Phillip Jr.; Cheadle, Clarissa; 6 Aug. 1829; (230); 231
Shrader, William (W.C.); Ellis, Martha (W.C.); 31 Aug. 1837; (256); 382
Shults, Jacob; Lewis, Caroline; 30 Aug. 1840; (123); 466
Shuster, Isaac; Price, Margaret; 16 Aug. 1838; (305); 410
Shute, Oliver (Wf); Devol, Mrs. Rachel (Wf); 6 Oct. 1821; (214); 123
Shuttlesworth, Joshua (Wo); Fleharty, Nancy (Wo); 23 Aug. 1810; (249); 66
Shwank, Philip (Mg.C.); Dixon, Mrs. Elizabeth (Wf); 20 Sept. 1827; (192); 193
Sibley, Solomon, Esq. (Way.C.); Sproat, Sally (W.C.); 31 Oct. 1802; (317);
    NW-59
Siffers, Jacob (Ad); Willis, Sarah (Ad); 21 May 1821; (355); 119
Silliman, Willis; Cass, Deborah W.; 3 Feb. 1802; (45); NW-52
Simmons, John; Woods, Rebecke; 1 Apr. 1802; (354); NW-54
Simmons, Samuel; Tillson, Lydia; 4 Apr. 1790; (331); NW-3
Simons, Edmund; Judd, Lucy Charlotte; 4 Sept. 1831; (306); 269
Simons, Faulkner (Ad); Chandler, Sally (Ad); 7 Sept. 1820; (355); 116
Simons, Ruben (Ad); Wells, Esther (Ad); 9 Mar. 1828; (79); 205
Sims, Francis Jr. (Me.C.); Rathbun, Electa (Be); 25 Dec. 1831; (311); 277
Sinclair, Martin (Ma); Baldwin, Naomi J. (Za); 10 Apr. 1833; (291); A.F. &
    M.G.v-17 #20
SinClair, Wm. (Ma); Briley, Nancy (Ma); 21 Mar. 1810; (31); 65
Skeen, Strawder; Bartlett, Caroline; 23 Nov. 1833; (130); 313
Skidmore, Hickman; Showers, Phoebe A.; 24 June 1838; (33); 405
Skinner, David (Un); Chamberlain, Sarah (La); 15 Apr. 1834; (109); 329
Skinner, David C. (Ma); McFarland, Eliza P. (Ma); 28 Jan. 1827; (22); 183
Skinner, Henry Jr. (Un); Riley, Mary Ann (Ba); 7 Nov. 1838; (63); 412

Skinner, Jesse (Pe.C.); Smith, Esther T. (W.C.); 6 Sept. 1832; (300); 302
Skinner, Joseph (Mg.C.); Kayler, Julia Ann (Wf); 23 Sept. 1830; (199); 251
Skipton, Elijah (Wn); Corns, Mary (Ba); 20 Jan. 1831; (139); 260
Skipton, John 3rd. (Wt); Willis, Sarah (Un); 10 Feb. 1835; (98); 339
Slary, Joseph (Ma); Pratt, Mahepsa (Ma); 4 Nov. 1806; (197); 51
Slocomb, John M. (Sh.M.); White, Julina (Wr.Vt.); 5 Apr. 1837; (22); M.G.v-3
 #20
Slocomb, Silas (Ja.C.); Come, Deborah P. (Wn); 25 Mar. 1828; (22); 234
Slocomb, William; Buell, Sibe H.; 10 May 1840; (1); 456
Smith, Adam (Ma); Hungerford, Nancy (Ma); 9 Nov. 1815; (38); 87
Smith, Asa (Ma); McClintick, Nancy (Ma); 23 Aug. 1819; (349); 110
Smith, Benjamin; Barker, Almy; 5 Oct. 1797; (121); NW-24
Smith, Carmi; Bishop, Sarah; 20 Oct. 1831; (122); 271
Smith, Christopher C.; Davis, Orilla; 21 May 1835; (14); 347
Smith, David G. (Ma); Bradley, Sally (Ma); 26 Sept. 1806; (340); 52
Smith, Elihue (Be); Withington, Naomi (Be); 5 Oct. 1817; (3); 98
Smith, Elijah G. (Ma); Handley, Eliza (Ma); 20 Sept. 1834; (103); 329
Smith, George; Clements, Catharine; 24 Jan. 1839; (7); 425, 428
Smith, George W. (Wn); Shaffer, Cynthia (Wn); 7 Apr. 1839; (70); 435
Smith, Harvey; Dixon, Elizabeth; 1 Jan. 1828; (322); 199
Smith, Major Hezekiah (Fa.C.); Goodale, Susan (Be); 7 June 1802; (257); NW-55
Smith, James; Porter, Priscilla; 19 Dec. 1797; (121); NW-24
Smith, James (Oh.C.); Beel, Mary (Oh.C.); 12 June 1800; (358); NW-38
Smith, James; Goddard, Eliza A. (We); 19 Aug. 1830; (148); 248
Smith, James; Ludwig, Lethe M.; 24 Jan. 1839; (65); 420
Smith, John; Thomas, Philena; 24 July 1818; (326); 103M
Smith, John (Np); Williams, Eliza (Ma); 25 Apr. 1824; (27); 135
Smith, John; Preston, Harriet; 5 Jan. 1826; (189); 161
Smith, John; Bishop, Caroline (Ba); 18 Oct. 1827; (241); 194
Smith, John; Bee, Letitia; 3 Oct. 1839; (58); 440
Smith, John A. (We); Brewer, Sarah E. (De); 6 Mar. 1831; (155); 264
Smith, Joseph (Wf); Stump, Nancy (Wf); 22 Apr. 1810; (143); 65
Smith, Joseph T. (Ma); Mider (Meder?), Lucy (Ma); 25 Jan. 1814; (109); 79
Smith, Lanson; Goddard, Frances A.; 4 Sept. 1827; (322); 192
Smith, Milton (Be); O'Brien, Susan (Be); 25 Apr. 1822; (367); 124
Smith, Nathaniel (Ma); Broom, Jemima (Ma); 13 Feb. 1814; (38); 79
Smith, Salmon (Ma); Mays, Catharine (Ma); 9 July 1813; (31); 77
Smith, Samuel (Mi); McDaniels, Isabella (Mi); 19 July 1804; (135); 44
Smith, Samuel (Ro); VanClief, Lavina (Wf); 26 Feb. 1824; (347); 132
Smith, Samuel B.; Dilley, Jane; 22 Dec. 1833; (4); 319
Smith, Samuel Royal (Wn); Pattin, Eleanor (Wn); 27 Jan. 1820; (57); 111
Smith, Stephen (Ma); Racer, Susan (Ma); 6 Nov. 1834; (118); 332
Smith, Stephen (Ma); Marshall, Sarah J. (Ha); 13 Feb. 1840; (129); 450
Smith, Vincent (W.C.); Hougland, Eleanor (W.C.); 19 Feb. 1822; (308); 122
Smith, William (Be); Gates, Sabra (Be); 16 Feb. 1795; (16); O.C.
Smith, William (Wn); Davis, Jane (Ma); 10 Sept. 1835; (103); 350
Smith, William; Hupp, Rachel (Au); 1 Oct. 1840; (305); 468
Smith, William Jr.; Corp, Sophia; 28 Feb. 1839; (324); 431

Smith, Wm. J. (Ma); Clarke, Elmina (A.); 24 Oct. 1839; (370); M.G.v-2 #47
Smithers, Wm.; Leavens, Matilda E.; 3 Mar. 1833; (144); 300
Smithson, John (Au); Campbell, Jane (Sa); 24 June 1829; (44); 229
Snider, William; Edwards, Rachel; 29 Oct. 1835; (119); 357
Snodgrass, Aaron; Taylor, Louisa; 7 May 1829; (326); 226
Snodgrass, Beniah; McKibben, Ann E.; 25 Nov. 1825; (326); 158
Snodgrass, Hiram (Gr); Oliver, Drusilla (Gr); 21 Apr. 1819; (97); 108
Snodgrass, Joseph; Parden, Maria; 12 Apr. 1827; (326); 187
Snyder, Peter; Nixon, Rosanna P.; 4 July 1833; (368); 306
Snyder, Theobold; Gerber, Caroline (Fe); 19 June 1838; (332); 408
Snyder, Thomas J.; Dickson, Jemima; 12 Sept. 1837; (180); 393
Solinger, John (Un); Johnson, Sally (Un); 9 Mar. 1824; (40); 133
Solomon, John (Wn); Havens, Margaret H. (Wn); 1 Mar. 1827; (241); 180
Sottle, John (Fe); Rood, Matilda (Fe); 1 Jan. 1829; (85); 218
Soul, Almond Jr. (Fe); McClure, Dolly K. (Fe); 25 Mar. 1819; (90); 108
Soule, Asa (Wf); McDonald, Mahala (Wf); 7 May 1829; (192); 223
Soule, Benjamin (Ma); Shanklin, Lucinda (Ma); 7 Sept. 1826; (27); 173
Soyes, Lewis (Ma); Protzman, Ann (Ma); 30 Jan. 1817; (38); 93
Sparhawk, Nathan (Be); Burroughs, Mrs. Susan (Be); 1 Dec. 1833; (174); 315
Sparling, John (W.C.); Collins, Joanna (W.C.); 6 Oct. 1816; (3); 92
Spears, Anis (W.C.); Ladd, Hannah (W.C.); 5 Aug. 1830; (71); 247
Spears, Charles; Spears, Polly; 5 Dec. 1826; (261); 179
Spears, Daniel; Johnson, Lovena; 4 July 1839; (71); 439
Spears, Ebenezer Jr. (Lu); Barnhart, Fanny (Lu); 4 July 1827; (261); 192
Spears, Gideon (Un); Ladd, Susan D. (Ad); 20 July 1837; (63); 380
Spencer, Isaac (W.C.); Wagner, Mary Ann (W.C.); 24 Feb. 1818; (271); 102
Spencer, Selden (Wf); Waterman, Polly (Wf); 9 July 1812; (143); 72
Spencer, William; Greene, Eliza; 2 Feb. 1825; (57); 144
Spinks, Jabez; Morris, Anna; 24 Feb. 1811; (90); 67M
Spooner, Dr. Cyrus (Ad); Wing, Mary (Ma); 23 Apr. 1817; (278); 96
Sprague, Anson (Wf); Sprague, Susanna (Wf); 11 Nov. 1806; (91); 53
Sprague, Augustus H. (Ad); Morris, Rowana (Ad); 1 Aug. 1839; (80); 456
Sprague, Elijah; Palmer, Betsy; 7 Oct. 1824; (306); 140
Sprague, Elijah (Ad); Morris, Harriet (Ad); 7 Aug. 1839; (80); 456
Sprague, Frederick; Starlin, Asenatha; 8 Sept. 1825; (306); 155
Sprague, George (Ad); Mason, Jane (Ad); 2 Aug. 1813; (138); 77
Sprague, George (Ad); Hunter, Lydia (Ad); 21 June 1831; (48); 268
Sprague, James; Owen, Polly (Ad); 13 Apr. 1826; (40); 166
Sprague, John G. (Ad); Beach, Eliza (Wf); 12 July 1838; (284); 407
Sprague, Jonathan (W.C.); Seamons, Sabra (W.C.); 18 Sept. 1792; (132); NW-25
Sprague, Jonathan (Ad); Owen, Susanna (Ad); 11 Feb. 1816; (138); 88
Sprague, Jonathan (W.C.); Lynch, Susan (W.C.); 14 Feb. 1824; (194); 132
Sprague, Jonathan Jr.; Smith, Malissa; 20 Apr. 1827; (306); 187
Sprague, Jonathan Sr.; Morris, Mrs. Hannah (Ad); 6 Mar. 1834; (87); 321
Sprague, Joshua (Ad); Brown, Phebe G. (Ad); 2 Jan. 1817; (138); 93
Sprague, Samuel (Wf); Delong, Hannah (Wf); 15 May 1795; (245); NW-14
Sprague, Simmons (Ad); Devol, Mary (Wf); 22 Nov. 1840; (2); 471
Sprague, Wayne (Ad); Devol, Lucinda (Ad); 4 Dec. 1815; (138); 87

WASHINGTON COUNTY MARRIAGES

Sprague, Wilber (Wf); Hollcraff, Gratry (Wf); 18 Aug. 1796; (245); NW-18
Sprague, William (Ad); Davis, Sally (Ad); 28 Dec. 1826; (40); 178
Sprague, Wm.; Emerson, Arta; 5 Mar. 1811; (90); 67M
Spraklin, John (W.C.); Goss, Lydia (W.C.); 9 July 1819; (279); 111
Springer, Clark W. (Wo); Wilson, Polly (Wo); 11 Jan. 1816; (9); 88
Springer, Harris (Wt); Starlin, Philinda (Wt); 1 July 1829; (63); 225
Springer, Humphrey H.; Havens, Jerusha; 21 Aug. 1827; (311); 192
Springer, Jacob (Be); Kearns, Catherine (Be); 2 Dec. 1823; (142); 131
Springer, Jacob; Johnson, Nancy; 23 Aug. 1838; (58); 407
Springer, Peleg; Welles, Sally; 17 Feb. 1791; (331); NW-3
Springer, Rufus; Wilson, Pamelia (Wt); 12 Sept. 1837; (360); 389
Spurgin, Uriah (Mu.C.); Queen, Nancy (Ro); 21 Aug. 1824; (347); 139
Squires, George (Wf); Rose, Jane (Wf); 3 Nov. 1803; (110); 39
Squires, Nathan (Wn); Havens, Charity (Wn); 1 Dec. 1822; (57); 127
Staates, Joseph (Nt); Daugherty, Margery (Nt); 14 Apr. 1801; (45); NW-50 O.C.
Staats, Abraham; Huges, Elizabeth; 23 Dec. 1798; (203); NW-39
Stackhouse, John; Powel, Sarah; 12 Aug. 1838; (213); 409
Stacy, Alvin (Un); Merriam, Julia (Un); 9 Jan. 1840; (2); 459
Stacy, Aurelius R. (Un); Ross, Sally M. (Un); 15 Dec. 1839; (70); 447
Stacy, Erastus W.; Gates, Amy; 17 Dec. 1834; (98); 333
Stacy, Flavins; Millard, Susanna; 14 Nov. 1839; (319); 444
Stacy, Gideon; Hays, Asenath W.; 20 Sept. 1838; (70); 413
Stacy, Joel; Howe, Lovella; 1808; ; X
Stacy, Joel 2nd; Elston, Sally (Un); 1 Jan. 1840; (129); 450
Stacy, John (Un); Rice, Luceby (Un); 8 June 1824; (316); 134
Stacy, John (Un); Frost, Louisiana W. (Ad); 10 Apr. 1828; (316); 205
Stacy, John; Frost, Claryna P.; 14 Apr. 1839; (88); 432
Stacy, Joseph (Ad); Perkins, Cynthia (Sa); 1 June 1808; (197); 58
Stacy, Joseph Jr. (Un); Williams, Frances (Un); 29 Dec. 1812; (197); 76
Stacy, Lyman; Perrin, Elizabeth; 5 Sept. 1830; (276); 250
Stacy, Samuel (Ad); Rice, Elizabeth (Ad); 28 Aug. 1809; (91); 62
Stacy, William; Sheffield, Hannah; 29 July 1790; (331); NW-3
Staden, John (Nt); Green, Elizabeth (Nt); 5 Jan. 1801; (303); NW-46
Stage, John; Williams, Rebecca; 25 July 1839; (29); 436
Stangler, Charles (Ky); Cooper, Hannah (Be); 20 Sept. 1832; (85); 293
Stanley, Daniel G. (Sa); Putnam, Rosella (Sa); 17 Dec. 1807; (197); 56
Stanley, Francis R.; Payne, Nancy; 1 Dec. 1814; (49); 83M
Stanley, George; Lankford, Elizabeth; 17 Mar. 1836; (162); 366
Stanley, James (Fe); Hill, Urania (Sa); 25 Mar. 1813; (73); 73
Stanley, James (Sa); Racer, Grace (Ma); 20 Apr. 1837; (87); M.G.v-3 #23
Stanley, Thomas F. (Fe); Goldsmith, Angelinia (Fe); 31 Oct. 1816; (278); 95
Stanton, Joseph; Johnson, Sophia; 8 Dec. 1831; (130); 277
Stanton, Nathan; Conkright, Lydia; 24 Sept. 1840; (70); 473
Stanton, William; Olney, Eliza; 2 Aug. 1832; (130); 287
Stanton, William; Barr, Rachel; 27 Aug. 1840; (7); 469
Starks, David (Be); Cannon, Susanna (Be); 5 Nov. 1818; (3); 106
Starlin, Erastus (Wo); Cowen, Mary (Wo); 3 Apr. 1823; (47); 129
Starlin, James M.; Morris, Hannah; 21 Aug. 1834; (87); 328

Starlin, John (Ad); Mason, Rachel (Ad); 4 Oct. 1810; (218); 66
Starlin, John (W.C.); Sprague, Polly (W.C.); 11 Nov. 1815; (246); 87
Starlin, Joseph (Wo); Sprague, Betsey (Wf); 2 May 1822; (10); 125
Starlin, Marvel; Smith, Polly; 20 Mar. 1814; (9); 84M
Starlin, Salathael; Cram, Margaret; 11 Jan. 1838; (240); 392
Starlin, Samuel (Wf); Woodard, Rebeckah (Ad); 24 Nov. 1805; (218); 47
Starlin, William (Wo); Collins, Margaret (Wo); 7 Nov. 1813; (47); 78
Starlin, William (Un); Taylor, Betsey (Wf); 5 Feb. 1824; (10); 132
Steadman, Alexander (Ho); Crespin, Comfort (Ho); 22 May 1805; (318); 48
Steadman, Bial (Be); Miles, Mary P. (Be); 14 Jan. 1807; (278); 56
Steadman, Lyman (Chs.); McClanathan, Samary (Wn); 1 Nov. 1823; (349); 130
Stealy, Jacob; Stewart, Jane; 1 Jan. 1815; ; 83M
Steed, James (Ad); Francis, Elizabeth (Np); 20 Nov. 1838; (116); 414
Steele, Wm. (Be); Lebody, Margaret (Be); 7 Nov. 1821; (308); 122
Stenson, James W. (Wo); Colby, Sally (Wo); 2 Feb. 1823; (362); 128
Stephen, Peter B. (Be); Ball, Maria (De); 10 Sept. 1835; (155); 350
Stephens, Hanson; Robinson, Mary; 3 Jan. 1815; (145); 83M
Stephens, Josephus (Ma); (Williams) (Slave of Isaac Williams of Williams-
town (W.) Va.), Amelia (Ma); 26 Oct. 1810; (31); 66
Stephens, Michael (Wt); Fletcher, Martha (Ma); 25 Sept. 1834; (360); 331
Stephens, Nathan; Miner, Betsy; 10 Sept. 1818; (271); 104M
Stephens, Peter B. (W.C.); Coggeshall, Abigail (W.C.); 16 Sept. 1822; (311);
127
Stephenson, John (Ma); Gray, Louisa (Ma); 13 July 1824; (38); 135
Stevens, David (Wf); Bentley, Elinor (Wf); 17 Mar. 1803; (41); NW-65
Stevens, Elijah; Bumgarner, Sarah; 3 Sept. 1840; (70); 473
Stevens, Isaac; Hains, Ellis; 2 Oct. 1831; (306); 271
Steward, Robert S.; Magee, Diantha; 18 Nov. 1836; (65); 374
Stewart, Alexander T. (Ma); Littlefield, Mrs. Eleanor (Ma); 23 Sept. 1827;
(63); 193
Stewart, Falander B. (Oh.C.); Scott, Sarah (Oh.C.); 28 May 1801; (358); NW-47
Stewart, James (Ma); VanCamp, Jane (Ma); 4 Sept. 1836; (63); 366
Stewart, Lemuel S. (Np); Coldwell, Jane (Np); 2 May 1801; (358); NW-48
Stewart, Valentine; Perkins, Elizabeth; 15 July 1838; (17); 404
Stewart, Wm. H.; Morton, Cynthia A.; 15 Nov. 1838; (70); 413
Stifle, Stephen (A.C.); Misner, Polly (Be); 25 Dec. 1826; (311); 180
Stiles, William (A.C.); Jarvis, Elizabeth (W.C.); 29 Dec. 1836; (256); 372
Still, Ebenezer (Sa); Hughs, Mary (Wf); 6 Feb. 1800; (245); NW-38
Still, Ebenezer (Sa); Fenn, Huldah (Ma); 16 Dec. 1830; (63); 254
Still, James (Sa); Offe, Peggy (Sa); 1 Jan. 1833; (44); 299
Still, Samuel; Fowler, Theressa; 14 Mar. 1830; (44); 244
Still, William (Sa); Reed, Sophrena (Sa); 8 May 1825; (90); 151
Stokely, David (Nt); Hulbert, Abigal (Wf); 3 July 1799; (245); NW-35
Stokes, Andrew T. (Mg.C.); Biggins, Polly (W.C.); 16 July 1840; (186); 462
Stone, Col. Augustus (Ma); Putnam, Charlotte (Be); 2 July 1829; (163); A.F.
& M.G.v-13 #40
Stone, Benj. F. (Ad); Devol, Rosanna (Wf); 1 Mar. 1810; (197); 64
Stone, Benjamin F. (Be); Cartwright, Hannah (Be); 21 Feb. 1813; (278); 79

Stone, Benjamin F. (Be); O'Neal, Betsey (Be); 7 Oct. 1830; (184); 253
Stone, Israel (W.C.); Corner, Mary (W.C.); 20 Aug. 1796; (132); NW-27
Stone, James (Np); Ashcroft, Mary (Np); 14 Jan. 1810; (242); 65
Stone, James; Ashcraft, Ruth; 4 Oct. 1802; (41); NW-59
Stone, Jasper (Ad); Converse, Polly L. (Ad); 11 Oct. 1801; (91); NW-51
Stone, John (Be); Loring, Charlotte P. (Be); 26 Sept. 1819; (3); 111
Stone, Noyes (Ad); Hanson, Peggy (Ad); 13 Apr. 1801; (317); NW-47
Stone, Rufus P. (Be); Barker, Eliza (Un); 2 Jan. 1814; (167); 78
Stone, Samuel (Be); Stedman, Nabby (Be); 1 Jan. 1809; (203); 60
Stone, Sardine (Ra); Smith, Polly (Hr.C.); 6 Dec. 1796; (203); NW-18
Stoneman, Isaac Q. (Ro); Shrader, Susan (We); 12 Jan. 1834; (149); 318
Stoneman, William; Shrader, Katharine; 21 Mar. 1837; (334); 376
Stonestreet, Aaron (Np); Armstrong, Narcissa (Np); 14 Feb. 1838; (178); 395
Story, Charles (Wf); Andres, Betsy (Wf); 3 Mar. 1829; (106); 218
Story, Charles (Wf); Devol, Hannah (Wf); 28 Feb. 1840; (2); 459
Story, Michael (Wf); Morris, Hetty (Ma); 2 Nov. 1820; (278); 117
Story, Michael (Wf); Wilson, Clarissa (Wf); 29 Dec. 1825; (258); 164
Stow, James Smith (Un); Merriam, Anna (Ad); 19 Apr. 1830; (274); 241
Straight, John (W.C.); Phelps, Sally (W.C.); 25 Dec. 1813; (312); 78
Strait, Aron; Rasor, Elizabeth; 11 Nov. 1800; (354); NW-42
Stroble, John Frederick (Ma); Snyder, Elizabeth (Ma); 23 Ja. 1831; (63); 259
Stroud, William; Lindsey, Mary; 6 Feb. 1798; (121); NW-28
Stump, Jacob; Parke, Sarah; 10 Sept. 1840; (192); 466
Stump, Joseph (Ba); Woodruff, Nancy (Ba); 26 Mar. 1840; (186); 454, 455
Sturgen, Martin L. T.; Young, Elizabeth; 26 Sept. 1839; (58); 440
Suber, Abner (W.C.); Parker, Sarah (W.C.); 8 Mar. 1813; (9); 75
Sullivan, Charles (Mu.C.); Devol, Mrs. Clarissa (Wf); 8 Sept. 1812; (143); 73
Sutton, Amariah; Jackson, Sally; 19 Oct. 1817; (90); 99M
Sutton, Robert (W.C.); Cline, Elizabeth (W.C.); 29 Dec. 1796; (238); NW-19
Sutton, William (Sa); Hartshorn, Statira (Sa); 26 Nov. 1818; (90); 115
Swan, Abner (We); Daniels, Mary Ann (De); 12 Apr. 1838; (7); 401
Swan, Henry; Bickford, Mary; 19 July 1840; (320); 463
Swan, Lawrens B.; Dustin, Emily; 1 Oct. 1840; (320); 467
Swan, Levi (Be); Springer, Margaret (W.C); 28 Mar. 1823; (311); 130
Swan, Levi (Be); Terrill, Mrs. Ann (Wn); 9 Jan. 1825; (311); 146
Swan, Levi (Wn); Greene, Dorinda (Wn); 9 June 1836; (85); 365
Swan, Levi K. (?R.); Harris, Charlotte; 20 May 1830; (311); 246
Swan, Marvin; Calder, Margaret; 19 Apr. 1827; (311); 186
Swan, Mila (Wn); Harris, Emeline (Wn); 21 Oct. 1836; (85); 372
Swan, Nathan (De); Gates, Beulah (De); 20 Feb. 1824; (28); 134
Swaney, Hiram (Gr); Sellers, Elizabeth (Gr); 22 Oct. 1835; (200); 353
Swanson, John; Griffith, Elizabeth; 3 June 1838; (247); 402
Swany, William (Gu.C.); Cook, Susanna (Ro); 17 Feb. 1836; (256); 360
Sweasey, Samuel; Hickman, Mary; 7 Dec. 1838; (248); 419
Swezey, Thomas (We); Preston, Mary (Wf); 24 Jan. 1839; (8); 430
Swift, Charles; Hinckley, Mrs. Elizabeth (Wf); 8 Nov. 1827; (66); 198
Swift, Gordon (Ma); Tucker, Mrs. Elizabeth (Ma); 18 Dec. 1828; (63); 216
Swift, Guy; Hinkley, Mary; 20 Dec. 1836; (54); 376

WASHINGTON COUNTY MARRIAGES

Sylvester, Charles (Ma); Bodwell, Rhoda (Ma); 26 Mar. 1820; (27); 114

Talbot, John; Sheets, Polly (Gr); 29 Jan. 1824; (353); 133
Talbot, William (Ma); Smith, Jemima (Ma); 8 Aug. 1819; (27); 109
Talbott, Wells; Cline, Elizabeth; 24 May 1835; (229); 345
Tallage, Jean Baptiste Nicholas (Ga); Warth, Catherine (Ma); 23 Apr. 1795; (132); NW-26
Taylor, Ebenezer S. (Fe); Tuttle, Phebe (Mrs.) (Fe); 25 Nov. 1821; (332); 121
Taylor, Edward H.; Barstow, Lydia (Ma); 13 Aug. 1823; (349); 130
Taylor, James (W.C.); Gibbs, Elizabeth (W.C.); 25 Feb. 1816; (314); 90
Taylor, Jasher (Np); Hill, Elizabeth (Np); 1 June 1813; (197); 77
Taylor, John (Ma); Harrison, Mary (Ma); 10 May 1806; (31?); 50
Taylor, John (Ma); Pell, Mahitabel (Ma); 13 Nov. 1806; (260); 51
Taylor, John (Sa); Kipple, Mary (Sa); 25 Mar. 1819; (90); 108
Taylor, John (O.G.,Mg.C.); Bacon, Mary (Wf); 16 Jan. 1825; (48); 148
Taylor, Joseph (Mg.C.); Sherman, Diana (W.C.); 16 Aug. 1840; (234); 466
Taylor, Milton; Stotts, Emily; 29 Mar. 1838; (130); 397
Taylor, Peter (W.C); Ashcroft, Margaret (W.C.); 6 Sept. 1815; (197); 88
Taylor, Stephen (Ma); Rathbone, Lovice (Ma); 21 June 1804; (296); 42
Taylor, Thomas; Jackson, Nancy; 27 Oct. 1815; (330); 86M
Taylor, Townley (W.C.); Jones, Polly (W.C.); 27 June 1816; (3); 92
Taylor, William H.; Talbert, Susan H.; 28 Oct. 1838; (255); 412
Teas, William (Ma); Miller, Nancy (Ma); 24 Feb. 1825; (27); 146
Teater, David T. (Mg.C.); Lang, Angeline (W.C.); 19 Oct. 1837; (287); 388
Templeton, William; Dye, Anna H.; 25 Dec. 1834; (119); 334
Tenil, John (Mn.C.); Buck, Jane (W.C); 10 Apr. 1828; (150); 205
Tenna, James Augustus (Ma); Fay, Beaulah S. (Ma); 18 Dec. 1838; (198); 416
Terman, William (Ma); Hoff, Eliza (Ma); 22 Jan. 1829; (63); 217
Test, John (Ma); Smith, Huldah (Wn); 25 Oct. 1832; (184); 289
Tewel, Daniel (Gr); Main, Polly (Gr); 6 Aug. 1812; (176); 75
Tharp, James (Be); Bellows, Susan; 6 May 1835; (144); 344
Tharp, Silas; Dyar, Harriet; 27 Mar. 1839; (70); 427
Thevenin, Nicholas; Maldon, Hannah Mion; 24 Nov. 1800; (285); 427
Thierry, Francis; Blake, Fanny; 25 May 1815; (145); 85M
Thistletwaite, Isaac (Ma); Price, Mary (Fe); 30 Jan. 1833; (332); 301
Thomas, Charles (Wf); Sprague, Sarah (Wf); 17 Dec. 1807; (91); 56
Thomas, Francis (Oh.C.); Ancrum, Nancy (Oh.C.); 14 Aug. 1800; (358); NW-41
Thomas, Lyard (Wn); French, Eliza (Wn); 14 Apr. 1825; (311); 149
Thomas, Weston (Ma); McFarland, Maria (Ma); 20 Apr. 1820; (278); 113
Thompson, Amaziah D.; Philips, Elizabeth; 25 Mar. 1838; (364); 396
Thompson, Amos (Mi); McBane, Jenne (Mi); 20 Oct. 1803; (110); 39
Thompson, Arthur (Ma); Fulton, Betsey (Ma); 15 July 1823; (27); 130
Thompson, Eli (Be); Barstow, Maria (Be); 22 Oct. 1816; (145); 93
Thompson, Enos; Higgins, Elizabeth; 16 May 1801; (151); NW-50
Thompson, Henry (Be); Cole, Dolly (Be); 8 July 1821; (76); 119
Thompson, Hugh (Np); Middleswart, Emily (Np); 26 July 1816; (326); 91

72

Thompson, James (Za); Doan, Julia Ann (Sa); 17 Nov. 1836; (87); M.G.v-3 #1
Thompson, Joseph (Ma); Record, Margaret (Ma); 31 May 1820; (349); 114
Thompson, Samuel (Ma); James, Ann (Ma); 30 Nov. 1812; (86); 75
Thorla, Richard (Ma); McAllister, Cammilla (Ma); 12 Apr. 1817; (38); 94
Thorn, Martin (Ma); Williams, Polly (Ma); 3 July 1806; (31?); 50
Thorniley, John Jr.; Temple, Jane P.; 19 Mar. 1840; (319); 448
Thorniley, Phillip V. (Ma); Martin, Nancy (Ma); 28 Mar. 1830; (12); 238
Thorniley, William (Np); Rowland, Eliza Jane (Np); 6 Mar. 1834; (116); 320
Thorniley, William J. (Ma); Smith, Esther (Ma); 11 Nov. 1829; (12); 232
Thornilly, Caleb (W.C.); Erwin, Tabitha (W.C.); 25 Apr. 1824; (205); 134
Thornly, Samuel (W.C.); Putnam, Sarah (W.C.); 2 Nov. 1796; (238); NW-19
Tice, David; Oliver, Nelly; 3 Sept. 1818; (84); 104M
Tice, David; Miller, Leana; 16 Apr. 1829; (326); 225
Tice, John (Lu); Peyton, Christianna (Lu); 25 May 1820; (97); 115
Tice, Solomon (Gr); Cline, Rosanah (Gr); 16 May 1809; (277); 62
Tice, Solomon 3rd; Payne, Henrietta; 24 Sept. 1835; (180); 357
Tidd, Charles; Lloyd, Eliza; 5 Nov. 1839; (319); 444
Tillton, Joseph (Be); Dunham, Bathsheba (Be); 21 Aug. 1797; (257); NW-21
Tilton, Austin (Ba); Pond, Julia Ann M. (Ba); 23 Nov. 1837; (337); 389
Tilton, Daniel (Be); Hiett, Deborah (Ba); 4 June 1829; (248); 224
Tilton, David (Wf); McAnninch, Anna (Wf); 11 Nov. 1824; (244); 141
Tilton, John; Ellenwood, Marilla; 13 Dec. 1832; (56); 293
Tilton, Joseph (Mg.C.); Hand, Mary D. (Au); 30 Mar. 1828; (69); 206
Tinkham, Cornelius (Ma); Plummer, Hetty (Ma); 7 Feb. 1820; (278); 113
Tippy, Uriah (Wf); Chadwick, Susanna (Wf); 31 Jan. 1805; (151); 44
Todd, Billy (Ma); Joline, Helen (Ma); 4 Sept. 1828; (327); 212
Todd, John (Wf); Todd, Sally (Wf); 18 Mar. 1806; (195); 49
Todd, Robert (Wf); Williams, Martha (Wf); 14 June 1805; (195); 46
Todd, Robert (Ro); Bundy, Susannah (Ro); 29 Dec. 1840; (123); 475
Toleman, Chester (Sa); Fowler, Betsey (Sa); 23 Nov. 1817; (134); 98
Tolman, Benjamin; Lewis, Mrs. Susanna (Au); 20 Mar. 1825; (90); 151
Tomley, John H. (Un); Merriam, Sally (Un); 15 Oct. 1835; (287); 351
Tough, Linus; Hagerman, Hannah; 19 Feb. 1840; (192); 446
Townsend, Stephen; Osgood, Amelia; 24 July 1829; (148); 230
Tracey, Moses (A.C.); Rathbone, Mercy (Be); 2 Dec. 1838; (168); 415
Travis, Asa (Ro); Johnson, Eleanor (Ro); 20 July 1833; (127); 307
Travis, Daniel; Turner, Betty S.; 1809; ; X
Travis, Daniel Jr. (Ro); Hallet, Hannah Jane (We); 2 Mar. 1837; (248); 374
Treadaway, Jeremiah; Hoff, Harriet; 30 Mar. 1826; (326); 167
Treadaway, Jonathan; Hoff, Mary; 11 Feb. 1836; (326); 360
Treadaway, Zetthu; Votaw, Elizabeth; 8 Nov. 1836; 371
Trever, Dr. Hugh; Holden, Maria; 24 Dec. 1835; (343); 356
Trobridge, David (Un); Howe, Sophronia (Un); 7 Mar. 1813; (167); 75
Trobridge, Philo; Blake, Martha; 30 Sept. 1815; (283); 85M
Trotter, William; Cooper, Polly; 16 Dec. 1800; (285); NW-48
Trowbridge, Jacob; Broome, Polly (Un); 29 Feb. 1824; (283); 133
Trowbridge, Morgan (Mg.C.); Marett, Mary (Ad); 17 Feb. 1840; (2); 458
True, Amlin (Sa); Brown, Martha (Sa); 29 May 1834; (330); 326

WASHINGTON COUNTY MARRIAGES

True, Ephraim (Sa); Amlin, Elizabeth (Fe); 16 Mar. 1808; (310); 61
True, Ephraim; Amlin, Betsey; 27 Apr. 1827; (322); 187
True, Jabez (Ma); Mills, Sarah (Ma); 11 Dec. 1806; (278); 53
True, John (Sa); Toleman, Jerusia (Sa); 7 Oct. 1811; (261); 70
True, Josiah (Am); Tuttle, Almira (Am); (1804/1805); (253); 46
True, William; Dutton, Jane (Sa); 9 Mar. 1834; (330); 322
Tubbs, Frederick (Ma); Sawyer, Dorcas (Ma); 21 Oct. 1804; (296); 46
Tucker, Daniel W. (Ma); Cory, Elizabeth (Ma); 16 Nov. 1826; (118); 177
Tucker, John R. (Fe); Broadhurst, Sally Ann (Fe); 11 Mar. 1827; (85); 185
Tucker, Joshua (W.C.); Bohannon, Matilda (W.C.); 10 Feb. 1824; (205); 133
Tucker, Thomas (A.); Dunbar, Sarah (W.C.); 9 Nov. 1826; (328); 176
Tuell, Presley; Bell, Mary; 14 Jan. 1830; (79); A.F. & M.G.v-14 #15
Tupper, Benjamin (Ma); Putnam, Patty (Ma); 25 Mar. 1802; (317); NW-53
Tupper, Edward W. (Ma); Putnam, Bethia L. (Ma); 3 May 1804; (296); 42
Turner, Col. George; Lincoln, Frances; 28 Oct. 1817; (278); 99M
Turner, George (Wa); Fleming, Janet (Ba); 29 Mar. 1822; (278); 126
Turner, George (Ba); Breakenridge, Sarah (Be); 24 Mar. 1831; (184); 262
Turner, Walker (Ma); Moore, Mrs. Catherine (Ma); 28 Nov. 1827; (79); 204
Turrell, Charles G.; Perdue, Susan; 17 Jan. 1836; (103); 358
Tuthill, Phineas (Be); Horner, Amanda (Be); 4 Mar. 1838; (344); 296
Tuttle, Augustus C. (Fe); Flanders, Martha (Fe); 27 Feb. 1823; (332); 129
Tuttle, Elisha (Am); Pugsley, Mary (Am); 13 Feb. 1804; (36); 41
Tuttle, Joel; Sandford, Huldah; 13 July 1790; (331); NW-2
Tuttle, Linus (W.C.); Tolman, Mary (W.C.); 8 Nov. 1796; (238); NW-19
Twiggs, Andrew (Fe); Miller, Maria (Sa); 28 June 1827; (261); 192
Tyler, Charles D.; Cathwright, Elizabeth; 12 Aug. 1838; (33); 406
Tyler, George W. (Ma); Allen, Mary (Ma); 21 Dec. 1834; (63); 334
Tyson, John (Ma); Fortner, Sarah (Ma); 6 May 1811; (86); 70

Udell, Nathan (Mn.C.); Payne, Eliza (W.C.); 30 June 1840; (1); 461
Ulen, John; Frazier, Harriet; 22 Aug. 1815; (278); 86M
Usher, Thomas (Ma); Bird, Catherine (Fe); 4 Mar. 1817; (309); 95

Valentine, Jonathan (Ma); Mees, Theodosia (Ma); 3 July 1822; (27); 126
Valodin, Francis (Ga); LaForge, Maria Gabriel (Ga); 18 Sept. 1798; (285); NW-34
VanCamp, Alex; Kahler, Lydia; 15 June 1837; (32); 381
VanCamp, John H. (Ma); Broadhurst, Jane (Ma); 5 May 1834; (259); 323
VanClief, Daniel (Ro); Jervis, Hannah (Ro); 3 June 1824; (222); 134
VanClief, Peter (Ro); Newton, Sally (Ro); 29 June 1815; (52); 87
VanColer, Garret (Ro); Rardin, Hannah (Ro); 20 Sept. 1832; (222); 290
Vangilder, Amasa (Be); Chappell, Elizabeth H. (Be); 24 Sept. 1833; (174); 315
VanGilder, Jesse H.; Miles, Mary G. (Be); 2 Oct. 1838; (184); 403
Vangilder, Thomas; Beebe, Caroline; 7 Mar. 1831; (360); 264
Vantassel, Henry (Ad); McCollum, Rachel (Gr); 16 Apr. 1832; (48); 283

74

WASHINGTON COUNTY MARRIAGES

Vanvaley, Solomon; Hudson, Elizabeth; 19 Dec. 1840; (29); II-1
Vanvaly, Solomon (Wt); Ackerson, Catharine (Wt); 8 Feb. 1827; (346); 181
Varner, Benjamin (We); Abbott, Sarah (We); 18 Dec. 1834; (67); 336
Varner, Samuel (We); Lake, Margaret (We); 27 Apr. 1820; (199); 114
Vaughan, Robert (Wf); Drury, Eliza (Wf); 29 Mar. 1832; (192); 275
Vaughan, Thomas; Baird, Anna; 1800; (78); E.C.
Vaughan, Thomas; Rodgers, Margaret; 8 Jan. 1835; (54); 339
Vaughn, Alexander (Wf); McMillan, Jane (Wf); 5 Aug. 1806; (195); 51
Vaughn, Alexander (Wf); Hill, Mary M. (Fe); 19 Nov. 1840; (59); II-10
Viall, Daniel (Fe); Hildebrand, Mary (Fe); 6 Mar. 1820; (278); 113
Vincent, Anthony Claudius (W.C.); Barthilot, Florence (W.C.); 23 Jan. 1799;
   (238); NW-32
Vincent, George (W.C.); Wilson, Rachel (W.C.); 15 Apr. 1830; (66); 240
Vincent, Henry (Wt); Wood, Elizabeth (Wt); 22 Aug. 1838; (192); 407
Vincent, Henry E. (Ba); Clark, Rhoda E. (Be); 18 Nov. 1830; (139); 257
Vincent, John; Duston, Elizabeth; 27 Sept. 1832; (139); 290
Vincent, John Jr. (Wf); Bacon, Mary Ann (Ro); 4 Dec. 1839; (192); 442
Vincent, Wm. (Ba); Eddy, Sarah (Ro); 24 Aug. 1826; (258); 172
Vinent, John (Ro); Olney, Rachel (Ro); 26 Jan. 1809; (292); 61
Vining, Luther (Wf); Webster, Sibbel (Wf); 2 Oct. 1814; (289); 82
Vinton, Francis (Bev); Fox, Harriet M. (Wf); 1 Oct. 1840; (209); 467
Visinier, Charles N. (Ga); Carteron, Sophia (Ga); 30 May 1793; (254); NW-10
Voshel, Ebenezer (Wt); Dolen, Sarah (Wt); 11 Nov. 1834; (297); 331
Voshell, Peter (Ma); Wayson, Jane (Wo); 25 June 1812; (197); 76
Votial, Peter (Be); Stover, Mary (Ba); 18 Dec. 1838; (337); 424
Vovus (Vorus?), William (W.C.); Bradley, Peggy (W.C.);17 Nov.1798; (238); NW-31

Wagner, Theobold; Semore, Margret; 17 May 1838; (247); 402
Wait, Henry; Wells, Sophia; 1 Jan. 1818; (223); 101
Waits, Jacob; Sailor, Catharine; 1 Mar. 1838; (247); 398
Walbridge, John (A.C.); Smith, Esther (W.C.); 6 Nov. 1818; (145); 107
Waldo, John (Be); Goldsbrough, Polly (Be); 1 Mar. 1810; (203); 64
Walker, Dougal (Wo); Wells, Elizabeth (Fe); 16 May 1812; (266); 74
Walker, Dugal (Wf); VanValey, Mary (Wf); 28 Dec. 1815; (289); 89
Walker, James (Sa); Bird, Nancy (Sa); 14 Jan. 1813; (227); 73
Walker, John (W.C.); Sawyer, Lydia (W.C.); 14 Mar. 1802; (257); NW-51
Walker, John (Ma); Waterman, Polly (Ma); 20 Jan. 1805; (197); 43
Walker, Jonathan (Mon.C.); Lowe, Betsey (Au); 28 Nov. 1837; (330); 392
Walker, Lewis; Hughes, Phebe; 10 Jan. 1815; (292); 83M
Walker, Obadiah (Be); Halsey, Cassandra (Be); 6 June 1805; (203); 47
Walker, Wm. R. (A.C.); Howe, Abigail P. (Be); 13 Nov. 1825; (82); 158
Wallace, James; Nott, Samantha; 25 Aug. 1833; (127); 308
Waller, Jesse; Talbot, Mrs. Sarah; 17 May 1837; (65); 379
Waller, Lewis C.; Carmichel, Rebecca; 13 Dec. 1838; (65); 417
Ward, Benjamin; Burns, Nancy; 5 July 1833; (224); 306
Ward, Henry (Sa); Babson, Ruth (Sa); 3 June 1832; (332); 281

WASHINGTON COUNTY MARRIAGES

Ward, Israel (Va); Barker, Rhoda (Mi); 2 Apr. 1800; (21); NW-37
Ward, James; Kidwell, Nancy J.; 30 Mar. 1834; (162); 323
Ward, Nahum; Skinner, Sarah; 20 Oct. 1817; (278); 99M
Ward, Robert (Fe); Tuttle, Lucy Maria (Fe); 23 Sept. 1827; (332); 194
Ward, Thomas Jr. (Fe); Fulton, Jane (Sa); 1 Nov. 1827; (61); 197
Warner, Christopher (Fe); Loge, Maria (Fe); 6 Apr. 1820; (210); 113
Warren, Elijah (Ma); Davenport, Patty (Ma); 8 Dec. 1793; (220); NW-7
Warren, Wm. Jr. (Ma); McAllister, Nancy (Ma); 19 Oct. 1823; (27); 131
Warth, Robert (Ma); LaLance, Katherine (Ma); 31 Jan. 1794; (132); NW-26
Washburn, Seth (Ma); Loring, Bathsheba (Be); 4 Dec. 1803; (257); O.C.
Wason, Thomas; Hunter, Mary Ann (Be); 23 Aug. 1836; (4); 365
Waterman, Aden; Lott, Frances; 20 Oct. 1825; (189); 160
Waterman, Ferrand Jr.; Wilson, Mary (Wt); 6 Nov. 1828; (248); 214
Waterman, Flavius (Wo); Walker, Polly (Wo); 2 Apr. 1820; (362); 113
Waterman, Horace (Wo); Wilson, Lydia (Wo); 18 Oct. 1819; (362); 110
Waterman, Ignatius (Be); Crawford, Nelly (Be); 16 June 1805; (270); 49
Waterman, John (Wf); Potts, Margaret (Wf); 12 Jan. 1804; (245); 41
Waterman, Dr. Joseph; Dana, Susan; 10 Mar. 1828; (187); 203
Waterman, Levi; Adams, Patty; 9 Jan. 1814; (9); 84M
Waterman, Levi L. (Ch); Cutler, Mary Ann (Wn); 28 Nov. 1820; (278); 117
Waterman, Reuben R. (Mg.C.); McAtee, Mary Ann (Wf); 11 Feb. 1830; (274); 236
Waterman, Sherman (Wo); Wilson, Nancy (Wo); 18 Mar. 1822; (10); 123
Waterman, William (Ma); Sharp, Abigail (Ma); 12 Feb. 1820; (27); 112
Watkins, David (W.C.); Chad, Margaret (W.C.); 26 July 1803; (140); NW-64
Watkins, Joseph W. W. (W.C.); Sage, Silinda (W.C.); 27 July 1837; (13); 382
Watrous, William (Ma); Bodwell, Priscilla (Ma); 12 June 1814; (38); 81
Watson, John; Johnston, Elizabeth; 10 June 1840; (123); 462
Way, Joshua (Ma); Bishop, Lucinda (Ma); 7 Jan. 1834; (259); 318
Wayson, James; Havens, Matilda; 10 Nov. 1831; (139); 271
Wayson, John (Be); Robbins, Abigail (Be); 7 Dec. 1817; (3); 98
Wayson, William; Hunter, Sally; 28 Mar. 1830; (139); 242
Waytes, John (Gr); Massie, Eliza (Gr); 22 Apr. 1820; (353); 116
Webb, James (Mg.C.); Coleman, Mary (Ro); 21 Mar. 1833; (66); 301
Webster, Adelphia (Ro); Coburn, Mary (Ro); 17 Nov. 1814; (347); 82
Webster, Andrew (Wf); Brown, Sally (Wf); 3 Apr. 1794; (245); NW-8
Webster, John L. (Wf); Burris, Mary (Wf); 14 Jan. 1821; (252); 118
Webster, Orin; Harrison, Lorana; 1 Aug. 1839; (157); 436
Wedge, Chester O.; Ellenwood, Polina; 1 July 1833; (368); 306
Wedge, Homer L. (Be); Whiting, Mary B. (Be); 28 Oct. 1830; (82); 253
Weethee, Daniel (Am); Wilkins, Lucy (Mi); 11 Feb. 1803; (21); NW-61
Welch, Robert; Perry, Nancy; 29 Jan. 1818; (323); 100M
Welles, David; Corey, Polly; 17 Apr. 1791; (331); NW-4
Wells, Barton A.; Barnhart, Mrs. Nancy; 19 July 1836; (119); 366
Wells, Daniel (Oh.C.); Ancrum, Elizabeth (Oh.C.); 12 Mar. 1801; (358); NW-44
Wells, Harris; Legrange, Sally; 10 Dec. 1829; (316); 233
Wells, Joseph (Mg.C.); Simons, Elizabeth (Ad); 11 Dec. 1836; (2); 374
Wells, Joseph C. (Ad); Fall, Amanda (Ad); 27 June 1819; (355); 109
Wells, Nicholas (Oh.C.); Wittin, Rachell (Gr); 7 Jan. 1810; (176); 64

Wells, Robert; Case, Hannah; 22 Dec. 1815; (278); 86M
Wells, Thomas (Ad); Patterson, Peggy (Ad); 4 Feb. 1801; (91); NW-46
Wells, Varnum G. (Ad); Davis, Sarah (Ad); 7 Nov. 1805; (91); 48
Wells (alias Patchell), Warren; Sheets, Actious; 4 Dec. 1834; (229); 335
Wells, William W. (Ha); Hill, Eliza (Ha); 14 Apr. 1839; (70); 435
Wesson, Joseph (Wf); Wilson, Abigail (Wf); 26 Apr. 1819; (252); 109
West, Edwin (Ma); Gardner, Mary (Ma); 20 Feb. 1827; (12); 182
West, Lucius; Gardner, Catharine; 5 June 1831; (224); 266
West, William (Ma); Kenada, Melinda (Ro); 1 Oct. 1831; (36); 270
Westbrook, Chester; Marvin, Lucinda; 1 Apr. 1829; (34); 221
Westcott, Samuel A. (Ma); Edgerton, Sarah L. (Ma); 1 Jan. 1821; (278); 117
Westfall, Isaac; Solomon, Betsey Ann; 20 Sept. 1833; (94); 309
Westfall, Newton E. (Ma); Frazer, Annaliza (Ma); 14 Mar. 1814; (197); 80
Westgate, Abner D. (Wn); Waterman, Calrina (Wn); 27 May 1830; (241); 243
Westgate, Thomas J. (Ma); Wheeler, Abigail (Ma); 15 Nov. 1832; (22); 291
Weston, Samuel; Record, Eliza Ann; 10 Oct. 1839; (319); 444
Westover, James (Ro); Parker, Rebecca (Ro); 15 Feb. 1835; (67); 339
Wharff, William; Clay, Deborah; 19 Apr. 1820; (90); 114
Wheatley, Hugh H. (Ma); Clogston, Deborah (Ma); 28 Nov. 1830; (38); 256
Wheeler, David A. (Ad); McGonnigal, Elzada (Ad); 28 Sept. 1820; (355); 116
Wheeler, Eliphalet (A.C.); Badget, Mrs. Elizabeth (Ma); 16 Aug. 1837; (85); 388
Wheeler, John B. (Ma); Dow, Nancy Ann (Ma); 3 Apr. 1828; (38); 205
Wheeler, Lovel P. (Ma); Gill, Angeline (Ma); 6 May 1838; (63); 398
Wheeler, Nathan W. (Ma); Hart, Elizabeth (Ma); 11 Jan. 1824; (38); 132
Wheeler, Otis (Ma); Moss, Diantha (Ma); 1 Jan. 1821; (278); 117
Wheeler, Otis (Ma); Cogswell, Abigal Ann (Wf); 16 Jan. 1828; (258); 204
Wheeler, Otis (W.C.); Foster, Nancy F. (W.C.); 25 Apr. 1833; (195); 302
Whipple, Samuel (Ma); Lincoln, Mrs. Margaret (Ma); 15 June 1825; (27); 151
Whiston, Jesse; Richardson, Esther; 29 Oct. 1835; (87); 353
White, Augustus (Wf); Webster, Lotia (Wf); 26 June 1840; (234); 464
White, David (W.C); Porter, Rebecca (W.C.); 28 Feb. 1802; (121); NW-53
White, David (Ro); Briggs, Catharine (Ma); 22 Jan. 1809; (278); 60
White, David; Miller, Nancy; 18 Apr. 1833; (144); 307
White, Ephraim (Wf); Waterman, Rhoda (Wf); 6 Nov. 1812; (55); 75
White, Harris; Stull, Frances (Wf); 30 Dec. 1830; (66); 259
White, Henry; Coleman, Lovisa; 16 June 1836; (54); 363
White, Rev. James H. (W.C.); Guitteau, Emeline M. (W.C.); 5 July 1838;
    (61); 403
White, John (Ma); Devoll, Presilla (Ma); 11 Oct. 1789; (311); NW-1
White, John; Leavens, Matilda; 19 Dec. 1802; (317); NW-60
White, John S. (W.C.); Boudinot, Sarah R. (W.C.); 14 Feb. 1816; (197); 88
White, Matthew; Merrick, Phebe; 22 Oct. 1837; (351); 389
White, Nathaniel (Ken.C.); Thornton, Nancy (Ken.C.); 23 July 1799; (285); NW-34
White, Pelatiah; Welles, Susanna; 24 Feb. 1791; (331); NW-4
White, Samuel; Meek, Matilda; 26 Aug. 1840; (298); 464
White, Thomas; Renols, Nancy; 18 Aug. 1803; (354); 40
White, Thos. Haffield (Wo); Wood, Joanna (Wo); 28 Mar. 1821; (362); 119
White, Wells (W.C.); Evans, Sally (W.C.); 1 June 1820; (347); 115

White, William (Fe); Tucker, Lydia (Un); 22 Aug. 1813; (197); 78
White, William (Ma); Grant, Mary Ann (Ma); 17 July 1825; (27); 152
Whiteside, James (Be); Breakenridge, Margt. (Be); 26 Feb. 1840; (105); 452
Whitmore, Francis (W.C.); Stroud, Rebecca (W.C.); 14 Aug. 1798; (203); NW-30
Whitney, James (Ma); Greene, Ruth (Np); 14 Nov. 1807; (278); 56
Whitney, James, Esq.; Bowen, Rebecca; 10 Dec. 1833; (322); 315
Whitney, John (Wf); Chapman, Sarah (Wf); 1 Mar. 1821; (18); 118
Whitney, Thomas (Wf); Preston, Artimacy (Wf); 21 Oct. 1820; (271); 117
Whitney, Thomas; Preston, Hannah; 13 July 1826; (189); 172
Whitten, Peter (Gr); Bowen, Rachel (Gr); 20 Feb. 1807; (277); 52
Whittlesey, William A.; Hobby, Jane H.; 25 Oct. 1838; (129); 423
Whittock, John (Fe); Follett, Ann (Ma); 12 Mar. 1825; (85); 147
Whittock, Samuel (Fe); Stanley, Mixenda (Fe); 6 Oct. 1825; (85); 156
Whittock, William (Fe); Patten, Nancy (Fe); 19 Mar. 1840; (59); 464
Wick, Samuel (Gr); Wick, Maria L. (Gr); 8 Oct. 1837; (114); 390
Wickingham, Joseph (A.); Miller, Fanny (W.C.); 3 Apr. 1814; (269); 80
Widgen, William H.; Stage, Jemima; 25 June 1839; (319); 434
Widger, George; Keeder, Rossa; 27 Dec. 1838; (71); 422
Wiggins, Eli (Wh); Brockley, Ann (Np); 26 July 1835; (118); 347
Wilber, Ira (Mg.C.); Moore, Hannah (Fe); 28 May 1825; (332); 348
Wilcox, Warren (Ma); Morse, Emily (Ma); 23 June 1825; (27); 151
Wiley, Abraham; Mannahan, Sarah (Fe); 8 Mar. 1828; (161); 208
Wiley, Thomas (Mg.C.); Scott, Maria (Np); 16 July 1831; (116); 268
Wilhelm, John; Horner, Sarah; 9 Nov. 1837; (177); 393
Wilking, Peter; Hopp, Adaline; 1 Mar. 1838; (247); 399
Wilkins, Peter (Ha); Otten, Anna; 12 Aug. 1840; (59); 464
Willcox, Henry P. (Ma); Willard, Caroline (Ma); 24 Mar. 1822; (278); 125
Williams, Chester (W.C.); Moor, Eleanor (W.C.); 5 Sept. 1824; (109); 142
Williams, David (We); Lake, Anna (We); 4 Oct. 1832; (36); 286
Williams, Henry (Wf); Abbot, Lydia (Wf); 15 Feb. 1816; (289); 89
Williams, John (W.C.); Lewis, Roxana J. (W.C.); 29 Oct. 1835; (63); 353
Williams, John; Toulson, Sophia; 2 Aug. 1838; (168); 408
Williams, Joseph (Wf); Stephens, Sally (Wf); 14 July 1806; (195); 51
Williams, Nathaniel (Ho); Hoyt, Anna (Ho); 22 May 1804; (64); 42
Williams, Othniel (Ma); Lord, Temperance (Ma); 26 Feb. 1804; (317); 45
Williams, Parker; Lowe, Maria; 11 June 1826; (109); 172
Williams, Reuben (La); Johnson, Betsy (La); 17 Apr. 1823; (109); 130
Williams, Robert (Ma); Needham, Mrs. Mary (Ma); 5 Aug. 1817; (38); 96
Williams, Samuel G. (We); Wilson, Eliza (Ad); 13 Nov. 1832; (332); 292
Williams, Thomas (Fe); Guitteau, Jane M. (Fe); 15 Mar. 1832; (22); 289
Williamson, Hannibal A. W. (Gr); Hubbard, Temperance (Gr); 14 Jan. 1841;
    (5); 474
Williamson, Moses (Oh.C.); Linn, Hannah (Np); 31 Mar. 1801; (354); NW-49
Williamson, Moses (Gr); Riggs, Jenne (Gr); 17 Sept. 1805; (358); 48
Williamson, Moses; Tice, Mrs. Liddey; 3 Oct. 1833; (180); 311
Williamson, Samuel, Esq. (Np); Dickerson, Deborah (Np); 10 June 1800;
    (358); NW-38
Willis, George (W.C.); Dolin, Betsy (W.C.); 16 June 1816; (347); 90

WASHINGTON COUNTY MARRIAGES

Willis, George 2nd (Un); Skipton, Christiana (Wt); 9 Apr. 1835; (297); 345
Willis, John (Un); Ware, Jane (Wn); 29 Dec. 1831; (98); 275
Willis, Reason; Skinner, Mary; 11 May 1830; (367); 249
Willis, Sampson (Un); Harrison, Eliza (Wt); 2 Nov. 1830; (98); 253
Willis, Samuel; Harris, Candis; 1 Mar. 1840; (320); 451
Willis, Warden (Un); Weir, Mary (Wn); 19 Aug. 1830; (98); 248
Willson, David (Wf); Convis, Easter (Wf); 26 Sept. 1791; (331); NW-6
Willson, Jeremiah (Wf); Hindley, Mary M. (Wf); 1 Feb. 1821; (18); 118
Wilson, Amos, Esq. (Ad); Perrin, Betsy (Ad); 30 Oct. 1823; (18); 131
Wilson, Andrew (Sa); Hagans, Betsy (Sa); 27 July 1821; (90); 120
Wilson, Armstrong; Travis, Louisa; 6 Mar. 1834; (127); 320
Wilson, Charles; Andrews, Hannah; 15 Aug. 1833; (2); 309
Wilson, Daniel G.; Palmer, Margaret A.; 17 July 1834; (2); 326
Wilson, Edward; Merow, Ageline; 12 Dec. 1839; (88); 443
Wilson, Elijah (Wo); Wilson, Cynthia (Wo); 27 June 1821; (362); 120
Wilson, Ephraim; Flowers, Mary; 22 Jan. 1839; (29); 419
Wilson, John (Wt); Gosset, Harriet (Wt); 29 Mar. 1832; (297); 280
Wilson, John (Sa); Hallet, Hannah (Sa); 24 Jan. 1837; (274); M.G.v-3 #12
Wilson, John 2nd (Wt); Chadwick, Julia (Wt); 6 Dec. 1832; (360); 296
Wilson, John D. (Wt); Lawrence, Rosamond (Wf); 10 June 1830; (106); 245
Wilson, John S.; Grant, Melvina; 12 Oct. 1840; (65); 469
Wilson, Johnston; Scott, Eliza; 29 Dec. 1825; (189); 161
Wilson, Joseph (Ro); Sells, Hester (Ro); 19 Dec. 1827; (243); 197
Wilson, Mills; Nott, Hannah; 9 Sept. 1828; (243); 213
Wilson, Noah L. (Ma); Waters, Kezia R. (Col); 20 May 1840; (163); M.I.v-1 #40
Wilson, Robert C.; Chadwick, Unity; 22 Jan. 1835; (123); 337
Wilson, Smith; Carmichael, Susanna; 23 Aug. 1840; (65); 469
Wilson, Stephen (Ro); Sills, Ann (Ro); 26 Feb. 1835; (123); 340
Wilson, William; Hartshorn, Pamela; 16 Apr. 1829; (148); 224
Wilson, Wm. 2nd; Chadwick, Irena; 23 Dec. 1827; (346); 198
Winans, Ezekiel (Be); Nelson, Margaret (Be); 7 Sept. 1834; (42); 331
Winans, Solomon (We); Staunton, Sally (We); 23 July 1833; (127); 307
Winchel, Lewis; Decker, Catharine; 8 Oct. 1837; (247); 390
Winchell, William (Wo); Coffman, Deborah (Wo); 7 Aug. 1821; (10); 120
Winchell, William; Byram, Susan; 16 Aug. 1835; (123); 348
Winsor, Henry (Cuy.C.); Payne, Anna (Wo); 17 Mar. 1820; (362); 112
Winsor, Jacob; Flarnernan, Cintia; 3 Oct. 1802; (354); NW-58
Winsper, Matthew; Tracy, Mary Jane; 2 July 1835; (162); 348
Wire, Michael O. (Ba); Oliver, Sarah (Ba); 4 Oct. 1840; (186); 470
Wires, John; Henning, Amelia Ann; 11 Aug. 1835; (4); 352
Wiser, John (Ma); Briggs, Hannah (Ma); 18 June 1819; (349); 109
Witham, Benjamin (Ad); Ogle, Ann (Sa); 8 Feb. 1808; (310); 56
Witham, Benj. (Wo); Willson, Jane (Wo); 11 Jan. 1816; (62); 87
Witham, Elias (Un); Rice, Zilpha (Un); 24 Apr. 1814; (316); 80
Witham, Elisha (Ro); Gates, Lydia (Ro); 15 Dec. 1831; (66); 275
Witham, Henry; Gates, Pamelia; 23 July 1839; (13); 437
Withee, James (Wn); Cole, Deborah (Wn); 15 May 1811; (57); 69
Withington, Francis; Bridges, Rebecca; 20 May 1824; (311); 136

Withrow, James; Locker, Elizabeth; 5 Dec. 1839; (263); 445
Witten, James (Gr); Scott, Margaret (Gr); 13 Feb. 1814; (295); 79
Wolbridge, Fraor (Ad); Newton, Betsy (Ad); 1 Jan. 1810; (197); 63
Wolcott, Alinson; McCluer, Caroline; 23 July 1831; (276); 268
Wolcott, Augustus S. (Guy.); Byard, Susan (Ma); 5 Mar. 1840; (364); 452
Wolcott, Elias H. (Wt); Starlin, Lorena (Wt); 18 Mar. 1827; (362); 184
Wolf, Christopher (Am); Dorr, Rhoda (Mi); 20 Mar. 1804; (36); 41
Wood, Anselm (Sa); Record, Lucy (Sa); 2 Jan. 1808; (310); 56
Wood, Caius M. (Un); Hall, Sophia (Un); 15 Apr. 1821; (316); 119
Wood, Francis; Clark, Sarah; 17 June 1830; (79); 258
Wood, Jacob; Longfellow, Merinda; 18 Oct. 1840; (305); 469
Wood, Jesse (Ma); Blake, Ladotia (Ma); 18 Nov. 1816; (367); 92
Wood, John (Ro); Kirby, Elizabeth (Ro); 25 Apr. 1839; (256); 435
Wood, Joseph (Wd.C.Va.); Cook, Lavina A.; 20 Sept. 1832; (224); 286
Wood, Manuel; Hawkins, Lucinda; 24 Nov. 1831; (56); 272
Wood, Morgan (Ad); Allison, Betsey (Ad); 11 Dec. 1823; (316); 132
Wood, Rasellus (Wo); Bartlett, Keziah (Wd); 7 Feb. 1821; (47); 118
Wood, Samuel Jr. (Wt); Coley, Caroline (Wf); 30 Aug. 1837; (207); 383
Wood, Shadrach; Kennedy, Elizabeth (La); 7 Apr. 1831; (109); 266
Wood, William; Kennedy, Sarah; 10 Dec. 1832; (109); 298
Wood, William (Wt); Buzzard, Phebe (Wt); 30 Oct. 1834; (297); 330
Woodard, William (Un); Frost, Nancy A. (Ad); 9 Dec. 1830; (306); 257
Woodbridge, Dudley Jr. (Ma); Gilman, Jane R. (Ma); 28 Nov. 1807; (278); 56
Woodford, William (W.C.); Ford, Diana (W.C.); 13 Oct. 1799; (310); NW-39
Woodford, William (Wt); Winsor, Anna (Wt); 8 Dec. 1831; (297); 277
Woodford, Wm. G. (Wt); Shields, Sophia (Wt); 27 Sept. 1832; (36); 286
Woodrough, Isaac; Green, Margaret; 13 Jan. 1811; (141); 67M
Woodruff, Abner Jr. (Ba); Gilmore, Mary H. (Ba); 25 Nov. 1827; (139); 196
Woodruff, Elias (We); McGuire, Eleanor (We); 18 Aug. 1817; (367); 97
Woodruff, Moses (We); Herrington, Mary (We); 4 Sept. 1817; (62); 97
Woodruff, Moses; Rardin, Phebe; 24 Sept. 1829; (230); 232
Woodruff, Silas (Ba); Stump, Mary (Ba); 21 Nov. 1833; (337); 313
Woods, Ephraim (Np); Rion, Margaret (Np); 5 Nov. 1815; (116); 87
Woodward, Oliver (W.C.); McGrath, Mary (W.C.); 26 Jan. 1816; (197); 88
Woodward, Oliver 3rd; Cook, Louisa P.; 29 Dec. 1831; (224); 274
Woodward, Wm.; Davis, Jemima; 22 Dec. 1825; (74); 161
Worstell, Vincent (Mn.C.); Hupp, Cynthia (Au); 20 Nov. 1834; (204); 333
Worth, James; Vaughn, Polly; 1799; (78); E.C.
Worthington, Isaac (Ma); Bacon, Sarah (Wo); 7 Nov. 1816; (346); 92
Worthington, Jesse (Be); Bickford, Sally (Be); 23 Dec. 1824; (311); 146
Worthington, Josiah; Taylor, Almyra; 16 Aug. 1837; (290); 384
Worthington, Thomas (Ma); Dye, Sally (Np); 30 July 1811; (197); 72
Wright, Henry (Un); Otis, Luvina (Un); 19 Apr. 1821; (279); 119
Wright, Horace (W.C.); Davidson, Calista (W.C.); 23 Nov. 1832; (191); 293
Wright, Simeon (Be); Dunham, Ruth (Be); 24 July 1791; (331); NW-5
Wright, Simeon (W.C.); Whitham, Mehitabel (W.C.); 5 Oct. 1797; (238); NW-23
Wright, Simeon (W.C.); Otis, Olive (W.C.); 30 Mar. 1831; (131); 267
Wyer, Garrett; Hall, Sarah; 8 Dec. 1833; (130); 316

Yates, Samuel (Ga); Brion, Phebe (Ken.C.); 10 June 1799; (285); NW-34
Yoho, Henry; Adams, Rebecca; 8 Oct. 1840; (290); 467
Young, Aaron (Mi); Picket, Mary (Mi); 27 Jan. 1801; (21); NW-45
Young, Henry (Gr); Davis, Nancy (Gr); 26 Oct. 1809; (277); 63
Young, John (Gr); Crouse, Eleanor (Gr); 28 May 1835; (114); 347
Young, Johnson (Pa); Middleswart, Susanna (Np); 29 Nov. 1829; (12); 232
Young, William (Mn.C.); Terrill, Elizabeth (W.C.); 24 May 1821; (330); 119
Youngkin, Abraham (Ma); Montgomery, Sally (Ma); 6 Nov. 1811; (197); 72
Youngs, Imbly (A.C.); Hamilton, Jane (W.C.); 2 Oct. 1837; (184); 387

Ziegler, Capt. David; Sheffield, Lucy Coggeshall; 22 Feb. 1789; ; **
Zimmer, Christian (Fe); Peters, Catharine (Fe); 15 Mar. 1835; (332); 342
Zimmer, Jacob (Fe); Meteer, Susanna (Fe); 2 July 1835; (332); 349

INDEX

Barton, Nancy 16
Batchelder, Eunice 63
Batchelder, Lucy 40
Batelle, Phoebe G. 9
Bateman, Sarah 6
Bayley, Barbara Ann 22
Beach, Anne 34
Beach, Eliza 68
Beach, Sabrina 47
Beals, Sarah 35
Beard, Margaret 9
Beard, Mary 64
Bebout, Catharine 49
Bechtold, Mary 45
Beck, Fanny 31
Bee, Letitia 67
Bee, Martha 27
Beebe, Caroline 74
Beebe, Elizabeth 26
Beebe, Eunice 41
Beebe, Frances Eliza 48
Beebe, Julia 56
Beebe, Mary 7
Beebe, Polly 6
Beebe, Rebecca 54
Beel, Jane 26
Beel, Mary 67
Beiber, Jane 4
Bell, Betsey 32
Bell, Charlotte 6
Bell, Elizabeth 6, 7
Bell, Isabelle 51
Bell, Jane 8, 56
Bell, Margaret 27, 39
Bell, Mary 74
Bellows, Anna 38
Bellows, Emeline 24
Bellows, Lucy 11
Bellows, Mahala 35
Bellows, Maria 6, 11
Bellows, Mary Ann 26
Bellows, Matilda 48
Bellows, Susan 72
Benedict, Irene 1
Benjamin, Dency 55
Benjamin, Mary 26
Bennett, Abigail 35
Bennett, Harriet 52
Bennett, Laurinda 31
Bennett, Prudence 38
Bennit, Margaret 52
Bens, Pamelia 38
Benson, Christianna 52
Bent, Dorcas 18
Bent, Elizabeth 59
Bent, Lucy R. 58
Bentley, Elinor 70
Bentley, Jane 53
Berkinsha, Anna 2
Berry, Jane 48
Berthe, Hannah M. 45
Beswick, Elizabeth 5
Bever, Katharine 18
Bickford, Mahala 23
Bickford, Mary 71
Bickford, Sally 80
Biddison, Drusilla 24
Biderson, Eliza Ann 1
Biers, Sally 10
Bigerstaff, Nancy 27
Bigford, Harriet 53
Bigford, Matilda 53
Biggerstaff, Sarah 1
Biggins, Elizabeth 6
Biggins, Nancy 60
Biggins, Polly 70
Billard, Sarah Ann 34
Bingham, Elizabeth 33

Bingham, Hannah 58
Bingham, Lucina 66
Bingham, Phoebe 32
Bingum, Flora 32
Birchard, Rebecca 30
Bird, Catherine 74
Bird, Nancy 75
Birth, Katharine 12
Bishannts, Louisa 62
Bishop, Caroline 67
Bishop, Hannah 14
Bishop, Jane 20
Bishop, Lucinda 76
Bishop, Sarah 67
Bizzants, Margaret 63
Blackmer, Mary 4
Blackmer, Polly 19
Blackmore, Laurany 53
Blake, Fanny 72
Blake, Hannah D. 11
Blake, Ladotia 80
Blake, Lucy 33
Blake, Martha 73
Blake, Sarah 57
Blough, Nancy 21
Blow, Nancy 21
Bobo, Betsey 38
Bobo, Letty 66
Bodkin, Mary 40
Bodkin, Nancy 62
Bodkin, Sarepta 29
Bodwell, Edith 18
Bodwell, Edney 9
Bodwell, Elizabeth 18
Bodwell, Priscilla 76
Bodwell, Rhoda 72
Boggs, Sarah 30
Bohannon, Matilda 74
Bohl, Mary Elizabeth 52
Bohling, Barby 3
Bois, Dorothy B. 28
Boling, Adeiheit 42
Boomer, Amy Ann 23
Boomer, Rachel 42
Booth, Lucy Sherman 37
Booth, Sarah Ann 64
Boothby, Sally 20
Borrowy, Johanna 63
Borrowy, Maria C. 61
Bosworth, Amanda 13
Bosworth, Lucy 37
Boudinot, Polly 13
Boudinot, Sarah R. 77
Bowen, Mary Ann 2
Bowen, Rachel 78
Bowen, Rebecca 78
Bowen, Sarah 64
Bowers, Elizabeth 34
Bowles, Martha 66
Bowrd, Martha 38
Brabham, Louisa M. 33
Brachbill, Catherine 45
Brackenridge, Elizabeth 61
Bradford, Sally 57
Bradley, Hannah 55
Bradley, Peggy 75
Bradley, Sally 67
Brady, Frances 32
Brady, Jane 52
Brady, Nancy 16
Brayton, Nelly S. 20
Brayton, Ruth 52
Breakenridge, Margt. 78
Breakenridge, Sarah 74
Breck, Anna 64
Breckenridge, Charlotte 22
Breckenridge, Mary 26, 48
Brewer, Sarah E. 67

Brewster, Deborah 42
Brewster, Martha 37
Brickmore, Eliza 39
Bridge, Lucy 43
Bridges, Minerva 32
Bridges, Rebecca 79
Bridges, Sally 58
Briggs, Abigail 50
Briggs, Catharine 77
Briggs, Hannah 79
Briggs, Rebecca 64
Briley, Nancy 66
Brion, Phebe 81
Briton, Mary 12
Briton, Nancy 12
Briton, Placy 59
Britton, Cyrene 58
Britton, Elizabeth 41
Britton, Hannah 64
Britton, Mary 36
Broadhurst, Jane 74
Broadhurst, Marietta 14
Broadhurst, Sally Ann 74
Brockley, Ann 78
Broocaw, Marietta 31
Brooker, Laura 22
Brooker, Sibyl 15
Brooks, Cynthia Ann 37
Brooks, Elizabeth 12
Brooks, Harriet 9
Brooks, Mary 53
Brooks, Mary M. 48
Broom, Betsy 3
Broom, Jemima 67
Broom, Ruth 48
Broome, Polly 73
Brough, Jane 25
Broun, Sophia F. 28
Brown, Ajubah 55
Brown, Apphia H. 35
Brown, Clarissa 18
Brown, Esther 61
Brown, Hannah 6
Brown, Harriet 31
Brown, Helen M. 65
Brown, Lydia G. 55
Brown, Margaret 65
Brown, Martha 73
Brown, Mary 22
Brown, Phebe G. 68
Brown, Polly 9, 65
Brown, Rachel 14, 30
Brown, Rebecca 32
Brown, Sally 76
Brown, Sarah Ann 18
Browning, Anne 38
Browning, Sarah 62
Brownwell, Patience 20
Brunie, Madalane 12
Bryan, Fanny 12
Bryan, Levina 15
Buck, Abigail 47
Buck, Eliza 3, 33
Buck, Jane 72
Buck, Lucretia 63
Buel, Sally M. 43
Buell, Eliza 10, 22
Buell, Frances S. 37
Buell, Helen A. 65
Buell, Maria 35
Buell, Sibe H. 67
Buell, Silena 21
Buell, Wealthy 1
Bukey, Mary 37
Bumgarner, Sarah 70
Bundy, Susannah 73
Burch, Betsy 13
Burch, Elvira 34

Burch, Gratia 51
Burch, Jerusha 18
Burch, Lucy 65
Burch, Mahala 40
Burch, Mary 40
Burch, Rhoda 2
Burchett, Elizabeth 50
Burchett, Hannah 30
Burchett, Jemimah 63
Burchett, Patty 62
Burchett, Sarah 26
Burchett, Susanna 62
Burden, Jane 49
Burker, Mary 6
Burlingame, Maria 32
Burlingame, Patty 62
Burlingame, Persis M. 49
Burlingame, Susanna 16
Burlinggame, Elizabeth P. 21
Burlinggame, Lucy 8
Burlinggame, Sarah 11
Burnham, Abigail H. 33
Burnham, Dolly 63
Burns, Elizabeth 25
Burns, Nancy 75
Burpey, Calista 60
Burrell, Nancy 51
Burris, Lavina B. 62
Burris, Mary 10, 76
Burroughs, Nancy 4
Burroughs, Susan 68
Buzelin, Elizabeth 43
Buzzard, Phebe 80
Byard, Harriet G. 49
Byard, Sarah 48
Byard, Sarah M. 3
Byard, Susan 80
Byram, Susan 79
Byran, Sarah Ann 27
Byrum, Angeline 58
Byser, Catharine 7
Bysor, Sally 63

Cable, Asphia 54
Caddington, Lydia 65
Caddot, Jean 22
Cady, Eliza 56
Cady, Fanny 41
Cain, Nancy 50
Calahan, Anna 28
Calahan, Dorcas 21
Calahan, Mary 12
Calder, Margaret 71
Callahan, Rebecca 15
Calman, Mary 6
Calvin, Sally 2
Calwell, Betsey 31
Cameron, Catherine 63
Camoren, Mary 23
Campbell, Jane 68
Campbell, Jean 2
Campbell, Margaret 11
Campbell, Martha 21
Campbell, Mary 25
Campbell, Nancy 2
Campbell, Rachel 55
Campbell, Rosanna 63
Campbell, Sally 22
Cannon, Rachel 3
Cannon, Susanna 69
Canor, Rachel 5
Capron, Marianne 63
Carl, Ruth 42
Carle, Sabina 56
Carlile, Elizabeth 15
Carlile, Frances M. 22

Carmeron, Margaret 44
Carmichael, Elizabeth 17
Carmichael, Susanna 79
Carmichel, Rebecca 75
Carmichel, Sarah 66
Carolle, Margaret 7
Carpenter, Barbara 49
Carpenter, Lydia 10
Carr, Abigail 21
Carter, Fortune 51
Carter, Margaret 40
Carteron, Sophia 75
Cartwright, Hannah 70
Carver, Mary 2, 32
Case, Eliza 1
Case, Hannah 77
Case, Polly 15
Casey, Seasy 11
Cass, Deborah W. 66
Cass, Narcissa 39
Cassidy, Didana 23
Castle, Amanda 42
Cathwright, Elizabeth 74
Catline, Adelphia 52
Caven, Jane 25
Cawood, Fanny 23
Cawood, Hannah 46
Chad, Margaret 76
Chadwick, Irena 79
Chadwick, Julia 79
Chadwick, Mary 47
Chadwick, Nancy 3
Chadwick, Susanna 73
Chadwick, Unity 79
Chamberlain, Amanda 16
Chamberlain, Anna B. 13
Chamberlain, Diana M. 18
Chamberlain, Fidelia 57
Chamberlain, Sarah 66
Chamberlin, Melisa 5
Chambers, Anna 59
Chambers, Eleanor 36, 56
Chambers, Harriet 20
Chambers, Isabella 7
Chambers, Mary 8
Chambers, Sarah Ann 39
Champlin, Nancy 20
Chandevert, Marie M. 6
Chandler, Sally 66
Chapin, Milly 44
Chapman, Anthea 32
Chapman, Betsey 31
Chapman, Clarissa 11
Chapman, Eliza 38
Chapman, Esther 21
Chapman, Harriet 3
Chapman, Hessibah 40
Chapman, Jerusha 21
Chapman, Maria 8
Chapman, Mary 3, 4
Chapman, Mary Ann 51
Chapman, Rhoda 56
Chapman, Ruth 42
Chapman, Sarah 78
Chapman, Sybil 21
Chappell, Elizabeth H. 74
Chappell, Matilda F. 14
Cheadle, Clarissa 66
Cheadle, Eliza 63
Cheadle, Lecty 19
Cheadle, Lucena 53
Cheadle, Pamela 62
Cheadle, Patty 16
Cheadle, Sally 33
Cheadle, Tryphena 54
Cherry, Christiana 30
Cherry, Eliza Ann 18
Cherry, Maria 61

Cherry, Mary Ann 26
Chiddester, Rhoda A. 19
Chidester, Sally 12
Churchill, Abigail 60
Churchill, Eunice S. 18
Cisler, Margaret 25
Cisler, Mary 53
Clark, Almira S. 14
Clark, Anna 1
Clark, Betsey 3
Clark, Catherine 13
Clark, Clarissa J. 63
Clark, Emily 45
Clark, Ethelinde 58
Clark, Fanny 47
Clark, Hannah 40, 61
Clark, Laura 12
Clark, Melinda B. 42
Clark, Polly 17, 27
Clark, Rhoda E. 75
Clark, Ruth 45
Clark, Sally 17
Clark, Sarah 80
Clark, Sarah Hayes 2
Clarke, Elmina 68
Clay, Deborah 77
Clements, Catharine 67
Cline, Cathrine 27
Cline, Christiana 55
Cline, Elizabeth 71, 72
Cline, Rosanah 73
Cline, Sarah 30
Cline, Susanna 45
Cline, Susannah 24
Clogston, Deborah 77
Close, Eliza Ann 50
Clutter, Rebecca 10
Cobern, Mary 20
Cobern, Susanna 46
Coburn, Lucy 27
Coburn, Mary 76
Cock, Rhoda 16
Cockshott, Ann 47
Cockshott, Elizabeth 28
Cockshott, Mary 22
Coffee, Lina 32
Coffman, Deborah 79
Coffman, Moriah 11
Coggeshall, Abigail 70
Cogswell, Abigal Ann 77
Colby, Lucy 52
Colby, Pamela 20
Colby, Sally 70
Coldwell, Jane 70
Cole, Ashia 25
Cole, Caroline 44
Cole, Clara 33
Cole, Cynthia 19, 42
Cole, Deborah 79
Cole, Diana 10
Cole, Diantha 20
Cole, Dolly 72
Cole, Eunice 55
Cole, Harty 45
Cole, Lydia 17
Cole, Mary 39
Cole, Mary Ann 4
Cole, Nancy 56
Cole, Phoebe 37
Cole, Polly 50
Cole, Sarah Ann 64
Cole, Susan 26
Coleman, Angeline 28
Coleman, Betsey 32
Coleman, Elizabeth 19
Coleman, Hannah 10, 64
Coleman, Lovisa 77
Coleman, Mary 76

Coleman, Peggy 52
Coley, Caroline 80
Coley, Charlotte 47
Coley, Sybyl A 64
Collans, Sarah 65
Collens, Nelly 26
Collins, Eunice 33
Collins, Joanna 68
Collins, Margaret 70
Colman, Rosanna 57
Colon, Ruth 37
Colwell, Hanna 47
Colwell, Mary 28
Combs, Ann 53
Come, Deborah P. 67
Comstock, Hannah 7
Cone, Martha S. 7
Conkright, Harriet 31
Conkright, Lydia 69
Converse, Hannah 20
Converse, Polly L. 71
Convis, Abigail 7
Convis, Easter 79
Cook, Lavina A. 80
Cook, Louisa P. 80
Cook, Mary A. 28
Cook, Rebecca 63
Cook, Rhoda 36
Cook, Rosannah 46
Cook, Sally 40
Cook, Susan 53
Cook, Susanna 35, 71
Cooke, Pheebe 38
Cooley, Easter 10
Coolidge, Hannah 25
Coon, Ann 61
Coon, Huldah 46
Cooper, Anna F. 57
Cooper, Hannah 69
Cooper, Mary 65
Cooper, Polly 73
Corey, Barbara 36
Corey, Elizabeth 39
Corey, Mary 63
Corey, Polly 76
Corner, Ann 53
Corner, Ann Maria 50
Corner, Lydia 57
Corner, Mary 13, 48, 71
Corner, Melissa 31
Corner, Olinda 37
Corner, Persis R. 5
Corner, Sarah 25
Corner, Sarah F. 25
Cornfield, Betsey 61
Corns, Louisa 30
Corns, Mary 67
Corns, Matilda 66
Corns, Polly E. 11
Corns, Rachel 14
Corp, Harriet 59
Corp, Sarah 67
Corvile, Nancy 9
Corwell, Catharine 22
Corwin, Susanna 48
Cory, Cynthia 15
Cory, Elizabeth 74
Cory, Ruth 41
Coss, Barbara 11
Coton, Lucy 56
Cotter, Margaret 37
Cotton, Susan B. 10
Coulter, Mary 20
Cousins, Elizabeth 59
Covey, Mary Ann 37
Covey, Polly 3
Cowee, Calista 10
Cowee, Sally 60

Cowen, Mary 69
Cowre, Tabitha 17
Cozens, Mary 25
Cradlebaugh, Anna 41
Cradlebaugh, Catherine 60
Craft, Sarah 60
Cram, Clarrissa Ann 28
Cram, Margaret 70
Cram, Rebecca D. 54
Cram, Sally 31
Crandall, Huldah 62
Crane, Frances E. 61
Crane, Lydia 38
Crawford, Catharine 39
Crawford, Eliza 9
Crawford, Florilla 29
Crawford, Mary Ann 14, 55
Crawford, Nelly 76
Cree, Eliza Ann 48
Creighton, Isabella 61
Crespin, Comfort 70
Cromer, Margaret 7
Crosby, Margaret 25
Crosby, Telitha 26
Cross, Bridget 9
Cross, Julia Ann 28
Cross, Mary 52
Cross, Ruth B. 20
Crouse, Eleanor 81
Cuddington, Anna 14
Cuddington, Jane 59
Culver, Avis 17
Culver, Catherine 43
Cunningham, Delilah 33
Cunningham, Elizabeth 30
Cunningham, Sally 51
Cunningham, Sarah 25, 34
Currier, Mary 35
Curtis, Clarissa 42
Curtis, Lucinda 12
Curtis, Lucy W. 13
Curtis, Maria Adelaide 64
Curtis, Mary 7
Curtis, Nancy 44
Curtiss, Louisa 61
Cushing, Bersheba 6
Cushing, Betsey 8
Cushing, Betsy 26
Cushing, Sally 30
Cusick, Mary Jane 19
Cutler, Mary Ann 76
Cutler, Sarah 19
Cyphert, Nancy 2

Dailey, Mary 23
Dailey, Nancy 56
Daley, Sally 21
Dallorson, Martha 38
Daly, Sarah 15
Dana, Amanda F. 53
Dana, Charlotte 1
Dana, Eliza 25
Dana, Elizabeth H. 34
Dana, Emily W. 21
Dana, Frances 66
Dana, Frances F. 2
Dana, Grace 24
Dana, Hannah P. 12
Dana, Maria 48
Dana, Mary 24, 59
Dana, Mary B. 22
Dana, Mary P. 15
Dana, Seraph D. 55
Dana, Sophia B. 37
Dana, Susan 76
Daniel, Jenny 61

Daniels, Mary Ann 71
Danker, Anna 44
Danley, Betsey 44
Danley, Eliza 31
Danley, Polly 16
Daugherty, Margery 69
Davenport, Mary Ann 8
Davenport, Patty 76
Davenport, Sally 54
Davidson, Calista 80
Davis, Anna 27
Davis, Betsey 11
Davis, Charlotte 31
Davis, Cynthia 49
Davis, Drusilla 2
Davis, Eliza 47, 57
Davis, Elizabeth 9, 36, 61
Davis, Hannah 42
Davis, Jane 67
Davis, Jemima 80
Davis, Lucena 20, 45
Davis, Martha 14
Davis, Mary 18, 23
Davis, Nancy 81
Davis, Orilla 67
Davis, Phebe 23
Davis, Polly 10
Davis, Reschal 29
Davis, Rhoda 51
Davis, Sally 69
Davis, Sarah 13, 77
Davis, Susan 21
Davous, Francis 7
Davrange, Constance 19
Day, Eliza 50
Day, Nancy 48
Dean, Eleanor 49
Deaver, Eleanor 46
Decker, Catharine 79
Delano, Cynthia 19
Delano, Julia Ann 37
Delano, Lucy A. 23
Delano, Sarah 14
Delley, Harriet 14
Delong, Hannah 68
Delong, Lydia 34
Delong, Matilda 29
Delong, Olive 39
Delong, Polly 34, 51
Delong, Rachel 48
Delong, Rebeckah 65
Delong, Sally 29
Demier, Jeanette 6
Deming, Betsy 26
Deming, Honor 33
Deming, Lucy 26
Deming, Rebecca 30
Dempsey, Sarah 7
Denher, Betsey 64
Dennis, Lydia 13
Detterly, Louisa 49
Devin, Catharine 24
Devol, Bathsheba 17
Devol, Betsey B. 46
Devol, Charlotte 58
Devol, Clarissa 16, 71
Devol, Cynthia 57
Devol, Electa 11
Devol, Elizabeth 9
Devol, Emeline 4
Devol, Hannah 71
Devol, Harriet 22, 56
Devol, Lucinda 68
Devol, Lucy 61
Devol, Maria 4
Devol, Mary 68
Devol, Nancy 9, 22, 64
Devol, Nancy C. 51

Devol, Polly 2, 30
Devol, Rachel 66
Devol, Rosanna 70
Devol, Sarah 20, 40
Devoll, Elizabeth 31
Devoll, Presilla 77
Dewees, Mary 17
Dewees, Sally 57
DeWitt, Margaret 60
Dick, Julia 62
Dickenson, Elizabeth 7
Dickenson, Harriet 64
Dickerson, Deborah 78
Dickerson, Elizabeth 40
Dickerson, Margaret 61
Dickerson, Nelly 24
Dickeson, Susanna 55
Dickey, Lucy 1
Dickey, Maria 5
Dickey, Martha 14
Dickey, Pamela 19
Dicks, Mary Ann 53
Dickson, Anna 64
Dickson, Jemima 68
Dickson, Lavina 19
Dickson, Sarah 30, 43
Diggans, Betsy 50
Dilley, Betsey 6
Dilley, Elizabeth 16
Dilley, Fanny 32
Dilley, Jane 67
Dilley, Julia 29
Dilley, Lucy 41
Dilley, Minerva 35
Dilley, Nancy 51
Dilley, Rebecca 7
Dilley, Sarah A. 17
Dilley, Sophia 23
Dilley, Susan 64
Dills, Saloame 29
Dilly, Eliza 40
Dilly, Susan 6
Divens, Sally 13
Dixon, Elizabeth 66, 67
Dixon, Jane 54
Dixon, Mary 45
Doan, Anna 13
Doan, Diana 51
Doan, Jerusha 36
Doan, Julia Ann 73
Doan, Linda 38
Doan, Sarah A. 62
Dodd, Elizabeth 16
Dodge, Anna 31
Dodge, Elizabeth 58
Dodge, Hannah 7
Dodge, Katharine 21
Dodge, Mary M. 9
Dodge, Polly M. 40
Dodge, Susanna M. 4
Dolen, Sarah 75
Dolin, Betsy 78
Dolin, Polly 15
Dorr, Rhoda 80
Doubleday, Mary 43
Douthitt, Calista 28
Douthitt, Nancy Ann 16
Dow, Mary Virginia 22
Dow, Nancy Ann 77
Dowdell, Elizabeth 51
Doyl, Mary 4
Drain, Catharine 25
Drake, Rhoda Jane 32
Drake, Sarah 58
Drigs, Mary 35
Driscoll, Lucy 11
Drown, Mary 13
Drury, Eliza 75

Druse, Anna 28
Druse, Lucy 16
Druse, Melissa 3
Dufer, Sally 56
Dufur, Rhoda 58
Dufur, Sally 29
Dunbar, Anna 66
Dunbar, Emily 49
Dunbar, Nancy 7, 20
Dunbar, Sarah 74
Duncan, Polly 15
Duncan, Sally 15
Dunham, Bathsheba 73
Dunham, Ruth 80
Dunlap, Rachel 60
Dunsmoor, Ataline 28
Dunsmoor, Mary K. 55
Duraille, Jeanne F. 13
Durfee, Adaline 44
Durfle, Abigail 37
Durham, Margaret 45
Dustin, Emily 71
Dustin, Eunice 34
Duston, Elizabeth 75
Dutton, Abigal 22
Dutton, Elizabeth 28
Dutton, Hannah 37
Dutton, Jain 29
Dutton, Jane 74
Dutton, Margaret 2
Dutton, Nancy 18
Dutton, Polly 18
Dutton, Srah 18
Dyar, Esther Ann 62
Dyar, Harriet 72
Dyar, Rosanna D. 64
Dyar, Sally 55
Dye, Abigail 33
Dye, Anna H. 72
Dye, Elisa 19
Dye, Elizabeth 23
Dye, Emily 35
Dye, Emma B. 12
Dye, Hannah 12
Dye, Harriet 45
Dye, Mary 15, 20, 36, 39
Dye, Patience 1
Dye, Polly 25, 49
Dye, Ruth 43
Dye, Sally 80
Dye, Sophia 23
Dye, Susan 57

Eastman, Hannah 49
Eastman, Lucy 37
Eastman, Mary G. 59
Eastman, Sally 49
Eaton, Nancy 2
Eddleblute, Amanda 53
Eddleblute, Elizabeth 24
Eddleblute, Hannah 60
Eddlebute, Rebecca 54
Eddy, Sarah 75
Edelblute, Polly 53
Edgerton, Abby S. 59
Edgerton, Elizabeth 31
Edgerton, Eunice 66
Edgerton, Mary Ann 66
Edgerton, Sarah L. 77
Edson, Berilla 33
Edwards, Hannah 15
Edwards, Mary 26, 64
Edwards, Priscilla 26
Edwards, Prusha 26
Edwards, Rachel 15, 68
Edwards, Ruth 18

Elder, Margaret 34
Ellenwood, Elizabeth 45
Ellenwood, Frances 53
Ellenwood, Marilla 73
Ellenwood, Martha 6
Ellenwood, Mary 41
Ellenwood, Polina 76
Ellinwood, Lucy 6
Elliot, Maria 34
Elliot, Sarah 32
Ellis, Diana 10
Ellis, Elizabeth 58
Ellis, Lucy 22
Ellis, Martha 66
Ellis, Mary 40
Ellis, Roxana 8
Ellison, Nancy 27
Ellison, Sally 51
Elston, Sally 69
Emerson, Amazilla G. 60
Emerson, Arta 69
Emerson, Mary S. 46
Emerson, Sarah 37
Emerson, Susanna 28
Emmons, Dorcas 26
Emmons, Nelly 63
English, Elizabeth 22
Eoff, Rachel 65
Erwin, Tabitha 73
Euitlebus, Mary C. 57
Evans, Jane 10
Evans, Martha 14
Evans, Polly 2
Evans, Sally 77
Eveland, Amy 20
Eveland, Catharine 18
Eveland, Lucy 62
Evens, Elizabeth 16
Everley, Catharine 41
Evritt, Maria 31
Ewing, Sally 14

Fairchild, Lucy 29
Fairchild, Monday 34
Fairchild, Polly 22
Fairlee, Margaret 33
Fall, Amanda 76
Fall, Lydia 63
Farley, Elizabeth 49
Farley, Margaret 46
Farley, Nancy 4
Farmen, Anna 21
Farmer, Sarah 3
Farnham, Elizabeth 13
Farnham, Lydia 7
Farnham, Philena 29
Farris, Jane 30
Farris, Lavina 24
Farris, Susan 43
Fay, Beaulah S. 72
Fearing, Lucy W. 46
Fearing, Mary 22
Fearing, Rebecca 9
Featherston, Sarah 33
Featherston, Susanna 43
Featherstone, Sally 25
Fenn, Huldah 70
Fenn, Jerusha 16
Fenn, Sarah 26
Ferguson, Grace 19
Ferguson, Mary A. 10
Ferguson, Matilda 55
Ferris, Eliza 39
Ferris, Rebecca 24
Finch, Samantha 7
Findley, Margaret 65

Firman, Hannah 36
Fish, Sarah 5
Fisher, Amanda M. 21
Fisher, Deborah 18
Fisher, Hannah 27
Fisher, Jane C. 45
Fisher, Maria 44
Fisher, Mary Ann 53
Flagg, Cynthia 41
Flagg, Editha 57
Flagg, Edna P. 62
Flagg, Mary 12
Flake, Elizabeth 11
Flanders, Ann 19
Flanders, Hannah 25
Flanders, Maria 56
Flanders, Martha 74
Flanders, Mary 37
Flarnernan, Cintia 79
Fleharty, Nancy 66
Fleming, Agnes 8
Fleming, Eliza 28
Fleming, Isabella 34
Fleming, Jane 8
Fleming, Janet 74
Fleming, Mary 34
Fleming, Mary Jane 40
Fleming, Welthy 63
Flemming, Cynthia 37
Fletcher, Clarrissa 24
Fletcher, Martha 70
Fletcher, Mary 39, 57
Fletcher, Nancy 26
Fletcher, Sally 4
Flint, Elizabeth 25
Flint, Lucy 31
Flowers, Elizabeth 25
Flowers, Margaret 29
Flowers, Mariam 25
Flowers, Mary 79
Follett, Ann 78
Forby, Amy 28
Force, Bridgart 17
Ford, Diana 80
Ford, Farnetta 43
Ford, Harriet 7
Ford, Julia A. 47
Ford, Mary A. 20
Ford, Sarah 26
Forshey, Betsey 24
Forst, Mahala 29
Fortner, Betsy 44
Fortner, Sarah 74
Fosburn, Rachel 65
Foster, Betsey M. 18
Foster, Deborah L. 48
Foster, Esther 18
Foster, Hannah G. 13
Foster, Mary 5
Foster, Mary 10
Foster, Matilda W. 27
Foster, Nancy F. 77
Foster, Olive 18
Foster, Olivia 48
Foster, Polly 18
Foster, Sarah 36
Foutch, Eliza 52
Fowler, Betsey 73
Fowler, Deborah 64
Fowler, Jane 20
Fowler, Miriam 57
Fowler, Senith 35
Fowler, Theressa 70
Fox, Harriet M. 75
Fox, Harriet P. 27
Francis, Elizabeth 70
Francis, Susanna 6
Franks, Margaret 2

Fraser, Christian 43
Fraser, Elizabeth 25
Frazer, Annaliza 77
Frazer, Margaret 34
Frazer, Margaret A. 8
Frazier, Harriet 74
Frazier, Mary 44
Freemire, Hannah 11
Freemire, Margaret 40
Freemyer, Elizabeth 42
French, Delila 58
French, Electa 37
French, Eliza 72
French, Leafy 40
French, Melissa 21
French, Nancy 33
Friend, Mary 50
Frizel, Sarah 33
Frost, Claryna P. 69
Frost, Louisiana W. 69
Frost, Nancy A. 80
Fulcher, Eliza 33
Fulcher, Nancy 40
Fulcher, Roxanna 27
Fuller, Almira 52
Fuller, Augustina 46
Fuller, Betsey 44
Fuller, Elizabeth 36, 52
Fuller, Experience 50
Fuller, Lucretia 8
Fuller, Marietta 50
Fuller, Minerva C. 41
Fuller, Theodosia 17
Fuller, Zeppora 63
Fullerton, Elizabeth 27
Fullerton, Jennet 22
Fulmer, Margaret 61
Fulsome, Temperance 27
Fulton, Betsey 72
Fulton, Eleanor 49
Fulton, Elinor 2
Fulton, Elizabeth 3
Fulton, Jane 76
Fulton, Jane H. 58
Fulton, Lydia 48
Fulton, Sarah F. 32
Furr, Mary Ann 58

Gabandan, Josephine 61
Gable, Anna 48
Gage, Marion 35
Gage, Susan H. 58
Galand, Katharine 21
Gard, Charity 22
Gard, Eleanor 38
Gard, Lucy 38
Gard, Mahala 41
Gard, Margaret 41
Gard, Maria 9
Gard, Martha E. 22
Gard, Polly 4
Gard, Priscilla 41
Gard, Rebecca 45
Gard, Rowena 11
Gard, Sophia 55
Gardiner, Sally 43
Gardiner, Sarah 65
Gardner, Catharine 77
Gardner, Hannah 15
Gardner, Lucinda 61
Gardner, Lydia 54
Gardner, Mary 77
Gardner, Silence 54
Garnett, Jane 9
Gates, Amy 69
Gates, Betsy 44

Gates, Beulah 71
Gates, Bittsa 19
Gates, Elizabeth 32
Gates, Frances 44
Gates, Hester 32
Gates, Lydia 79
Gates, Maria 51
Gates, Mary 10, 29, 33
Gates, Pamela 43
Gates, Pamelia 79
Gates, Phoebe 17
Gates, Ruby 1
Gates, Sabra 67
Gates, Sally 17
Gates, Susanna 29, 52
Gay, Elizabeth 56
Gaylor, Elizabeth 46
Gaylord, Mary 46
Gearing, Jane 52
Geddings, Hannah 39
Gedins, Elizabeth 24
Geering, Hannah 36
Gellison, Hannah 28
George, Sarah Ann 53
Gerber, Caroline 68
Geren, Jane D. 12
Geren, Mary G. 52
Gerrard, Elizabeth 5
Gevrez, Felicity 43
Gevrez, Mary Ann 6
Gibbs, Elizabeth 72
Gibson, Harriet 31
Gibson, Jane 36
Gibson, Lovina 32
Giddings, Ann 53
Gifford, Roxana 35
Giles, Elizabeth 7
Gill, Angeline 77
Gill, Elizabeth 39
Gill, Lucy 56
Gilman, Catherine 23
Gilman, Jane R. 80
Gilmore, Mary H. 80
Gilmore, Rebecca 35
Gilpin, Anna Maria 59
Gilpin, Eliza D. 5
Gilpin, Eunice 38
Gilpin, Sally 35
Gitteau, Jerusha 59
Glidden, Lydia 2
Glidden, Mary 11
Glover, Priscilla 51
Goddard, Eliza A. 67
Goddard, Frances A. 67
Goddard, Julia 22
Gold, Esther 30
Gold, Sarah 29
Goldsbrough, Polly 75
Goldsmith, Angelinia 69
Goldsmith, Elizabeth 41
Goodale, Cynthia 5
Goodale, Elizabeth 12
Goodale, Sarah 19
Goodale, Susan 67
Gooding, Zelinda 11
Goodwin, Margaret 11
Goodwin, Sarah 29, 34
Goodwin, Sarah E. 13
Goold, Alizabeth 33
Gordon, Ann 35
Gorman, Jane 31
Gorman, Letitia 11
Goss, Eliza 65
Goss, Elizabeth 42
Goss, Lydia 69
Gosset, Harriet 79
Gossett, Elizabeth 10
Gossett, Margaret 10, 62

Gossett, Matilda 56
Gossett, Sarah 43
Gossett, Sarah Ann 56
Gould, Elizabeth G. 23
Gould, Mary A. 41
Graham, Betsy 54
Graham, Margaret 7
Graham, Mary 16
Granden, Rhoda 3
Grant, Leafy 47
Grant, Mary Ann 78
Grant, Melvina 79
Gray, Betsy 14
Gray, Charlotte 34
Gray, Clarissa 33
Gray, Deborah 44
Gray, Elizabeth 50
Gray, Louisa 70
Gray, Mary Ann 41
Gray, Phebe 14
Gray, Polly 25
Gray, Rebecca 34
Greathouse, Mary 24
Green, Eliza 57
Green, Elizabeth 69
Green, Harriet 24
Green, Lucy 31
Green, Margaret 80
Green, Pamela 61
Green, Rowena 59
Green, Susan 9
Greene, Catharine 57
Greene, Dorinda 71
Greene, Elisa 31
Greene, Eliza 68
Greene, Harriet 33
Greene, Isabella 37
Greene, Louisa 37
Greene, Mary A. 46
Greene, Nancy 39
Greene, Phebe H. 61
Greene, Phoebe 34
Greene, Ruth 78
Greene, Susanna 11
Greene, Sylvina 21
Greenleaf, Lucy 37
Greenlee, Rachel 6
Greenlees, Mary 56
Greenwood, Elizabeth 5
Gregg, Jane 55
Gregory, Maria 48
Gridley, Caroline 22
Griffith, Elizabeth 71
Griggs, Catherine 64
Griggs, Jane 36
Grigsby, Leah 4
Grimes, Catharine 44
Groves, Eleanor 14
Groves, Susanna 63
Grubb, Elizabeth 43
Grubb, Sally 43
Guitteau, Eliza Ann 27
Guitteau, Emeline M. 77
Guitteau, Jane M. 78
Guitteau, Julia 41
Guitteau, Patience 51
Guitteau, Sarah 60
Gushing, Alimira 5
Guthrie, Almira 17
Guthrie, Laura M. 22

Hagans, Betsy 79
Hagerman, Hannah 73
Hagerman, Latetia 33
Hagerman, Maria 11
Hagerman, Rebecca 51

Hahn, Hannah 41
Haight, Mary 7
Hains, Ellis 70
Hait, Jerusha 2
Hait, Sarah Ann 30
Hale, Elizabeth 39
Hale, Margaret 36
Hall, Amanda 22
Hall, Eliza T. 44
Hall, Elizabeth 44
Hall, Eunice 2
Hall, Jane 15
Hall, Louisa 42
Hall, Martha 60
Hall, Mary 11, 21
Hall, Polly 49
Hall, Sarah 6, 80
Hall, Sophia 80
Hall, Theodocia 10
Hallet, Hannah 79
Hallet, Hannah Jane 73
Hallet, Ruth 18
Hallett, Margaret 56
Hally, Anne 28
Halsey, Cassandra 75
Hambelton, Rebecca 49
Hamilton, Barbara 13
Hamilton, Jane 81
Hamilton, Lucy F. 11
Hamilton, Mary 57
Hamlin, Eliza 65
Hamlin, Harriet 8
Hammon, Anna 64
Hammond, Hannah 47
Hammond, Meribah 26
Hammond, Phila 45
Hancock, Elizabeth 61
Hand, Mary D. 73
Hand, Sarah 13
Handley, Eliza 67
Hanes, Mary 40
Hanley, Elizabeth 3
Hanson, Nancy 41
Hanson, Peggy 71
Hanson, Susanna 56
Hanway, Eliza 37
Harden, Mary 55
Harden, Nancy 15, 41
Harper, Christina 4
Harper, Isabella 4
Harper, Mahala 11
Harper, Nancy G. 26
Harpig, Catherine 39
Harrington, Charity 60
Harris, Candis 79
Harris, Charlotte 71
Harris, Cynthia 49
Harris, Elizabeth 11
Harris, Emeline 71
Harris, Hannah 19
Harris, Irene 10
Harris, Laura Ann 63
Harris, Mary Ann 64
Harris, Peggy 45
Harris, Romantha 15
Harris, Sally 17
Harris, Susanna 7
Harrison, Eliza 79
Harrison, Jane 15
Harrison, Lorana 76
Harrison, Mary 72
Harrison, Nancy 21
Hart, Betsey 10
Hart, Clara 21
Hart, Elizabeth 77
Hart, Margaret 51
Hartshorn, Pamela 79
Hartshorn, Statira 71

Hartshorne, Clarissa 40
Hartshorne, Elizabeth 19
Harvey, Catharine 47
Harvey, Elizabeth 2
Harvey, Margaret 8
Harvie, Martha 8
Harvie, Mary 65
Hase, Elizabeth 42
Hase, Valeriah 26
Haskell, Eliza W. 43
Haskell, Elizabeth H. 47
Haskell, Maria 43
Haskell, Rebecca 50
Haskins, Mary 16
Hatch, Anna 20
Hatch, Hannah P. 20
Hatch, Ida 10
Haven, Abigail 36
Havens, Charity 69
Havens, Dorcas 34
Havens, Jerusha 69
Havens, Margaret H. 68
Havens, Mary 51
Havens, Matilda 76
Havens, Sophia 16
Haver, Nancy 59
Hawkins, Lucinda 80
Hawkins, Margaret 52
Hayden, Eleanor 52
Haynes, Abigail 62
Haynes, Elivira D. 24
Haynes, Minerva 66
Hays, Asenath W. 69
Hays, Hannah 9
Hayze, Polly 63
Heaney, Delaney 9
Hearn, Hetty Ann 27
Hearn, Polly 43
Heck, Mary 35
Hee, Sarah 52
Heirin, Patty 34
Heit, Sally 19
Hempstead, Esther 47
Henderson, Louisa 40
Henderson, Lucy 52
Hennan, Eunice 45
Henning, Amelia Ann 79
Henry, Ann 20
Henry, Betsy 35
Henry, Hannah 35
Henry, Polly 31
Henry, Shabariah 33
Henton, Ann 12
Henton, Eliza 12
Herington, Elizabeth 51
Herrin, Susanna 56
Herrington, Mary 80
Herrington, Patty 14
Herrod, Mary 56
Herron, Theresa S. 54
Hersey, Mercey 13
Hewit, Sally 35
Hewitt, Bethial 5
Heywood, Anna 41
Hickman, Martha 2
Hickman, Mary 71
Hiett, Deborah 73
Higgins, Elizabeth 72
Higgins, Mary 45
Hilar, Elizabeth 44
Hildebrand, Mary 75
Hilderbrand, Jane 30
Hilderbrand, Sarah 56
Hildreth, Louisa 2
Hildreth, Mary A. 59
Hildreth, Mary B. 10
Hildreth, Rebecca Ann 46
Hill, Anna 33

Hill, Eliza 10, 50, 77
Hill, Elizabeth 23, 36, 72
Hill, Hannah 43
Hill, Jane 2, 22, 29, 50
Hill, Julinda 56
Hill, Lucinda N. 3
Hill, Margaret 49
Hill, Maria 3, 8
Hill, Martha 41
Hill, Mary 4, 41
Hill, Mary G. 12
Hill, Mary Jones 61
Hill, Mary M. 75
Hill, Matilda 50
Hill, Nancy 19, 29
Hill, Peggy 17
Hill, Polly 29, 31
Hill, Ruth 13, 60
Hill, Sarah 49
Hill, Urania 69
Hilliard, Amy 27
Hinckley, Elizabeth 71
Hindley, Mary M. 79
Hinds, Amy 36
Hinkley, Betsy 35
Hinkley, Lydia 34
Hinkley, Mary 24, 71
Hinkley, Ruth 36
Hisem, Catharine 49
Hisum, Sarah 14
Hobby, Jane H. 78
Hoff, Angeline 27
Hoff, Eliza 72
Hoff, Elizabeth 46
Hoff, Eve 45
Hoff, Hannah 54
Hoff, Harriet 73
Hoff, Lucy 58
Hoff, Lydia N. 27
Hoff, Margaret 16
Hoff, Mary 73
Hoff, Mary Ann 19
Hoff, Polly 1
Hoff, Prudence 11
Hoff, Sarah 39
Hoff, Sophia 28
Hoff, Susanna 54
Hoffman, Lavina 59
Hoffman, Louisa 59
Hoit, Sally 37
Holburt, Lucy 29
Holden, Harriet 21
Holden, Julia 34
Holden, Maria 73
Holden, Mary 60
Holdren, Betsey 47
Holdren, Grace 25, 56
Holdren, Ruth 42
Holdren, Susanna B. 60
Hollcraff, Gratry 69
Holleburt, Lydia 40
Hollister, Sibel M. 15
Hook, Hannah 29
Hook, Lydia B. 30
Hook, Polly 22
Hooks, Nancy 25
Hoops, Sarah Ann 21
Hopkins, Ann 56
Hopkins, Eunice 64
Hopp, Adaline 78
Horner, Amanda 74
Horner, Sarah 78
Horton, Eliza 24
Hoskins, Mary 62
Hoskinson, Delila 55
Hoskinson, Sarah 45
Houghland, Anna 55
Houghland, Margaret 55

Houghland, Polly 48
Hougland, Eleanor 67
House, Farlana 64
Howe, Abigail P. 75
Howe, Betsey Eluira 15
Howe, Harriet R. 27
Howe, Lovella 69
Howe, Lucinda 1
Howe, Lucy W. 28
Howe, Minerva 30
Howe, Orinda 44
Howe, Rachel 16
Howe, Sally Adaline 15
Howe, Sophronia 73
Howell, Maria 45
Howlet, Charlotte 37
Hoyt, Anna 78
Hoyt, Cynthia 53
Hubbard, Temperance 78
Hudson, Elizabeth 75
Huff, Polly 36
Huges, Elizabeth 69
Huges, Sarah 10
Hughes, Drusilla 41
Hughes, Phebe 75
Hughs, Margaret 29
Hughs, Mary 70
Hulbert, Abigal 70
Hull, Elizabeth 42
Hull, Mary 40
Hull, Rachel 12
Humiston, Juliana 12
Humiston, Lavina 47
Humiston, Sally 12
Humiston, Wealthy 33
Humphrey, Harriet 52
Humphrey, Lydia 55
Humphreys, Mary Ann 20
Hundberry, Mary 45
Hungerford, Nancy 67
Hunter, Lydia 68
Hunter, Mary Ann 76
Hunter, Ruth 32
Hunter, Sally 76
Hupp, Cynthia 80
Hupp, Elizabeth 65, 66
Hupp, Mary 11
Hupp, Rachel 41, 67
Hurlbut, Mary M. 3
Hurty, Susanna 19
Hussay, Lydia 56
Hussay, Phoebe 36
Hutchins, Louis 51
Hutchins, Nancy 18
Hutchins, Rosanna 19
Hutchinson, Catharine 35
Hutchinson, Eleanor 62
Hutchinson, Elizabeth 1
Hutchinson, Lucinda 55
Hutchinson, Sally 37

Ice, Ann E. 21
Inbody, Catharine E. 49
Inbody, Mary M. 17
Ingals, Fanny 23
Ingle, Catharine 64
Ingles, Elizabeth 17
Ingles, Mercy 53
Ingram, Comfort 60
Ingram, Neoma 33
Inman, Deborah 30
Inman, Eliza 47
Ireland, Susan 32

Jackson, Clarissa 23
Jackson, Electra M. 11
Jackson, Elizabeth 9
Jackson, Jane 61
Jackson, Margaret 32
Jackson, Mary 32
Jackson, Nancy 72
Jackson, Phoebe 50
Jackson, Ruhanna 28
Jackson, Sally 71
Jadding, Nancy 49
James, Ann 73
James, Anne 3
James, Hannah 39
Jameson, Margaret 39
Jarrett, Elizabeth 42
Jarrett, Louisa 14
Jarrett, Sally 2
Jarvis, Elizabeth 70
Jarvis, Jane 1
Jemason, Abigail 34
Jenkins, Sally 9
Jennings, Delilah 61
Jennings, Eliza 53
Jennings, Elizabeth 27
Jennings, Margaret 52
Jennings, Nancy 15
Jennings, Rhoda 48
Jervis, Hannah 74
Jett, Eliza B. 61
Jett, Lucena 55
Jett, Maria H. 27
Jett, Rowena 60
Johnson, Abigail 61
Johnson, Asenath 3
Johnson, Betsy 78
Johnson, Drusilla 48
Johnson, Eleanor 58, 73
Johnson, Elizabeth 7
Johnson, Fanny 17
Johnson, Hannah 64
Johnson, Huldah 53
Johnson, Lovena 68
Johnson, Mary 59
Johnson, Matilda 63
Johnson, Nancy 69
Johnson, Nancy T. 41
Johnson, Sally 53, 68
Johnson, Sarah 24
Johnson, Sophia 69
Johnston, Amy 44
Johnston, Elizabeth 50, 76
Johnston, Jane 55
Johnston, Molly 62
Joline, Helen 73
Jolly, Liddy 21
Jolly, Mary 51
Jolly, Rachel 2
Jolly, Rebecca 46
Jones, Abigail 34
Jones, Betsey 13
Jones, Mary 5, 49
Jones, Nancy 44
Jones, Polly 19, 72
Jones, Rebecca 34
Jordan, Polly 54
Judd, Amanda 1
Judd, Catharine 44
Judd, Lucy Charlotte 66
Judd, Milly 54
Judge, Mary 17
Judge, Nancy 56

Kahler, Lydia 74
Kayler, Julia Ann 67
Kearns, Catherine 69

Keath, Catharine 52
Keath, Elizabeth 66
Keating, Elizabeth 32
Keeder, Rossa 78
Keirns, Catherine 38
Keirns, Sally 60
Keith, Polly 10
Keller, Betsey 64
Keller, Rachel 62
Kelly, Abigail 4
Kelly, Margaret 4
Kelly, Mary 57
Kelly, Nancy 26
Kelly, Nelly 41
Kelly, Polly 40
Kemple, Lucretia Ann 4
Kenada, Melinda 77
Kenady, Sally 53
Keneda, Delilah 53
Kennedy, Elizabeth 80
Kennedy, Jane 13
Kennedy, Mary 5
Kennedy, Nancy 46
Kennedy, Sarah 80
Kensor, Betsey 41
Kent, Eleanor 1
Kent, Harriet 38
Kent, Katharine 54
Kent, Phebe 53
Kent, Sally 53
Kent, Selestia 53
Kerr, Hannah 48
Kerr, Margaret 61
Kidwell, Eliza 59
Kidwell, Harriet A. 40
Kidwell, Julia Ann 65
Kidwell, Mary Ann 49
Kidwell, Nancy 28
Kidwell, Nancy J. 76
Kidwell, Sarah 14
Kimberly, Elizabeth 4
Kimberly, Maria 29
Kimberly, Mary Jane 46
Kincade, Catharine 42
Kincade, Christiana 25
Kincade, Phebe 8
Kincade, Sally 8
King, Anne 48
Kinney, Abigail 2
Kinney, Elizabeth 2
Kinney, Sally D. 5
Kinzer, Mary 19
Kinzier, Margaret 41
Kinzor, Lucinda 64
Kipple, Mary 72
Kirby, Elizabeth 80
Knapp, Eliza 25
Knight, Elizabeth 8
Knight, Welthy 28
Knott, Patty 17
Knowles, Cynthia Ann 32
Knowles, Esther 17
Knowles, Hannah 32
Knowlton, Betsey 34
Knowlton, Eunice 32
Knowlton, Lucy 32
Koon, Rhoda 33

Lackey, Desdemona 36
Ladd, Hannah 68
Ladd, Susan D. 68
Lafield, Mary Ann 17
Laflin, Huldah 61
Lake, Anna 78
Lake, Hannah 65
Lake, Jane 18

Lake, Margaret 75
Lake, Martha 51
Lake, Mary C. 22
Lake, Sally 50
Lakin, Amarillas 44
Lamna, Rebecca 62
Lancaster, Betsey 14
Lancaster, Polly 64
Lane, Hannah 35
Lane, Jamima 47
Lane, Rhoda 53
Lane, Sally 24
Lang, Angeline 72
Lang, Jane 13
Langley, Nancy Ann 53
Lankford, Elizabeth 69
Lankister, Nancy 19
Lapham, Polly 51
Laughery, Jane 52
Law, Sarah 64
Lawrence, Elizabeth 21
Lawrence, Hannah 43
Lawrence, Lydia 16
Lawrence, Olive 57
Lawrence, Pamela 65
Lawrence, Rebecca 18
Lawrence, Rosamond 79
Lawson, Hannah 38
Lawton, Rebecca 31
LaForge, Maria Gabriel 74
LaGrange, Edith 20
LaGrange, Elizabeth 61
LaGrange, Harriet N. 9
LaLance, Katherine 76
Learned, Laura 19
Leavens, Betsey 46
Leavens, Esther 64
Leavens, Matilda 77
Leavens, Matilda E. 68
Lebody, Margaret 70
Lee, Mary 54
Lee, Nancy 24
Leget, Hannah 16
Leget, Melissa M. 63
Legget, Sarah 25
Legrange, Sally 76
Leineson, Janet 50
Lenhart, Catharine 19
Leonard, Lydia 28
Lett, Keziah 50
Lett, Susannah 31
Levins, Frances 44
Lewis, Betsey 39
Lewis, Betsey M. 20
Lewis, Caroline 66
Lewis, Francis 21
Lewis, Hannah 51
Lewis, Jane W. 20
Lewis, Lucy Ann 16
Lewis, Mary 7
Lewis, Roxana J. 78
Lewis, Sally 36
Lewis, Sarah 60
Lewis, Susanna 73
LeSunior, Marie 44
Lightfritz, Betsey 63
Lincoln, Frances 74
Lincoln, Margaret 77
Lincoln, Sarah 5
Lincoln, Susan 49
Lindsey, Mary 71
Linn, Christiana 14
Linn, Hannah 78
Linn, Mary 14
Linnel, Bethiah 33
Little, Catharine 59
Little, Emma 42
Little, Jane 50

Little, Nancy 44
Little, Rebecca 12
Little, Wealthy 36
Littlefield, Eleanor 70
Littlefield, Mahitable 27
Littlefield, Phebe 22
Littleton, Elizabeth 6
Livermore, Mary 27
Lloyd, Eliza 73
Lloyd, Maria 9
Lobdell, Annis 29
Lobdell, Matilda 40
Lobdille, Rebecca Ann 28
Locker, Elizabeth 80
Locker, Sarah Ann 44
Locoe, Rachel 47
Loge, Maria 76
Lognachan, Catharine 49
Longfellow, Lydia 40
Longfellow, Merinda 80
Longfellow, Sarah 38
Longworth, Mary P. 59
Lord, Betsey 27
Lord, Polly 32
Lord, Sophia 12
Lord, Temperance 60, 78
Loring, Bathsheba 76
Loring, Charlotte 59
Loring, Charlotte P. 71
Loring, Mary 6
Lott, Frances 76
Lovekin, Sally 35
Low, Polly 39
Lowe, Betsey 75
Lowe, Maria 78
Lucas, Elizabeth 38
Lucas, Mary Ann 5
Lucas, Nancy 24
Lucas, Peggy 30
Luckey, Rachel 12
Lucky, Elizabeth 42
Ludwig, Lethe M. 67
Lumpkins, Lucy A. 1
Lund, Abigail S. 21
Lund, Katharine 29
Lund, Nancy A. 13
Lutere, Victore C. 49
Lyles, Elizabeth 34
Lynch, Susan 68
Lyon, Lucy 58
Lyons, Charlotte 18, 23
Lyons, Elizabeth 39
Lyttle, Mary Ann 59

Madison, Experience 45
Magee, Diantha 70
Magee, Electa Ann 48
Magee, Nancy 48
Magruder, Sally 29
Main, Katherine 47
Main, Polly 72
Malder, Margaret 29
Maldon, Hannah Mion 72
Male, Margaret 65
Mallecy, R. 15
Manahan, Catharine 15
Manahan, Nancy 13
Manchester, Anna 21
Mann, Margaret 52
Mannahan, Sarah 78
Marett, Mary 73
Margeret, Margarette 6
Marhew, Mary 38
Marriette, Martha 22
Marsh, Sally 31
Marshall, Sarah J. 67

Martin, Cynthia 40
Martin, Nancy 15, 73
Martin, Sally 55
Marvin, Lucinda 77
Mash, Lydia 38
Mason, Betsey 51
Mason, Betsy 63
Mason, Clerinda 20
Mason, Eliza 47
Mason, Harriet 60
Mason, Jane 68
Mason, Nancy 47
Mason, Pamela 62
Mason, Rachel 20, 70
Mason, Rebecca 62
Mason, Sophonia 56
Mason, Susanna 18
Massie, Eliza 76
Masters, Eleanor 60
Matheny, Jane 26
Matthews, Betsy 42
Matthews, Catharine 54
Matthews, Lucy Ann 53
Matthews, Martha 12
Matthews, Mary Ann 44
Matthews, Sally A. 19
Maxon, Sarah 16
Maxon, Susan Eliza 35
Maxson, Harriet 12
Maxson, Laurana 1
Maxson, Lydia 13
Maxson, Mary 16
Maxson, Phebe 58
Maxson, Sophia 17
Maxson, Sophronia 3
Mayhew, Deborah 57
Mayhew, Mehitable 39
Mayhew, Minerva 54
Mayhew, Sarah 56
Mays, Catharine 67
MaGee, Nancy 13
McAllister, Cammilla 73
McAllister, Irene 33
McAllister, Nancy 76
McAllister, Polly 15
McAninch, Nancy L. 53
McAnninch, Anna 73
McAtee, Amelia 61
McAtee, Betsey 29
McAtee, Harriet 16
McAtee, Lavina 9
McAtee, Louisa 47
McAtee, Mary Ann 76
McBane, Jenne 72
McBride, Mary 1
McCabe, Hannah 39
McCabe, Margaret 6
McCabe, Patience 19
McCaig, Margaret 47
McCall, Peggy 13
McCarley, Betsey 47
McClanathan, Samary 70
McClimans, Esbel 37
McClimans, Jean 60
McClintick, Nancy 67
McClintick, Polly 15
McCluer, Caroline 80
McCluer, Hannah 30
McCluer, Sarah 30
McCluer, Sarah D. 3
McClure, Dolly K. 68
McClure, Maria T. 63
McCollum, Eleanor 9
McCollum, Rachel 74
McCoy, Ann C. 36
McCoy, Betsey 21
McCoy, Elizabeth 32, 62
McCoy, Jane B. 45

McCoy, Latitia 31
McCullouch, Mary 7
McCulluch, Lavinia 21
McCullum, Elizabeth 51
McCune, Mary 47
McCune, Peggy 44
McDaniel, Elizabeth 25
McDaniels, Catherine 48
McDaniels, Isabella 67
McDonald, Henrietta 46
McDonald, Mahala 68
McDonald, Maria 47
McDonald, Mary Ann 65
McDonald, Nancy 33
McFarland, Eliza P. 66
McFarland, Hannah 26
McFarland, Maria 72
McFarland, Sally 38
McFarlin, Lydia 38
McFarlin, Peggy 55
McGee, Elizabeth 46
McGeehan, Mary 33
McGeehan, Nancy 6
McGonnigal, Elzada 77
McGrath, Mary 80
McGrath, Mary B. 8
McGrew, Hannah 16
McGuire, Eleanor 80
McIntire, Lydia 42
McIntire, Margaret 36
McIntosh, Deborah 8
McIntosh, Rhoda Ann 12
McKee, Sally 43
McKewer, Sally 9
McKibben, Ann E. 68
McKibben, Letty 54
McKibben, Susan 58
McKibbin, Margaret 54
McKinly, Eliza Ann 42
McKinney, Mary S. 38
McLean, Keziah 14
McLeane, Polly 16
McMasters, Catharine 31
McMeekon, Margaret 49
McMillan, Jane 64, 75
McMullen, Betsy 2
McNeal, Mary 34
McNeal, Susana 47
McNitt, Margaret 35
Mead, Abigail 34
Mead, Ann 9
Mead, Mina 40
Meder, Lucy 67
Medley, Elizabeth 34
Medley, Harriet 23
Medly, Mariah 26
Meek, Matilda 77
Mees, Cynthia 58
Mees, Mary 63
Mees, Theodosia 74
Meigs, Mary Sophia 39
Mellor, Eleanor 3
Mellor, Love P. 57
Mellor, Sally 31
Mellor, Susannah 22
Melvin, Eliza Ann 66
Melvin, Louisa 31
Memund, Jane 62
Menair, Betsy 35
Merow, Ageline 79
Merriam, Anna 71
Merriam, Julia 69
Merriam, Mary 36
Merriam, Sally 73
Merrick, Phebe 77
Merrick, Sarah 34
Merrit, Unity 65
Merwin, Susan 17

Meteer, Susanna 81
Metheny, Rachel 25
Michael, Polly 34
Middleswart, Emily 72
Middleswart, Susanna 81
Mider, Lucy 67
Miles, Mary G. 74
Miles, Mary P. 70
Millard, Mary Ann 30
Millard, Susanna 69
Miller, Adaline 19
Miller, Amanda 52
Miller, Betsy 38, 65
Miller, Catharine F. 28
Miller, Elizabeth 24, 61
Miller, Fanny 78
Miller, Jane 42
Miller, Leana 73
Miller, Love P. 1
Miller, Magdelena 40
Miller, Maria 74
Miller, Mary 1
Miller, Nancy 72, 77
Miller, Polly 16, 44
Miller, Ruth H. 3
Miller, Zipporah 27
Mills, Caroline 65
Mills, Jane 29
Mills, Sally 32
Mills, Sarah 14, 74
Mills, Wnza 12
Miner, Betsy 70
Miner, Esther 33
Minton, Rebecca 60
Misner, Polly 70
Misner, Sally 1
Mitchel, Betsey 2
Mitchell, Nancy 60
Mitchell, Phebe 1
Mitchell, Sally 16
Mitty, Elizabeth 55
Mixer, Almonia 5
Mixer, Elizabeth 36
Mixer, Sally 10, 29
Mogrudge, Sally 17
Molton, Lydia 44
Monroe, Hannah 7
Montgomery, Sally 81
Moon, Susan 37
Moor, Eleanor 78
Moore, Barbary 31
Moore, Catherine 74
Moore, Hannah 78
Moore, Mary 14
Moore, Mary C. 39
Moore, Nancy 10
Moore, Rachael 50
More, Azuba 2
More, Betsy 65
Moreland, Elizabeth 62
Moreland, Nancy 62
Morey, Elizabeth 47
Morey, Julia 38
Morgan, Elizabeth 23
Morrel, Louise N. 45
Morris, Anna 68
Morris, Betsey 38
Morris, Elizabeth 2
Morris, Hannah 68, 69
Morris, Harriet 68
Morris, Henrietta 13
Morris, Hetty 71
Morris, Mary 43
Morris, P. 46
Morris, Rachel 58
Morris, Rebecca 51
Morris, Rowana 68
Morris, Sarah 21

Morris, Selina 21
Morrison, Eliza Jane 48
Morrison, Mahala 58
Morse, Elvira 26
Morse, Emily 78
Morse, Louisa M. 3
Morse, Sarah M. 57
Morton, Cynthia A. 70
Moss, Anna M. W. 7
Moss, Diantha 77
Mosser, Sarah 6
Moulton, Anna 33
Mulcher, Betsey Ann 17
Mullen, Jane 60
Mullen, Mary 60
Munro, Sally 15
Munro, Susanna 42
Murdough, Aritia 36
Murphey, Nancy 65
Murphy, Dorcas 17
Murphy, Elizabeth 23
Murphy, Mary 36
Murphy, Providence 34
Murray, Elizabeth 36
Murray, Mary 48
Mutchler, Sylvina 58
Myers, Patty 24
Myers, Roesey 21
Myers, Sarah 51

Napier, Elizabeth 39
Nash, Elizabeth 1, 27
Nash, Malinda 66
Nash, Nancy 7
Neal, Abigil 64
Neal, Harriet 41
Nedick, Joanna 1
Needham, Mary 78
Needham, Mary S. 15
Needham, Sophronia S. 23
Neel, Patience 2
Nelson, Margaret 79
Nesmith, Nancy 27
Neushifen, Christiana 6
Newberry, Sally 62
Newell, Eliza 34
Newell, Hannah 51
Newell, Sarah Ann 13
Newton, Alice 12
Newton, Betsey 17
Newton, Betsy 80
Newton, Harriet 24
Newton, Salena 51
Newton, Sally 74
Newton, Sarah 4
Nicholl, Elizabeth 48
Nicholls, Elizabeth 36
Nicholls, Nancy 49
Nichols, Abigail 8
Nichols, Lucinda 51
Nichols, Sally 42
Nicholson, Polly 49
Nicoll, Catharine 47
Nixon, Betsey 54
Nixon, Harriet 62
Nixon, Julia Ann 42
Nixon, Laurana 10
Nixon, Margaret 57
Nixon, Rosanna P. 68
Nixon, Sarah 12
Noble, Rachel 14
Noland, Ann Elizabeth 53
Noland, Elizabeth 29
Noland, Lavina E. 62
Noland, Sarah 58
Norman, Clexanda 30

Norman, Harriet 4
Norman, Lucinda 4
Northorp, Huldah 48
Northrup, Jane 47
Nott, Elizabeth 39
Nott, Hannah 79
Nott, Julia 44
Nott, Julia Ann 44
Nott, Mary 15
Nott, Phebe 53
Nott, Philinda 8
Nott, Rhoda 6
Nott, Samantha 75
Nulton, Catharine 66
Nulton, Katherine 49
Nulton, Mary 4
Nulton, Nancy 44
Nulton, Susan 53
Nulton, Susanna 20
Nye, Panthea 34
Nye, Rowena 59
Nye, Sarah 58
Nye, Sophia 11
Nyghswonger, Sukey 41
Nyswonger, Sally 50

Oakley, Lydia 16
Oaks, Charlotte 32
Obleness, Elizabeth 23
Obleness, Maria 2
Obleness, Phebe P. 39
O'Bleniss, Gertrude 2
O'Blenness, Rachel 36
O'Blennis, Rachel 50
O'Brien, Susan 67
Offe, Peggy 70
Ogle, Ann 79
Ogle, Margaret 38
Ogle, Nancy Ann 31
Ogle, Polly 13
Ogle, Ruhama 27
Oliver, Amy 8
Oliver, Christian 10
Oliver, Drusilla 68
Oliver, Elanor 44
Oliver, Eliza 62
Oliver, Elizabeth 62
Oliver, Isabella 9
Oliver, Liza 54
Oliver, Lucinda 59
Oliver, Lucretia 52
Oliver, Mahala 65
Oliver, Mary 40
Oliver, Nelly 73
Oliver, Peggy 58
Oliver, Sarah 23, 79
Olney, Anna 43
Olney, Apphia 47
Olney, Chloe 43
Olney, Drusilla 18
Olney, Eliza 69
Olney, Elizabeth 24
Olney, Huldah 65
Olney, Joanna 18
Olney, Lois 15
Olney, Mary 15
Olney, Patience 14
Olney, Rachel 75
Olney, Sally 18
Olney, Sarah 26
O'Neal, Betsey 71
O'Neale, Mary 56
Oppe, Sarah 5
Orison, Mary 30
Orison, Sarah 7
Ortt, Elizabeth 44

Osgood, Amelia 73
Otis, Caroline M. 19
Otis, Luvina 80
Otis, Olive 80
Otis, Rosanna 63
Otten, Anna 78
Owen, Olive F. 47
Owen, Polly 68
Owen, Sally 25
Owen, Susanna 68
Owens, Azaba 4
Owens, Susanna 47

Pain, Lydia 42
Painter, Susannah 53
Palmer, Achsah 32
Palmer, Betsey 48
Palmer, Betsy 68
Palmer, Ivah F. 4
Palmer, Jerusha 31
Palmer, Julia Ann 66
Palmer, Margaret A. 79
Palmer, Martha 32
Palmer, Mary 5, 22, 58
Palmer, Polly 55
Palmer, Rebe 29
Palmer, Rebecca 5
Palmer, Sarah 37, 41
Parden, Maria 68
Parke, Hannah 26
Parke, Mary 35
Parke, Sarah 71
Parke, Susan 31
Parker, Charity 24
Parker, Fanny 26
Parker, Hannah 11
Parker, Polly 41
Parker, Rachel 63
Parker, Rebecca 77
Parker, Sarah 71
Parker, Sarah Ann 33
Parks, Electa 30
Parmentier, Jean 20
Parr, Catharine 27
Parr, Lucretia W. 65
Parr, Rebecca 65
Patten, Elizabeth B. 15
Patten, Harriet 60
Patten, Nancy 53, 78
Patten, Rebeckah 14
Patten, Ruth 38
Patterson, Betsy 64
Patterson, Esther 32
Patterson, Peggy 77
Pattin, Eleanor 67
Pattin, Mary 46
Pattin, Sally 30
Payne, Anna 79
Payne, Eliza 74
Payne, Hannah 59
Payne, Henrietta 73
Payne, Lucy 13
Payne, Nancy 69
Pearl, Hannah 61
Pearson, Mary Ann 50
Pearsons, Anna 29
Peck, Lavina 7
Peck, Matilda 50
Peek, Rachel 20
Peese, Eliza 14
Peirce, Lois 63
Pell, Mahitabel 72
Pennell, Sarah 5
Penney, Mary 41
Penny, Catherine 47
Penny, Mahala 57

Penny, Sally 8
Penny, Sophia 45
Perdieu, Rebecca 54
Perdue, Susan 74
Perking, Phebe 22
Perkins, Ann 57
Perkins, Anna 22
Perkins, Asenath 27
Perkins, Betsy 54
Perkins, Cynthia 27, 69
Perkins, Elizabeth 1, 70
Perkins, Elvira 22
Perkins, Jane 22
Perkins, Mary 1, 56
Perkins, Matilda 56
Perkins, Sally 13
Perrin, Betsy 79
Perrin, Charlotte 37
Perrin, Elizabeth 69
Perry, Betsey 25
Perry, Catharine 16
Perry, Mary 18
Perry, Nancy 76
Perry, Rebecca 35
Perry, Sally 36, 53
Perry, Susanna 31
Peters, Catharine 81
Peters, Mariah 9
Petty, Lydia 3
Petty, Margaret 43
Petty, Maria 23
Pewthers, Matilda 52
Peyton, Christianna 73
Peyton, Drusilla 16
Pfaff, Elizabeth 55
Phelps, Sally 71
Philip, Mary 9
Philips, Elizabeth 72
Philips, Peggy 34
Phillips, Anna 12
Phillips, Elizabeth 48
Phillips, Mary 63
Phillips, Polly W. 8
Phillips, Tabitha 12
Pickering, Winnefred 51
Picket, Elizabeth 50
Picket, Mary 81
Pilcher, Ann 53
Pilcher, Catharine 30
Pilcher, Maria 40
Pinny, Cordealy 40
Pixley, Cynthia 57
Pixley, Philomela 56
Place, Hannah 37
Place, Jane 39
Place, Lucy 63
Place, Lydia 58
Platter, Lucretia C. 25
Plumer, Ann 50
Plumer, Catherine 65
Plummer, Clarissa 10
Plummer, Esther W. 8
Plummer, Hannah R. 57
Plummer, Hetty 73
Plummer, Nancy B. 18
Plummer, Sarah 58
Poe, Clarinda 6
Pond, Elida 13
Pond, Eliza 55
Pond, Julia Ann M. 73
Pond, Louis 8
Pond, Pamela 18
Pool, Charlotte 38
Pool, Elizabeth 34
Pool, Jane 34
Pool, Nancy 6, 10
Pool, Polly 28
Pope, Catharine 6

Pope, Elizabeth 14
Porter, Catharine 12
Porter, Hannah 19
Porter, Jerusha 19
Porter, Lois 30
Porter, Lydia 49
Porter, Mary 37, 42, 43, 51
Porter, Nancy 2
Porter, Priscilla 67
Porter, Rebecca 77
Porter, Ruth 34
Porter, Sarah 12
Posey, Frances 1
Posey, Louisa 48
Posey, Marian 12
Posey, Mary A. 48
Posey, Nancy 35
Posey, Polly 48
Posey, Sally 1
Posey, Sidnah 60
Potts, Elizabeth 21
Potts, Hannah 34
Potts, Margaret 76
Potts, Mary 59
Potts, Polly 59
Powel, Aney 57
Powel, Sarah 69
Powell, Eliza 1
Powell, Meriam 46
Powell, Nancy 60
Pratt, Anna T. 18
Pratt, Elizabeth 63
Pratt, Louisa Jane 56
Pratt, Mahepsa 67
Pratt, Maria 46
Pratt, Mary 47
Pratt, Parthenia 41
Prentiss, Mary C. 30
Preston, Artimacy 78
Preston, Artymisa 26
Preston, Hannah 78
Preston, Harriet 67
Preston, Mary 71
Prewitt, Rachel 36
Price, Margaret 66
Price, Mary 72
Price, Nancy 33
Price, Sarah 6
Price, Sarah S. 36
Prior, Sally 28
Pritchard, Betsy 49
Pritchard, Mary 14
Procter, Lovina 35
Procter, Sally 31
Proctor, Abigal 22
Proctor, Mary R. 37
Proctor, Phebe 35
Proctor, Polly 30, 37
Protsman, Catherine 12
Protsman, Margaret 29
Protzman, Ann 68
Protzman, Royall 65
Prouty, Rachel 10
Pruden, Achsah P. 9
Prunty, Mary 8
Pugh, Mary 16
Pugh, Nancy 16
Pugh, Sarah 30
Pugsley, Mary 74
Pugsley, Olive 59
Putnam, Abigail 9
Putnam, Bethia L. 74
Putnam, Betsey 17
Putnam, Catharine 10
Putnam, Catherine 60
Putnam, Charlotte 70
Putnam, Elizabeth A. 14
Putnam, Harriet 39

Putnam, Helen P. 21
Putnam, Julia H. 60
Putnam, Laura A. 13
Putnam, Lucy E. 29
Putnam, Martha W. 28
Putnam, Nancy 52
Putnam, Patty 74
Putnam, Persis 37
Putnam, Polly 46
Putnam, Rosella 69
Putnam, Sarah 73

Queen, Nancy 69
Quigley, Mary 59, 61
Quimby, Elizabeth 33
Quinn, Julian 56

Racer, Ann 58
Racer, Grace 69
Racer, Mary 49
Racer, Susan 67
Ralston, Sarah 4
Ramsey, Sarah M. 37
Randles, Nancy 5
Randols, Eessbeth 44
Ranger, Mary 51
Rankins, Rachael 36
Ransom, Mindwell 61
Ransom, Sarah 19
Rardin, Hannah 74
Rardin, Phebe 80
Rardin, Polly 25
Rardon, Mary 5
Raridin, Jane 15
Rarrdon, Rebecca 50
Rasor, Elizabeth 71
Rathbon, Elizabeth 51
Rathbone, Electa 27
Rathbone, Lovice 72
Rathbone, Mercy 73
Rathbun, Electa 66
Rathbun, Eley 11
Rathbun, Elsa 15
Rathbun, Mercy 27, 39
Rathburn, Frances 5
Ray, Mary 11, 14
Ray, Polly 60
Rayley, Content A. 9
Rea, Eliza 6
Rea, Margaret 19
Rea, Nancy 62
Read, Rowena 46
Record, Eliza Ann 39, 77
Record, Elizabeth 12
Record, Huldah 27
Record, Lucy 80
Record, Margaret 73
Record, Mary 28
Record, Mary Ann 57
Record, Susan 39
Rector, Sallie 55
Reece, Nancy Jane 1
Reed, Anna 48
Reed, Diantha 51
Reed, Elizabeth 12
Reed, Harriet 36
Reed, Nancy 36
Reed, Polly 64
Reed, Sally 25
Reed, Sophrena 70
Reeder, Sophia 5
Rees, Mary 28
Regnier, Hannah 48
Reinard, Elizabeth 15

Renolds, Margaret 64
Renols, Nancy 77
Reppert, Ann M. 61
Reynolds, Eliza Ann 57
Rhea, Rebecca 25
Rhodes, Lucy 46
Rice, Cynthia 39
Rice, Elizabeth 69
Rice, Luceby 69
Rice, Polly 3, 64
Rice, Sabrina 55
Rice, Zilpha 79
Richards, Diana 12
Richards, Fanny B. 29
Richardson, Esther 77
Richardson, Lucy S. 8
Richardson, Olive 5
Richardson, Prudy 60
Richarts, Sarah 26
Richmond, Phebe 53
Ridgeway, Mary A. 23
Ridgeway, Priscilla 23
Rieder, Betsey 30
Riggs, Jenne 78
Rightmire, Eliza 64
Riheldarfee, Julia A. 52
Riley, Betsey 48
Riley, Jane 9
Riley, Mary 27, 58
Riley, Mary A. 4
Riley, Mary Ann 66
Riley, Susan 30, 37
Rily, Betsy 41
Rinard, Cynthia 50
Rinard, Margaret 56
Rinby, Margaret 18
Rinney, Rosey 37
Rion, Margaret 80
Risley, Caroline 45
Ritchey, Patty 36
Roach, Mary Ann 3
Roach, Polly 47
Robbin, Jane 7
Robbins, Abigail 76
Robbins, Mary E. 23
Robbins, Sibul 2
Robenett, Susanna 24
Roberts, Eleanor 11
Roberts, Eliza 28
Roberts, Elizabeth 24
Roberts, Grace 31
Roberts, Kaziah 41
Roberts, Maria A. 46
Robertson, Elizabeth 45
Robertson, Eunice 23
Robertson, Hannah 40
Robinet, Sarah 27
Robinson, Anne 22
Robinson, Elizabeth 54
Robinson, Keziah 13
Robinson, Margaret L. 28
Robinson, Mary 70
Robinson, Phoebe 32
Robinson, Sarah C. 17, 47
Robinson, Sylvia 35
Roche, Mary 64
Rockey, Susanna 13
Rodgers, Margaret 38, 75
Roe, Rosanna 32
Rogers, Eleanor 61
Rogers, Lavina 10
Rood, Caroline 14
Rood, Charity 25
Rood, Cyrena 7
Rood, Matilda 68
Rood, Sylvina 7
Root, Lucinda 20
Root, Rosmer 39

Root, Sarah 39
Root, Susan 22
Rose, Clarissa 4
Rose, Fanny 52
Rose, Jane 69
Rose, Lydia 52
Rose, Ruth 44
Ross, Dorcas 23
Ross, Elizabeth H. 62
Ross, Narcissa 32
Ross, Phoebe 18
Ross, Sally M. 69
Ross, Sarah 7, 32
Roun, Betsey 4
Rouse, Bathsheba 31
Rouse, Catherine 43
Rouse, Cynthia 25
Rouse, Cynthia F. 62
Rowland, Betsey 6
Rowland, Eliza Jane 73
Rowland, Jane 38, 44
Rowland, Mary Ann 61
Rowland, Sarah 52
Rubel, Margaret 5
Ruble, Sarah 16
Rude, Mariah 42
Rumbold, Eleanor 35
Rump, Eliza Ann 35
Russell, Betsey 16
Russell, Lucy 17
Russell, Mary A. 20
Russell, Polly 16
Russell, Sarah Ann 26
Rutter, Susan 50
Ryan, Catharine 22
Ryan, Julia 51
Ryan, Mary Ann 37
Ryan, Mary E. 56
Ryder, Mary 50
Rynard, Sarah 23
Ryon, Jane 11

Saelor, Sophia 12
Sage, Silinda 76
Sailor, Catharine 75
Saltonstall, Nancy 44
Sandburn, Polly 1
Sanders, Elizabeth 53
Sanders, Mary A. 3
Sanders, Sarah 43
Sandford, Huldah 74
Sargent, Sarah 16
Sarot, Mary Catherine 43
Sawyer, Dorcas 74
Sawyer, Lydia 75
Sayles, Louisa 30
Schofield, Lydia 46
Schonover, Temperance 28
Schoonover, Charlotte 60
Scott, Almira 17
Scott, Celestina 27
Scott, Cynthia 24
Scott, Eleanor 8
Scott, Eliza 79
Scott, Elizabeth 19
Scott, Esther 24
Scott, Joanna 5
Scott, Malissa 38
Scott, Margaret 80
Scott, Maria 78
Scott, Martha 24
Scott, Mary 63, 65
Scott, Mary Ann 54
Scott, Mary T. 45
Scott, Patience 20
Scott, Polly 57

Scott, Sally 8
Scott, Sarah 70
Scritchfield, Catharine 47
Seaman, Serena E. 64
Seamans, Polly 3
Seamons, Patty 52
Seamons, Sabra 68
Sears, Mary 8
Sedlift, Julia 19
Seeley, Margaret 62
Seely, Elizabeth 48
Seely, Lusetta A. M. 7
Seely, Sarah 19
Seevers, Mary Ann 14
Seivers, Fanny 42
Selers, Phebe 28
Sellers, Christina 9
Sellers, Elizabeth 71
Sells, Hester 79
Semore, Margret 75
Severs, Margaret 61
Shafer, Polly Ann 10
Shaffer, Cynthia 67
Shakley, Sally 46
Shankland, Jane 51
Shanklen, Catherine 66
Shanklin, Louisa 51
Shanklin, Lucinda 68
Shannon, Jane 15
Sharp, Abigail 76
Sharp, Anna 51
Sharp, Anna Louisa 30
Sharp, Eleanor 36
Sharp, Eliza 2
Sharp, Marget 33
Sharp, Martha 45
Shaw, Betsy 25
Shaw, Catharine 48
Shaw, Charlott H. 9
Shaw, Margaret 38
Shaw, Sally 18
Shears, Rebecca 64
Sheets, Actious 77
Sheets, Balinda 56
Sheets, Elizabeth 14
Sheets, Mary 42
Sheets, Polly 72
Sheets, Ruth 56
Sheffield, Hannah 69
Sheffield, Lucy Coggeshall 81
Shekley, Mary 33
Sheldon, Elizabeth 63
Sheldon, Olive 65
Shepard, Eleanor 63
Shepard, Huldah 65
Shepard, Lorena 14
Shepard, Louisa 44
Shepard, Lydia 40
Shepard, Rachel 12
Shepard, Rhoda 48
Shepherd, Caroline 19
Sheppard, Sarah 60
Sheppart, Nelly 21
Shereman, Lucy 66
Sherman, Anna 64
Sherman, Clarissa 20
Sherman, Diana 72
Sherman, Mira 65
Sherwood, Thamur 56
Shettleworth, Eleanor 52
Shields, Anna 42
Shields, Louisa 15
Shields, Sarah 56
Shields, Sophia 80
Shipman, Joanna F. 7
Shipman, Julia 37
Shipman, Maria 66
Shipman, Mary Ann 4

Shipman, Polly 4
Shirley, Elizabeth 41
Shirley, Polly 54
Shockley, Betsey 41
Showers, Phoebe A. 66
Shrader, Jane 25
Shrader, Katharine 71
Shrader, Susan 71
Shrum, Catharine 15
Shuey, Sophia 4
Shukes, Mary 6
Sifers, Elizabeth 52
Sills, Ann 79
Sills, Sarah 13
Silva, Elizabeth 21
Silverton, Elizabeth 7
Silvey, Sarah 21
Silvius, Susanna 64
Simmons, Betsey 49
Simons, Elizabeth 76
Simons, Jane 55
Simons, Patience 46
Sims, Elizabeth 42
Sinclair, Nancy 2
Sinclair, Polly 1
Skinner, Letitia 33
Skinner, Mary 79
Skinner, Piety 7
Skinner, Rebecca 29
Skinner, Sarah 76
Skipton, Catharine 6
Skipton, Christiana 79
Skipton, Mary Ann 29
Skipton, Susan 52
Slaughter, Desdemonia 40
Sloan, Pamela 5
Smith, Adaline 2
Smith, Betsey 63
Smith, Betsy 24, 57
Smith, Caroline 9
Smith, Catherine 26
Smith, Charlotte 30
Smith, Diadama 35
Smith, Eliza 44
Smith, Esther 73, 75
Smith, Esther T. 67
Smith, Experience 31
Smith, Huldah 72
Smith, Jemima 36, 72
Smith, Julia A. 15
Smith, Katharine 51
Smith, Lavina 38
Smith, Lucy 3
Smith, Lydia A. 6
Smith, Lydia B. 58
Smith, Malissa 68
Smith, Mary 23, 54, 56
Smith, Matilda P. 54
Smith, Melinda 38
Smith, Polly 5, 62, 70, 71
Smith, Sally 43
Smith, Sarah 31, 52
Smithson, Jane 29
Smithson, Mary Ann 39
Snodgrass, Barbara 46
Snodgrass, Margaret 4
Snodgrass, Martha 19
Snyder, Eliza Ann E. 21
Snyder, Elizabeth 71
Snyder, Jane 44
Solomon, Betsey Ann 77
Solomon, Mary 3
Soul, Hannah C. 12
Spacht, Polly 38
Spears, Damaris D. 42
Spears, Phebe 41
Spears, Polly 68
Spears, Sarah 26

Spears, Susanna 41
Speck, Susanna 38
Speed, Nancy 45
Spencer, Polly 14
Sprage, Cynthia Ann 52
Sprague, Abigail 54
Sprague, Betsey 70
Sprague, Cynthia 51, 54
Sprague, Experience 21
Sprague, Lucinda 62
Sprague, Luny 46
Sprague, Mary M. 33
Sprague, Nancy 24, 46
Sprague, Phoebe 63
Sprague, Polly 70
Sprague, Rebecca 61
Sprague, Ruby 20
Sprague, Sally 46
Sprague, Sarah 72
Sprague, Susanna 68
Springer, Abigail 6
Springer, Lucy 38
Springer, Margaret 71
Springer, Mary Ann 46
Springer, Susannah 50
Sproat, Sally 66
Staats, Rebecca 43
Stacey, Abigail 47
Stacey, Susan 61
Stacy, Beulah 46
Stacy, Mary 8
Stacy, Mary L. 20
Stacy, Susanna 27
Stage, Ann E. 29
Stage, Jemima 78
Stanford, Eliza 24
Stanley, Abigail 20, 25
Stanley, Clarissa 37
Stanley, Elizabeth 13
Stanley, Lucy 7
Stanley, Martha 56
Stanley, Mary 58
Stanley, Mixenda 78
Stanley, Nancy 8
Stanley, Sarah W. 21
Stanley, Thirza 17
Stanton, Emily 24
Stanton, Frances 60
Stanton, Laura A. 39
Stanton, Mary 50
Stanton, Nancy Olive 27
Stanton, Sarah 31
Stark, Anna 54
Starks, Susanna 26
Starlin, Asenath 68
Starlin, Betsey 38
Starlin, Deborah 20
Starlin, Lorena 80
Starlin, Orinda 11
Starlin, Philinda 69
Starlin, Polly 18
Starling, Anna 35
Staunton, Sally 79
Stedman, Mary 28
Stedman, Nabby 71
Steel, Julia Ann 47
Stephens, Amirila 13
Stephens, Catharine 33
Stephens, Harriet 53
Stephens, Sally 62, 78
Stephenson, Sarah 3
Stevens, Delilah 57
Stevens, Melissa 30
Stevens, Nancy 19
Stevens, Sophia 41
Stewart, Amanda 34
Stewart, Elizabeth 17, 31
Stewart, Frances 45

Stewart, Jane 70
Still, Elizabeth 58
Still, Polly 58
Stillson, Cynthia 17
Stone, Colina 45
Stone, Eliza 58
Stone, Elizabeth 32
Stone, Esther C. 48
Stone, Grace 18
Stone, Lydia 37
Stone, Melissa W. 4
Stone, Rosanna D. 23
Stone, Susan 11
Stone, Vesta 63
Stoneman, Elizabeth 43
Storey, Relief 9
Story, Mary 58
Stotts, Emily 72
Stover, Mary 75
Stowell, Mary Ann 3
Straight, Sally 36
Strawsnider, Elizabeth 41
Stroble, Mary 63
Stroud, Rebecca 78
Stuck, Sarah 54
Stull, Anna 19
Stull, Catharine 14
Stull, Frances 55, 77
Stump, Cassandra 20
Stump, Joanna 58
Stump, Mary 43, 80
Stump, Nancy 67
Stutts, Hester 2
Sullivan, Emma 33
Sullivan, Nancy 23
Sutton, Betsey 24
Sutton, Mary 58
Sutton, Rhoda 58
Sutton, Sally 58
Swank, Pemelia 6
Swearingame, Phoebe 27
Swearingen, Sarah A. 35
Sweasey, Margaret 35
Sweet, Sarah 43
Swesey, Jane 5
Swett, Keziah 22
Swift, Deborah 55
Swift, Mary 50
Swift, Phebe 63

Talbert, Susan H. 72
Talbot, Michel 39
Talbot, Sarah 75
Taylor, Almyra 80
Taylor, Anna 57
Taylor, Betsey 70
Taylor, Catherine 50
Taylor, Charlotte 62
Taylor, Elizabeth 4, 57
Taylor, Ellin 26
Taylor, Fanny 50
Taylor, Jane 49
Taylor, Levina 30, 35
Taylor, Lois 49
Taylor, Louisa 68
Taylor, Maria 23, 29
Taylor, Mary 5
Taylor, Mary B. 28
Taylor, Phebe 17
Taylor, Sally 56
Temple, Hannah H. 10
Temple, Jane P. 73
Templeton, Eliza 5
Templeton, Jane 1
Templeton, Margaret 3
Terey, Mary 5

Terrill, Ann 71
Terrill, Elizabeth 81
Terrill, Laura Ann 33
Terry, Margaret 57
Tew, Sarah 52
Tewel, Lavina 53
Tewel, Polly 23
Tharp, Hannah 50
Thomas, Harriet 17
Thomas, Mary 20, 59
Thomas, Nancy 39
Thomas, Philena 67
Thompson, Elizabeth 35
Thompson, Esther E. 61
Thorn, Mary 21
Thornelly, Harriet 3
Thorniley, Augusta E. 6
Thorniley, Louisa 18
Thorniley, Mary 16
Thorniley, Mary Ann 37
Thorniley, Tabitha 62
Thornton, Nancy 77
Thurlo, Ruth 48
Tice, Catharine 50
Tice, Liddey 78
Tice, Margaret 57
Tice, Mary 19
Tillson, Lydia 66
Tilson, Eliza 14
Tilson, Ida 2
Tilson, Pamelia 61
Tilton, Lyda 53
Tilton, Mary 50
Tilton, Persis 55
Tilton, Sarah 49
Tinsley, Margaret 45
Todd, Sally 73
Toleman, Jerusia 74
Tollman, Mary M. 57
Tolman, Mary 74
Tolman, Urana 24
Tomlinson, Elizabeth A. 35
Tompkins, Emily B. 5
Toothaker, Eliza 27
Toothaker, Sarah 12
Totman, Polly 63
Toulson, Sophia 78
Towell, Margaret 42
Townsend, Betsey 32
Townsend, Nancy 17
Tracy, Mary 26
Tracy, Mary Jane 79
Travis, Louisa 79
Travis, Samantha 60
True, Elizabeth 58
True, Louisa 13
True, Real 56
Truesdale, Eliza 29
Tucker, Eleanor 35
Tucker, Elizabeth 71
Tucker, Frances 42
Tucker, Lydia 78
Tucker, Mary 43
Tucker, Nancy B. 40
Tupper, Rowena 64
Turner, Betty S. 73
Turner, Nancy 59
Tuttle, Almira 74
Tuttle, Ann Maria 64
Tuttle, Lucy Maria 76
Tuttle, Mary Ann 25
Tuttle, Phebe 72
Tuttle, Polly 55
Tuttle, Sally 46
Twiggs, Sarah 36
Twiggs, Jemima 35
Twitty, Amelia 7
Twomley, Deborah H. 26

Tyler, Abigail 37
Tyson, Esther 27
Tyson, Polly 52

Uhl, J. 59
Uhl, Phebe 9
Ulmer, Harriet 42

Vanclief, Elizabeth 51
Vanderventer, Jane 60
Vandevender, Nancy 52
Vanduyn, Rachel B. 5
Vanvaley, Hannah 16
Vanvaley, Hester 49
VanCamp, Jane 70
VanClief, Abigail 13
VanClief, Emme 53
VanClief, Lavina 67
VanGordon, Anna 10
VanPelt, Catharine 58
VanValey, Iatruda 58
VanValey, Mary 75
VanValey, Phebe 4
Varner, Ann 14
Varnum, Mary 4
Varnum, Rebecca 54
Vaughan, Betsey 22
Vaughan, Patty 43
Vaughan, Polly 16
Vaughn, Catherine 65
Vaughn, Polly 80
Vincent, Amy 23
Vincent, Clarinda 6
Vincent, Eliza 8
Vincent, Lucinda 1
Vincent, Maria 37
Vincent, Mary 15, 47
Vincent, Nancy 3
Vinton, Susan G. 21
Violet, Margaret 25
Voshel, Susan 10
Votaw, Elizabeth 73

Wadkins, Sarah 65
Wagner, Elizabeth 14
Wagner, Mary Ann 68
Wait, Lois 5
Walbridge, Elvira 24
Walker, Corrine 65
Walker, Eleanor 28, 30, 40
Walker, Elizabeth 43
Walker, Lucy 36
Walker, Margaret 54
Walker, Mary 3, 48, 54
Walker, Nancy 38
Walker, Nancy D. 54
Walker, Polly 12, 76
Wallace, Edith 19
Wallbridge, Roesea 38
Waller, Catherine 30
Waller, Eleanor 33
Walls, Malander 23
Walton, Nancy 23
Ward, Jemima 11
Ward, Maria 3
Ward, Mary 64
Ward, Matilda 55
Ward, Frances 57
Ward, Phebe 10, 43
Ward, Sarah 55
Ward, Tabitha 45
Ware, Jane 79

Warner, Patience 43
Warrell, Rebecca 29
Warren, Delia 12
Warren, Fanny 44
Warren, Larvina 49
Warren, Lucretia 40
Warren, Nancy 38
Warren, Rebecca 6
Warren, Sophia 18
Warth, Catherine 26, 72
Waterman, Calrina 77
Waterman, Lydia 8
Waterman, Polly 68, 75
Waterman, Rhoda 77
Waters, Kezia R. 79
Waters, Margaret 10
Waters, Rhoda A. 20
Waters, Sally 34
Watkins, Elizabeth 45
Watkins, Sally 57
Watrous, Sally 34
Wausil, Elizabeth 45
Wayson, Jane 75
Weakley, Catharine 23
Weatherbe, Deborah 48
Weatherby, Lydia 15
Weaver, Lavina 34
Webster, Avis 20
Webster, Caroline M. 5
Webster, Doshe E. 8
Webster, Lotia 77
Webster, Sally 47
Webster, Sibbel 75
Wedge, Betsey 4
Wedge, Eliza 46
Wedge, Lucinda 23
Weir, Mary 79
Welch, Abigail 5
Welch, Jane 13
Welch, Sally 21, 38
Welles, Nancy 16
Welles, Sally 69
Welles, Susanna 77
Wells, Amanda 65
Wells, Candace 33
Wells, Cynthia 4
Wells, Electa L. 46
Wells, Elizabeth 59, 75
Wells, Esther 66
Wells, Harriet 41
Wells, Louisa 65
Wells, Sally 1
Wells, Sarah 2, 40
Wells, Sophia 75
West, Phebe 45
Westcott, Susan A. 59
Westgate, Patty 15
Westgate, Roda 61
Weston, Mary 9
Whaley, Lucetta 15
Wharff, Eliza Ann 50
Wheeler, Abigail 77
Wheeler, Asenath 31
Wheeler, Betsey 49
Wheeler, Catharine Ann 8
Wheeler, Clarissa 26
Wheeler, Joanna 8
Wheeler, Maria 7
Wheeler, Mary T. 28
Wheeler, Rebekah 33
White, Anna 16
White, Cynthia 31
White, Experience 5
White, Joanna 54
White, Julina 67
White, Lydia 40
White, M. Eliza 9
White, Mary Ann 9

White, Polly 1, 24, 49
White, Rebecca 43
White, Sally Ann 62
White, Sophia 4, 7
White, Susanna 23
Whitehouse, Mary 37
Whitham, Mehitabel 80
Whiting, Mary B. 76
Whiting, Nancy 10
Whiting, Susan 5
Whitney, Sarah 35
Wick, Maria L. 78
Widger, Margaret 17
Widger, Mary 24
Wier, Sally 56
Wightman, Eliza A. 25
Wilcox, Rebecca 8
Wiley, Olive 30
Wilhelm, Elizabeth 16
Wilkins, Lucy 76
Willard, Caroline 78
Williams, Amanda E. 23
Williams, Amelia 70
Williams, Eleanor 22
Williams, Eliza 6, 67
Williams, Elizabeth 4, 64
Williams, Frances 69
Williams, Hannah 30
Williams, Jane 25
Williams, Mahala 22
Williams, Margaret 8
Williams, Maria 34
Williams, Martha 73
Williams, Mary 40
Williams, Nancy 41
Williams, Polly 73
Williams, Rebecca 69
Williams, Sarah 2
Williamson, Christina 40
Williamson, Deborah 6, 21
Williamson, Elizabeth 59
Williamson, Hannah 24
Williamson, Isabella 45
Williamson, Jane 49
Williamson, Maria 61
Williamson, Mary 40
Williamson, Narcissa 11
Willis, Betsey 66
Willis, Eleanor 66
Willis, Jane 54
Willis, Mary 5
Willis, Sarah 66, 67

Willis, Sophrona 48
Wills, Eliza 16
Wills, Sally 44
Wills, Sophrona 17
Willson, Jane 79
Willson, Mary 41
Wilmorth, Lucinda 55
Wilson, Abigail 77
Wilson, Almedia 9, 62
Wilson, Betsey 3
Wilson, Betsy 7
Wilson, Caroline 42
Wilson, Celestia 9
Wilson, Clarissa 71
Wilson, Cynthia 79
Wilson, Deborah S. 50
Wilson, Eliza 78
Wilson, Elizabeth 31, 61
Wilson, Esther 50
Wilson, Joan 10
Wilson, Lauranna 16
Wilson, Lydia 76
Wilson, Margaret 65
Wilson, Mary 33, 48, 76
Wilson, Nancy 1, 76
Wilson, Pamelia 69
Wilson, Pammelia 26
Wilson, Polly 44, 69
Wilson, Rachel 75
Wilson, Rebecca 20
Wilson, Sarah 43, 62
Wilson, Susannah 59
Winans, Sally 53
Winchell, A. M. 27
Winchell, Deborah 25
Wing, Docia 21
Wing, Mary 68
Winget, Rachel 34
Wingett, Cassinda 56
Winsor, Anna 80
Winters, Rachel 45
Wiser, Elizabeth 59
Witham, Luceba 53
Witham, Maria 46
Witham, Zilpha 9
Withington, Betsey 7
Withington, Naomi 67
Withington, Sally 52
Witighin, Hannah 18
Wittin, Rachell 76
Wolcott, Vilate S. 6
Wolf, Mary 59

Wonsiter, Elizabeth 20
Wood, Catharine 54
Wood, Catharine A. 59
Wood, Cynthia 14
Wood, Elizabeth 75
Wood, Joanna 77
Wood, Lucy 6
Wood, Mary Ann 14
Wood, Rebecca 39, 42
Wood, Ruth 65
Wood, Sarah 29
Woodard, Elimira 34
Woodard, Molly 46
Woodard, Rebeckah 70
Woodbridge, Jane G. 51
Woodbridge, Lucy 57
Woodbridge, Sally 46
Woodford, Laura 9
Woodmansee, Mary 2
Woodruff, Betsey 30
Woodruff, Caroline 46
Woodruff, Hannah 26
Woodruff, Maria 3
Woodruff, Nancy 27, 71
Woodruff, Polly 17, 52
Woodruff, Sarah Ann 65
Woods, Rebecke 66
Woodward, Caroline 5
Woodward, Eleanor 46
Woodward, Highley C. 8
Woodward, Sally 42
Worrell, Eleanor 51
Worstell, Mary Ann 16
Worth, Polly 46
Worthington, Amy P. 50
Wright, Corlinda 57
Wright, Huldah 45
Wright, Lauria 24
Wyor, Milia 4

Yant, Elizabeth 58
Young, Elizabeth 22, 50, 71
Young, Margaret 49
Young, Mary 31
Younge, Charity 57

Zigler, M. W. F. C. L. F. 5